LIMPING WITH GOD

Published by:
1517 Publishing
PO Box 54032
Irvine, CA 92619-4032

Publisher's Cataloging-In-Publication Data
(Prepared by The Donohue Group, Inc.)

Names: Bird, Chad, author.
Title: Limping with God : Jacob & the Old Testament guide to messy discipleship / Chad Bird.
Description: Irvine, CA : 1517 Publishing, [2022] | Includes bibliographical references and index.
Identifiers: ISBN 9781948969826 (hardcover) | ISBN 9781948969833 (paperback) | ISBN 9781948969840 (ebook)
Subjects: LCSH: Jacob (Biblical patriarch) | Bible. Old Testament—Criticism, interpretation, etc. | Christian life—Biblical teaching. | God (Christianity)—Mercy.
Classification: LCC BS580.J3 B57 2022 (print) | LCC BS580.J3 (ebook) | DDC 222/.11092—dc23

Printed in the United States of America.

Cover art by Brenton Clarke Little

LIMPING WITH GOD

JACOB & THE OLD TESTAMENT GUIDE TO MESSY DISCIPLESHIP

CHAD BIRD

Contents

Part 3. Coming Home: Fighting God and Limping Onward

Part 4. Growing Old: Colorful Coats and Saying Goodbye

Foreword

One of the most heartbreaking and liberating revelations that confronts us in our growing-up years is that all our heroes are characters in a tragedy. Those to whom we look up in devotion will, almost without exception, become those whom we look down upon in dismay. I remember, as a young man, being awed by a leader in our church. His character. His eloquence. The way he truly was a man of God. When later I heard the whispers about his philandering, then the growing volume of the rabid small-town gossip, my heart shrank within me. I felt stupid. How could I be so naïve as to look up to him?

If I were able to write a letter to the younger me, I would simply say, "Listen, you're not stupid. You just have yet to plumb the depths of humanity's radical frailty."

We have a tendency, in church circles, to close our eyes to this patent truth. We suppose that the best models of the Christian life are heroes or heroines of the faith. Sunday School material, of course, has mastered the art of inculcating this moralistic ideology, with various Old Testament paragons of this or that virtue held up before our children's eyes as the person they should aspire to be. Noah the Obedient. David the Brave. You know the predictable titles. Anyone with even a passing familiarity of these stories knows that our children are being lied to—or, to put it more charitably, half-lied-to. Biblical stars, like famous people today and of every generation, have a large pile of bones rattling around in their closets, and often spilling out onto the floor for all the world to gawk at. Or, to change the metaphor, in the dark basement of every human heart, heroic or otherwise, the wolves of evil scratch and growl—and often escape, with disastrous consequences.

One of the reasons I have devoted my life to studying and writing about the Old Testament is because, in these stories, there is a remarkable exposé of these wolves. Here we spy humanity's occasional beauty (yes) and ongoing ugliness (also yes). Rather than whitewashing the flaws of their characters, the biblical authors paint them in lurid and glowing colors. In fact, some of the narratives are so embarrassingly honest that I cringe to think that these poor souls have had their dirty underwear swinging in the breeze of Scripture for millennia. Yet there they are—unlaundered, raw, nasty, evil, and extraordinarily human. I can only hope that part of the heavenly bliss for these characters will be in *not* knowing that their lives have been the objects of sermon material for ages!

Or perhaps they do know. And are glad. Glad in this way: they are thankful that we can read their stories and (to borrow C. S. Lewis' famous phrase), say, "What? You too? I thought I was the only one." And they can smile from the page of Scripture and say, "Oh, no, friend. You are far from alone." Indeed, our flawed and frail friends of the Bible give us a profound hope. That hope is not built upon them, but upon the fact that the perfect God chose to use such profoundly imperfect people in his kingdom.

Among such people was a man whose life we will explore in this book, the man named Jacob.

There is much in Jacob's character, actions, and motives that I find extremely distasteful, which is exactly why I identify so closely with him. He is everything about myself that I wish I were not. Even in utero, he is looking out for #1. He takes full advantage of the disadvantages of others. He tells lies. He plays favorites. He fights with God. For all these reasons and more, Jacob is the model disciple. The model disciple in that there is no effort to clean him up and make him look more presentable to the world so as not to embarrass God for having chosen such a deceitful man to be not only his follower but the very man after whom the Old Testament community of believers was named: Israel.

Jacob's crimes and punishments are paraded in public, as is the Lord's stubborn and gracious commitment to him.

Jacob's story is the story of a God who doesn't select the sainted or pick the pious, but who regularly pans for gold in the sewers of this world. And, even there, he doesn't find gold but plain old stink-covered rocks that he washes, polishes, and gilds with grace.

Such is Jacob.

Such am I.

And such are you.

I have entitled this book, *Limping with God* instead of *Walking with God* or *Running with God*, not because there would be anything wrong with those metaphors, but because, as Jacob limped away from his famous wrestling match with God, so we all get by on bum hips and bad knees. Following Jesus, we gimp our way down the dark and slippery paths of life. As we do, we discover, ironically, that the longer we follow him, the weaker we become, and the more we lean on our Lord. Finally, at our most mature, our eyes are opened to realize that we've never run or walked or even limped a single day of our lives.

We've been on Christ's shoulders the entire time.

Part 1

The Early Years:
The Brothers Hairy and Heel

CHAPTER 1

Dear God, Any Day Now...

And Isaac prayed to the LORD for his wife, because she was barren.

Genesis 25:21

If there is any other certainty in life besides the proverbial "death and taxes," it is this: God will not do something when you want him to do it. He may do it earlier. He may do it later. But if you ask the Lord to do something at 7:00 on Wednesday night on March 14, don't be shocked when he shows up a week before or six months later, with neither his hat in his hand nor even a flimsy excuse. "Whatever the LORD pleases, he does" (Ps. 135:6). That's about as true as true can be. However, if God has a predilection, it is to be perpetually late. And not just a wee bit tardy, but ridiculously, almost laughably late. Just ask Sarah or her daughter-in-law, Rebekah.

Sarah held a full promise in her hand and an empty womb in her belly. As distressing as it is today for women who desire to bear children, but cannot, it must have been all the more painful for Sarah because, when she was sixty-five years old, God had promised her a child. Then he forgot about her for the next twenty-five years. Or so it seemed.

Earlier in life, she had turned twenty. No children. But there was plenty of time, right? Then thirty came and went. Still no children. She subsequently blew out forty, fifty, and finally sixty-four candles on her birthday cakes and, needless to say, by then she knew she would never be called Momma. Women joining the Mesopotamian equivalent of the AARP society don't shop for maternity dresses. Then, unasked and unsought, the Lord showed up on her doorstep one day to say, "You and Abraham will have a baby." Then he left, without explanation, without a timetable, with Sarah staring down at her wrinkled hands, a smile playing at the corners of her lips. Did she dare hope?

So, she and old Abe waited. What else could they do? They traveled from Haran to Canaan; from Canaan to Egypt; from Egypt back to Canaan. No baby. At one point, they grew tired of the Lord dragging his feet, so finding a loophole in the cultural law of that day, Abraham and the maidservant Hagar went into the baby-making business together. After that scheme totally blew up in their face, they hunkered down to wait. And wait they did. When God finally did pay them a visit to reaffirm his commitment to give them a son, and to actually set a date this time, old Sarah thought the whole affair so silly that she laughed aloud.

A year later, as everyone around them giggled, they named their son Yitzchaq, the Hebrew word for Laughter. We call him Isaac.

Fast-forward forty years. Baby Laughter is now a grown man, wed to Rebekah. As fathers are wont to do, around the campfire at night, I'm sure father Abraham had bored young Isaac to tears with the same old worn out stories—a favorite of which would surely have been that quarter-century of waiting for God to make good on his promise. "Yeah, yeah, Dad, I know. If you've told me once, you've told me a hundred times," Isaac probably thought to himself. Little did this promised son know at the time, however, that his pre-history was about to be replicated in his personal history.

Isaac loved Rebekah, we are told, and he certainly made love to her as well, as newlyweds are wont to do. But Mr. and Mrs. Isaac would have no honeymoon baby, nine months later. In fact, five years would pass, then ten, then fifteen, and still the crib would remain painfully empty, a vacant reminder of what might have been. Isaac, the man named Laughter, was yet to hear the infectious giggle of a little baby, cradled in his arms.

As God had forced Abraham and Sarah to wait, so he did with Isaac and Rebekah. And the Lord was just getting warmed up. As we will see later in the story of Jacob, this patriarch had to wait two decades in exile before packing up to head home. Exodus will tell us that Jacob's descendants, the people of Israel, languished for generations as slaves under Pharaoh before the Lord finally sent Moses to lead them into liberation. And we haven't even touched on the fact that untold centuries crawled by before the Seed promised in Genesis 3:15 was finally growing inside Mary's virgin womb.

Is it little wonder that, in the psalms, one of the most common questions to erupt from the lips of Israelites is, "How long, O Lord?"

For a few years, in my mid-30's, I felt the jagged edge of that prayer. My evenings were spent sitting on the back porch of a small rock house in Pampa, Texas. I was alone most of the time. My young son and daughter lived a few miles away with their mom and stepdad. My job as a truckdriver in the oil and gas fields kept a roof over my head and groceries in the fridge but did nothing to feed my starving hopes for a better future. The occasional girlfriend helped to pass the time and provided me with some female companionship, but, when I was brutally honest with myself, I knew these women were distractions to keep me from dwelling on what I had squandered and trashed: my relationship, my union, my connection to God. He seemed as remote from me as water from a desert, snow from a fire. There were nights, on that back porch, when I would look up at the stars and, from the rubble of my ruined soul, manage to choke out that ancient Israelite prayer, "How long, O Lord? How long?"

As it turns out, being a disciple of Jesus entails asking that question quite often. We follow a God who doesn't wear a watch or carry a smartphone. For him, punctuality is not a virtue. To tell you the truth, he often lets situations unravel and become a tangled mess before taking the time to act.

Two occasions in the life of Jesus illustrate this quite graphically. Once, while he and his disciples were crossing the Sea of Galilee, one of the severe storms that often bedevil that body of water fell upon the darkening sea. Winds howling. The vessel swamped as wave after wave vomited water over the side. No novice fishermen, these hearty men, gritting their teeth and straining their muscles, were giving it all they had just to stay alive.

And Jesus? Where was he when all this is going down? He was "in the stern, asleep on the cushion" (Mark 4:38). In my opinion, this is one of the most unforgettable images in the Gospels. In the vortex of panic and mayhem, about to be swallowed by the raging mouth of the sea, Jesus is just over there catching some z's. Only when his panicked disciples shake him awake, crying out, "Teacher, do you not care that we are perishing?" does he say, "Peace! Be still!" and the storm ceases its raging (4:39). You see what's happening? The Lord waits until external circumstances convince his disciples that he doesn't care before he shows them that he cared about them all along. He waits until their only hope was him before he showed them that their only hope had been him all along.

The other occasion is when Lazarus, a dear friend of Jesus, fell ill. Notice the startling disjunction of these two sentences: "Now Jesus loved Martha and her sister and Lazarus. So, when he heard that Lazarus was ill, he stayed two days longer in the place where he was" (John 11:5-6). Make sure you don't miss this: Because Jesus loved Lazarus, when he heard he was sick, he purposefully delayed coming to see him. Is that right? Yes. That is exactly what he did. And to really complicate matters, during Jesus' willful delay, Lazarus succumbed to the illness and his life slipped away. If Jesus had hightailed it to his friend's hometown of Bethany, would Lazarus have improved? Oh, yes, without a doubt. But Christ waited two more days precisely in order to make sure his friend was good and dead before he came to see him. Indeed, by the time Jesus rolls into town, Lazarus has been (presumably) decaying in the tomb for four days (11:17). Only as the story unfolds do we realize why Christ twiddled his thumbs. *His lack of punctuality was to prove the fullness of his power.* He appears on the home turf of death itself, in the graveyard, to speak resurrection power into the corpse of his friend. As Lazarus comes stumbling out of the tomb, his face and body still wrapped in burial cloths, he walks out as a witness to the God who works by no timetable save his own (11:44).

Isaac and Rebekah would discover this same truth. We read that "Isaac prayed to the LORD for his wife, because she was barren. And the LORD granted his prayer, and Rebekah his wife conceived" (Gen. 25:21). Only later, after the pregnancy is over, do we learn that "Isaac was sixty years old" when Rebekah gave birth (25:26). A husband at forty and now finally a father at sixty, Isaac was forced to wait twenty long years for God to act. Don't imagine, by the way, that the phrase "Isaac prayed" refers to a one-time petition, as if this man let nineteen years pass before he suddenly got the bright idea of asking God to intervene. If he's like most of us who struggle with the

Lord's turtle-paced timetable, Isaac poured out his soul before the Lord many a year, only to hear the deafening roar of silence.

"How long, O Lord? How long?" For Isaac and Rebekah, it was two decades. For me, it was about five more years of darkness and doldrums before I began to feel alive again. For Mary, Martha, and Lazarus, it was a few days. For the water-logged disciples on that storm-tossed sea, it was a brief time of struggle and terror. Each of us, in our own way, learned through that period of waiting that our only hope is God. Very often what he is doing is stripping away those things upon which we rely—especially our sense of control—so that we might learn the painful lesson of being grossly inadequate for this thing called life. Read a hundred libraries worth of self-help books. Train for triathlons and learn breathing techniques. Listen to the right life coaches and eat kale every day. Whatever you wish. All it takes is a lump in the breast, a drunk teen behind the wheel, or a short in the wires of your attic, to bring your little ideal world crashing down all around you. Life is that ridiculously fragile.

But our God is not. And he spends most of our lives showing us that. He is strong. He is powerful. And, most importantly, he is merciful. In fact, he gets a thrill out of demonstrating his power precisely in showing mercy. During those hard years of waiting, he is not absent but fully present in his grace. While we cry out, "How long, O Lord? How long?" he is answering us in his own way, filling us with this Spirit of hope, conforming us to the image of his Son, and holding us in his paternal arms until he is ready to say, "Now, my child. Now it's time."

DISCUSSION QUESTIONS

1. Read Genesis 12:1-4 and Hebrew 11:8-12. What was God calling Abram and Sarai to give up or leave behind? Hebrews 11 focuses upon what this couple did "by faith"—but specifically faith in what? Is faith just a leap in the dark or something else?
2. Read Genesis 16. Why did Abram and Sarai come up with this plan involving Hagar? What does it tell us about their faith? How does this story exemplify God's promise to cause everything to work together for his good (Rom. 8:28)?

3. Talk about the two stories from the Gospels discussed in this chapter: the stilling of the storm and the raising of Lazarus (Mark 4:35-41; John 11:1-44). What do these accounts tell us about the different understandings of time from the perspective of God and us? Why does the Lord frequently wait so long to answer our prayers? Provide other examples from Scripture, or your own life, where waiting for the Lord to act was extremely difficult.

4. Reflect on the stories of the barren women in the Bible, not just Sarah and Rebekah, but Hannah (1 Samuel 1) and Elizabeth (Luke 1:1-25) as well. In all these stories, everything hinges on God acting unexpectedly to provide a child, even when all hope seems lost. How does this intersect with the story of the conception and birth of Jesus? How is Mary similar and dissimilar to these other women?

5. What is the relationship between waiting and prayer? Does praying help us to wait? Yes or no, and why?

CHAPTER 2

Womb Wrestling

The children struggled together within her.

Genesis 25:22

Most mothers begin to feel the first flutters of movement inside their womb when their baby is 17-20 weeks old. This is called "quickening." Over time, as the child grows, these movements will increase and intensify. Later in the pregnancy, the father too will be able to feel the kicks and thrusts as he puts his hand on his wife's belly. I fondly recall doing this while awaiting the birth of my daughter and, later, my son. It's an amazing and marvelous experience.

Judging by the description of the pregnancy of Rebekah, however, she would not have described her sensations as either amazing or marvelous. The expected quickening accelerated into something resembling an all-out MMA fight inside her womb. The Hebrew verb translated here as "struggled together" is *ratzatz*. It is used when a woman "crushed" the head of Abimelech with a millstone she tossed off a tower (Judg. 9:53). Five times, it is paired with the verb *ashaq*, which means "oppress" (e.g., Deut. 28:33). Amos uses *ratzatz* to depict how the well-off "crush the needy" (4:1). In his translation, Robert Alter renders it, "the children clashed together within her."[1]

---

[1] I will frequently refer to or quote from the translation by Robert Alter, *The Hebrew Bible: A Translation with Commentary*, Three-Volume Set (New York: W. W. Norton, 2019), which will hereafter be referenced as "R. Alter."

I suppose unborn babies can't brawl, but something like that was happening inside this mother. The twin brothers clashed.

Keep in mind, however, that at this point, Rebekah didn't even know she was pregnant with twins. All she knew was that something was not right. When we translate her exclamation literally, her voice seems suddenly to break off halfway through the sentence (perhaps from a sharp kick inside her!), "If this is so, then why am I…." (Gen. 25:22).

As Isaac had prayed that Rebekah would become pregnant, so now Rebekah does some fervent praying of her own. She "went to inquire of the LORD" (25:22). To "inquire," *darash* in Hebrew, conveys the idea of "seeking out" or "looking for," especially during times of uncertainty. Rebekah is looking for answers. "Why is this happening to me? Is my baby okay? Dear God, tell me what's going on!" Rebekah does get her answer, but I'd bet the farm that it's not anything close to the response that she expected:

> And the LORD said to her,
> "Two nations are in your womb,
> and two peoples from within you shall be divided;
> the one shall be stronger than the other,
> the older shall serve the younger."
> (Gen. 25:23)

The first surprise, of course, is that her painful pregnancy is not caused by one rambunctious infant but two children. She's having twins! Not pausing a moment to let her recover from that shock, God goes on to say that these two babies will be much more than two individuals who grow up, settle down, marry, raise a family, and eventually fade from the world's memory. No, they are "two nations" or "two peoples." Each already embodies a national future. They will be the fathers of two different groups of people who, at some point, will "be divided [*parad*]." This verb, *parad*, was used earlier in Genesis to describe how Lot had "separated" from Abraham (13:11, 14). So, too, these twin brothers, like that uncle and nephew, will one day go their separate ways.

The real bombshell God saves for the last line: "the older shall serve the younger." The Hebrew is slightly more ambiguous than most translations suggest. The line could be rendered, "The older shall serve the younger" or "the older, the younger shall serve." Either is a possible translation. Since we are privileged to know the rest of the story, we realize "the older shall serve the younger" is the correct understanding, but did Rebekah realize this at the time? Did her future preference for the younger son influence her interpretation of the oracle? Or did the oracle influence her preference from the beginning? All we can say is that there is a built-in uncertainty in the narrative.

This episode may be brief—a mere two verses (Gen. 25:22-23)—but we could spend the next two years ruminating on the subtleties that the Spirit is teaching us in these words. And these subtleties are not some head-in-the-clouds, esoteric theology but down-to-earth, practical truths that directly affect how we understand both ourselves and the ways that God is active in our lives as his disciples. Let's concentrate on only two matters.

The first and most obvious is this: *the big things of God begin in such little places that it seems foolhardy to believe that anything will come of them.* The Lord's prophetic words to Rebekah entail the birth of nations, the upending of traditional arrangements, and the future clash of once-fraternal empires. All that seems way overblown when you consider he's talking about a couple of unborn babies the size of small bananas. God's words seem more than a little over-the-top. We can't build millennia-worth of upcoming history on two kids who weigh a few ounces each. True, we cannot. But God? He can. When he begins something big, he starts small.

The grain of sand between the Father's fingers will one day become a mountain.

Isn't that the foundational confession we make concerning the Lord we follow? Once, long ago, in Mary's womb, God was so small you would have needed a microscope to see him. The Creator became a two-celled human zygote who drifted down the fallopian tube of a virgin and eventually made his home insider her uterus. He was born like every infant: so utterly helpless that, left on his own, he would have died within hours. Later, even at his pinnacle of fame, less than 1% of the world's population had heard of Jesus of Nazareth. Then he was publicly executed in that quintessentially gruesome way of the Romans. And it was all over. Or, so it seemed.

God had big plans for Jacob. The Father certainly had big plans for Jesus. Both had their respective prophecies. But in the beginning, and even later in their lives, both seemed to be utter failures. Jacob had to flee into exile, penniless. Jesus was crucified as an enemy of the state. Judged by outer appearances, apart from God's word, it seemed nothing would come of them.

And that is exactly why, as disciples, we live by every word that proceeds from the mouth of God, not every sight that promenades before our eyes. What God says, not what we see—that is how we live and move and have our hope. We might see a grain of sand; the Lord sees a mountain in the making.

The second point is this: God's choosing is not based on our moral, intellectual, or spiritual credentials. The Lord did not wait until these boys were thirteen or twenty-one years old, have angels compile a dossier of their vices and virtues, interview them to ascertain their suitability to his cause, and then, based on all those criteria, select the morally and spiritually superior son to be the head of the chosen nation. Paul will later note that God's choice happened "though [the twins] were not yet born and had done nothing either good or bad" (Rom. 9:11). As we will see, the "good or bad" would come in time, but was all much later. Jacob, in fact, grows up to be an egotistical, self-serving, conniving, and deceitful jerk. He's hardly a paragon either of virtue or humility. In many ways, Esau, despite his notable faults, comes across in the big picture of the narrative to be a much more stable, forgiving, and likable character.

Yet it is Jacob whom God chooses. He picks one of questionable character, moral inferiority, and the father of a family that would be Norman Rockwell's nightmare come true. What does that tell us? It tells us that God, through his word and because of his mercy, calls people to himself regardless of their moral resume. As Jesus tells his disciples, "You did not choose me, but I chose you" (John 15:16). He chose rural fishermen. He chose a despised tax-collector. He chose a fiery zealot. And he chose one who would eventually betray him with a kiss. And he chose you.

You might be saying to yourself, "Yes, but...

...I have a felony on my record

...I have ruined marriages

...I am full of self-hatred

...I have screwed up everything in my life

...I have betrayed those closest to me

…I am filthy with shame on the inside

…I am not worthy that God should give me even a second's worth of thought."

To all that, God says, "I forgive you. I love you. My heart is yours. There is no condemnation for those who are in Christ Jesus. But there is a whole eternity worth of peace and love and hope."

Do you think the Lord was unaware of the scoundrel that Jacob would often be? Of course he knew. But Jacob's good or bad deeds had zero to do with God's choice of him for his future plan. The Lord is accustomed to working with sinners. That's the only material he has.

So, you're a sinner? Welcome to humanity. And welcome to the forgiven family of God in Jesus Christ, full of limping disciples.

DISCUSSION QUESTIONS

1. Read Genesis 25:21-23. Judging by the rough nature of the movements with her, what would have been going through Rebekah's mind? Her confusion and fears drove her to inquire of God. How does the Lord still work that way today (Ps. 18:6; James 5:13; Luke 18:1-8)?

2. God's response to Rebekah is brief but packed with promise and prophecy. List all the particulars in Gen. 25:23. How is this story similar or dissimilar to other biblical narratives about the Lord's promises regarding children still in utero or newly born? See Judges 13:1-5; Jeremiah 1:4-10; Luke 1:11-17; Luke 1:26-38.

3. Discuss how the big things of God begin in little places. What are some examples from the Bible or from your own life? What does this teach us about the Lord's ways? How does it call forth faith from us?

4. Talk about how God's choosing is not based on our moral, intellectual, or spiritual credentials. How is this fundamentally contrary to the way the world works? How does Paul use this story in Romans 9:6-13?

5. Describe how certain actions or sins make us feel "undesirable" to God, or one whom the Lord would not want. How does our Savior respond to such feelings?

CHAPTER 3

The Brothers Hairy and Heel

> His brother came out with his hand holding Esau's heel, so his name was called Jacob.
>
> Genesis 25:26

Most parents today have picked out a name for their son or daughter well before the child is welcomed into the world. It's not unusual, in fact, for names to be chosen before there is even a pregnancy—or a marriage, for that matter. For example, for as long as I can remember, even as a boy, I liked the name Luke. So I decided that, once I grew up and got married, should God give me a son, that is the name I would give him. And so I did. As of this writing, my son Luke is twenty years old. Recently, while we were on a hike in the Texas hill country, he told me that, should he too have a son, he already had a name picked out for him. So, it appears this tendency of early name-choosing runs in the Bird family.

It must not, however, have run in the family of Isaac and Rebekah. Judging by how the events unfolded, like other biblical couples, they chose names based upon events surrounding the birth of the boys. Given that the names they chose mean "Hairy" and "Heel," perhaps a little more forethought would have served them well! Or perhaps their father, Isaac, whose own name means "laughter," was just a guy with a healthy sense of humor. Here's the story:

> When [Rebekah's] days to give birth were completed, behold, there were twins in her womb. The first came out red, all his body like a hairy

cloak, so they called his name Esau. Afterward his brother came out
with his hand holding Esau's heel, so his name was called Jacob. Isaac
was sixty years old when she bore them. (Gen. 25:24-26)

First, there was Esau, who sounds like a top contender for ugliest
baby of the year. The word "red," *admoni*, can refer to red hair or a
ruddy complexion (David is the only other biblical figure described
in this way [1 Sam. 16:12]). In Esau's case, *admoni* must refer to his
hair. Being a ginger is fine, of course, but this kid had so much body
hair, he resembled a baby ginger bear. The name itself is bit of a
linguistic conundrum. Esau sounds very little like the Hebrew word
for hair (*se'ar*), though that will become the source of the name, Seir,
which will be Esau's eventual homeland. However, some connection
between shagginess and the name, Esau, seems to be assumed.

With the name of the second brother, however, we are on much
more solid ground—though even here, the subtleties of language are
at play. This boy is born "holding Esau's heel ['*aqev*]," so, riffing off
that unflattering part of the anatomy, his mom and dad christened
him *Ya'aqov* ("Jacob").[1] Something else is going on as well. Forms
of the name Jacob or Jacob-El are attested multiple times in other
ancient languages, besides Hebrew, all formed from the verb meaning
"protect." In these cases, the name means something like "may El
[God] protect him" or "God has protected him."

That being said, in the Bible, the former meaning connected
with "heel" dominates—and not in a positive way. The Hebrew verb,
'aqav, formed from the same root, carries the connotation of grabbing
someone by the heels so as to trip them up, hinder them, or betray
them. As we will see later, this is the angry pun that Esau uses when
he says, "Is he not rightly named Jacob [*Ya'aqov*]? For he has cheated
[*'aqav*] me these two times" (27:36). In other words, Jacob lived *down*
to his name.

But let's not get too far ahead of ourselves. Let's focus on what
is happening while Rebekah is in the throes of labor. The time has

---

[1] If you've wondered why the English spellings of biblical names so often
look very different from their original Hebrew counterparts, it's because our
English spellings are mainly influenced by the Greek and especially the Latin
spellings of the biblical names, not the Hebrew.

finally arrived. There is our tiny friend, Hairy, the primogeniture, making his grand entrance into the world. His head. His shoulders. His body. And just as he's almost all the way out of his mom, behold, the hand! Five little digits grasp, seize, hang on for dear life to the heel of his brother. What is he doing? It seems he's trying to pull his sibling back in. He wants to get ahead of him, to shift from beta into alpha position.

You might say, "Oh, come on, he's just an infant; he isn't thinking rationally or making conscious decisions." Of course, this is true. But here is something even truer: Jacob's birthday grasping is prophetic of his biography. In the very birth of these boys, the first flexing of the muscles of ambition has begun.

Ambition. There was a significant portion of my life, from around the age of sixteen to thirty-five, when one of the highest compliments I could receive was being labeled "ambitious." I would wear that adjective like a badge of honor. "You bet, I'm ambitious," I would say to myself as I surveyed the future landscape of my carefully orchestrated plans to rise up the ranks, achieve my dreams, and outdo all my brothers in the faith. I didn't smoke. I drank on occasion. But I became heavily addicted to an age-old drug: the opiate of ambition. And I snorted, smoked, and shot up that narcissistic narcotic day and night. What I wouldn't give to get ahead. What I wouldn't sacrifice to climb the ladder rungs of success. I was a man on a mission; and the ambitious mission was a self-absorbed self-advancement to self-glorification.

If someone were to call me ambitious today—it's happened once in the last ten years—it would feel like a slap in the face. The last time it happened, the word felt repellant, like someone had just insulted me to the core. It was unintended, of course, for it was meant as a compliment, but it had the opposite effect: it stung. Why? Because, through a long and dark series of catastrophic events, I came to realize that ambition had been the fuel of hell that powered my life into a head-on, flaming explosion of personal destruction.

An "ambitious disciple of Jesus" is as much an oxymoron as "a holy follower of Satan." Ambition is not the drive to do one's best to help others. It is the drive to do whatever it takes for me, me, me. It is the engine of egotism. It harnesses some good qualities in humanity—virtues such as hard work, commitment, and drive—and perverts them all into the vicious service of self. Ambition does not grab hold of the hands of others to pull them up. No, ambition grabs hold of the heels of brothers, friends, strangers, and enemies, to pull them back. All to get ahead. That's what matters. That's *all* that matters. Onward and upward to the glory of self.

Paul, in biting irony, tells the disciples in Thessalonica, "Make it your ambition to lead a quiet life" (1 Thess. 4:11). The apostle is saying, "Oh, so you want to be ambitious? Well, then, make it your ambition to be unambitious!" Or, as our Rabbi himself put it, "If anyone would be first, he must be last of all and servant of all" (Mark 9:35). "Blessed are the meek," Jesus says, alluding to Psalm 37:11, where we read that "the meek shall inherit the land and delight themselves in abundant peace." The "meek" in Hebrew is one who is *anav*: humble, lowly, unpretentious, one who patiently endures suffering. The "ambition" of the meek, the *anav*, is to serve in quietness and in the fear of the Lord.

But Jacob, he was ambitious. I was ambitious. And that demon, always skulking in the shadows of success, stares with glowing eyes at my weary soul still today. I hate it. And I kick at it every chance I get. But because it is so akin to pride, ambition will continue haunt me, as it haunts many others.

Isn't that the way sin works? We may hate a particular evil or vice. It may once have destroyed our lives. We may know its inner workings, its seductive traps, its deadly fruits, but that does not mean it goes away. I have known alcoholics, for instance, who stayed on the wagon for decades, only to fall off one day and shatter their lives once again. Did they not know what would happen? Of course, they knew. But such is the blinding power of evil.

We will see what dark times await Jacob, that ambitious young man. One truth, however, that will emerge repeatedly in his life—as it emerges over and over in our own—is this: were it not for the grace and mercy of the Lord, he would have ruined everything beyond the possibility of redemption. Were it up to Jacob to fix things, all would have remained broken.

But he, and we, worship a God who knows how to deal, both in severity and in kindness, with stupid sinners like ourselves. He breaks us. He breaks us down. Sometimes, if need be, he crushes us. And, dear God, that hurts. We are undone. But that is only the beginning.

Our Father is far more than a heavenly hammer for whom everything on earth looks like a nail. He breaks down and builds up. He shatters and shapes. He crucifies and resurrects.

Isn't it amazing to think that, while on the cross, dying for evil, dying for ambition, dying for all the sins of humanity, the humble Lord of love lifted up his heel and brought it down on the head of the serpent? In a splendid irony, the Father gave us a heel, a "Jacob," to whom we can hold fast as we emerge from death to life again in him.

DISCUSSION QUESTIONS

1. Read Genesis 25:24-26. As you reflect on the names that Isaac and Rebekah chose for their newborn twins, think also of the importance of names. Names are not just random words but usually carry some meaning or significance. Why is that? Discuss the intimate connection between people and their names.

2. Up until modern times, ambition was understood to be a vice not a virtue. How has that changed and what has changed? What is the significance of the fact that, today, looking out for yourself, focusing on yourself, pursuing success at all costs, is considered healthy?

3. Discuss 1 Thessalonians 4:9-12. What are the practical, real-life implications of these verses?

4. What does it mean that God breaks us down and builds us up, shatters and shapes, crucifies and resurrects? For biblical examples, look at how the Lord dealt with Nebuchadnezzar in Daniel 4 or the prodigal son in Luke 15:11-24.

CHAPTER 4
With Brothers Like That, Who Needs Enemies?

Jacob said, "Sell me your birthright now."

Genesis 25:31

In his short essay, "The Sermon and the Lunch," C. S. Lewis states this unwelcome truth: "charity begins at home; so does uncharity."[1] He illustrates this by recalling one particular Sunday, when, not five minutes into the preacher's sermon, everyone in the congregation had turned a deaf ear to the pulpit. Why? Because in his message about family life, the pastor was painting a flowery portrait of our homes as that place where we can retreat from the world, be ourselves, be renewed, be at peace.

Here's the thing: every person in the pew knew he was lying. They knew this not necessarily because this particular preacher's home life wasn't rosy (it wasn't; Lewis had seen its ugliness firsthand), but because they all knew their own family lives were anything but bliss. As Lewis says, if we want to redeem hearth and home, if we want to make it a place of blessing, then the first step is "to stop telling lies about home life."[2] Sure, domestic life can often be a welcome castle in our cruel and cutthroat world, but it's just as often a dark dungeon full of rattling chains of resentment, passive-aggressive poisons, and uncharitable favoritism.

---

[1] *God in the Dock* (San Francisco: HarperOne, 2014), 284.

[2] "The Sermon and the Lunch," 284.

The Bible offers us no shortage of stories to illustrate this point. And few are more illustrious than Jacob's family saga.

Up to this point, all has seemed relatively healthy in the household of Isaac and Rebekah. But, now, as we leap forward from the twin's birth to their adult years, the family fabric begins to tear. Here is the first thing we're told: "When the boys grew up, Esau was a skillful hunter, a man of the field, while Jacob was a quiet man, dwelling in tents. Isaac loved Esau because he ate of his game, but Rebekah loved Jacob" (Gen. 25:27-28). Esau is thus the rugged outdoorsman, a Hebrew Daniel Boone, keeping the family well-stocked with venison. Isaac loved this older son "because he ate of [Esau's] game." The Hebrew is literally, "because of the game in his mouth," which is an unflattering, almost bestial, portrait of Isaac. His stomach steered the direction of his heart.

What about Jacob? He was "dwelling in tents," which implies his vocation was shepherding (see Gen. 4:20, where the same Hebrew expression occurs). The Hebrew for "quiet man" is *ish tam*, the same phrase used twice to describe Job as an "upright man" (1:8; 2:3). Since Jacob is being contrasted with Esau, it might here carry the connotation of "civilized." Either way, Rebekah doted on her younger son. Why? Perhaps because of the oracle during her pregnancy. We don't know. What we do know is that this preferential parenting is a foreshadowing of the dramatic events of Genesis 27—not to mention Jacob's own preferential parenting of his son, Joseph, in Genesis 37:3, which will also lead to a fracture in the family. This is a vivid example of the sins of the fathers (and mothers) passed down to the next generation.

The next scene is perhaps the most well-known of Jacob's life. Indeed, it's become proverbial. If a person has backward priorities, so that he gives away something of immense value for an inconsequential pleasure or trifle, we say something like, "He sold it for a mess of pottage." The reference, of course, is to the "bowl of lentil stew" that Esau acquired by selling his birthright to Jacob (Gen. 25:29-34). The story is a bit more complicated that the standard moralizing of it suggests, so let's think about it for a moment, looking not only at Esau but Jacob.

First, Esau. Clearly, he made a rash and idiotic decision. If he were truly "about to die" from hunger, as he claims with all the fanfare of a drama queen, then scarfing down one bowl of soup and some bread is not going to give him the wherewithal to hop up and be on his merry way after the meal (25:34). Secondly, the whole scene (especially in the Hebrew) makes Esau appear as uncouth as a dog, almost unable to speak coherently. Literally, he says, "Let me gulp down this the red, the red," (25:30 [my translation]). The verb for "gulp down" (*la'at*) implies not human eating but animal eating (like *essen* vs. *fressen* in German). And he does not even say the word for "stew" or "soup" but only points out the color ("this the red, the red"). It is no shock, then, when the narrator passes his harsh judgment on the eldest son, "Thus Esau despised his birthright" (25:34). Yes, he most certainly did.

And Jacob? If Esau treated his birthright with contempt, then Jacob treated his older brother with equal if not greater contempt. Esau comes across as a dumb ox and Jacob as an ice-cold lawyer. He immediately sizes up the situation and goes for the jugular with legal precision, even saving "me" for the last word in the sentence, "Sell first your birthright to me" (25:31).[3] No, "Hey, brother, you look famished; here, eat a bowl of soup. Rest and eat up." There is no fraternity, no compassion, no hesitancy to treat a fellow human being with mercy. One commentator puts it: "Esau capitulates and Jacob capitalizes."[4] All that matters to Jacob is Jacob. This may not be the same as price-gouging after a hurricane, but it is equally despicable. And, in this case, successful. Now that he has the birthright, all he needs is the father's blessing.

There is a high likelihood that the person in the world who has hurt you the most, or will hurt the most, is a member of your own family. That's a hard pill to swallow, but unavoidably true. Parents abuse children—sexually, emotionally, psychologically. Children cut elderly parents out of their lives. Spouses cheat on each other and weaponize their sons and daughters against their respective ex's. The first two family stories in the Bible bear this out: Adam points his accusing finger at Eve when God confronts him (Gen. 3:12). And in a brother-versus-brother narrative strongly reminiscent of Jacob and

---

[3] My translation. The ESV renders it, "Sell me your birthright now."

[4] Victor Hamilton, *The Book of Genesis: Chapters 18-50*, NICOT (Grand Rapids, MI: Eerdmans, 1995), 186.

Esau, Cain will lure Abel into the field and begin the cycle of murder that has polluted the earth with blood to this day (4:8).

At one point in my life, I owned a home near the corner of Hatfield and McCoy Streets in the Texas town of Amarillo. I remember laughing at the names when I moved there, thinking how ironic it was that my own happy family lived near roads named after that old and infamous family feud. Later, when the divorce was impending and I was moving out, choked with bitterness and resentment and rage, those two names felt a little too close to home to strike me as comical anymore. The feud they represented was fitting, but in a sick and satanic sort of way. In biblical fashion, the one who had hurt me the most, struck the deepest blow I've ever received, had been a member of my own family.

And so, I began the long and painful process that all of you have been through, are going through, or will go through at some point: forgiving those who have sinned against us. There are times when uttering those three words, "I forgive you," can seem fairly easy, when the offense against us is slight and shallow. At other times saying "I forgive you" feels like we're being eviscerated, like some monster deep and ancient is being ripped from the cavity of our soul. It feels like we're going to die.

That is not surprising. It is, in fact, entirely predictable, because to forgive people means that we must die. There is no other way. And that is also, of course, why we don't want to forgive. To forgive is to die to the people we would become, and often do become, when we breed bitterness, conceive resentment, and nurse the desire for a pound or three of flesh from those who have hurt us. It consumes us. It eats at us like a cancer from within. To forgive is to kill the ungod within us for whom absolution is anathema and redemption reprehensible.

You may have noticed that, in the prayer that Jesus taught us to pray, there is only one line in the whole prayer that entails an action on our part. Our Father keeps his name holy. He brings his kingdom. He forgives us, gives us daily bread, guards us in times of temptation and evil. He is the doer of all those verbs. The only part of the Lord's Prayer that involves us doing something is this: "as we forgive those who trespass against us." The reason for this is obvious: there is arguably no more fundamentally Christian act than forgiving others.

Forgiveness is not an admission of innocence on the part of the forgiver. Quite the opposite. We do not forgive the innocent but the guilty. The pronouncement of absolution is an implicit acknowledgment that the absolved has done something in need of forgiving. Had Esau, for instance, forgiven Jacob—and we will get to that eventually—he would not thereby have pretended his brother's avarice was excusable. Esau would not be saying, "Well, I guess I could see how my brother treating me like an enemy was understandable." No, he would be saying, "That evil you did, I forgive. Or, rather, God forgives you in and through me. I do not hold it against you because God does not hold it against you."

Absolution is the beating heart of discipleship because Christ, our forgiveness, is the beating heart of discipleship. Every day he richly and prodigally forgives us, lavishing love upon us, undeserving though we be. And we, having received, do not build a dam within our hearts to stop the flow of mercy, but let it pass from us to others. We forgive, as we have been forgiven.

Forgiveness begins at home, for that is the place, as Lewis reminded us, where both charity and uncharity begin. The corner of Hatfield and McCoy is not a place fit for human habitation, much less family peace. Replace it with avenues of mercy and grace. It will hurt. You will die to things you thought were keeping you alive. But you will discover, in the arms of the resurrected Jesus, a new life of freedom and a capacity for joy in this Brother who will never sell you out.

DISCUSSION QUESTIONS

1. Why is it in families that we so often experience uncharity and meanness? Discuss the reasons we often see both the best and the worst of humanity in those closest to us.

2. Read Genesis 25:27-34. Compare and contrast the type of men that Jacob and Esau grew up to be. What kinds of words come to mind when you picture each of them?

3. What were the motivations of both Esau and Jacob over the matter of the birthright? Give modern examples of how these same motivations and kinds of sins still occur. Which of the Ten Commandments address this?

4. Talk about why it is so painful and difficult for us to forgive others. Use the parable in Matthew 18:21-35 to discuss the forgiveness we have in Jesus and the forgiveness we pass on to others.

Chapter 5

Isaac and Elephants

> Isaac said, "Behold, I am old; I do not know the day of my death."
>
> Genesis 27:2

On some of my milestone birthdays, I engage in a father/son comparison. Using memory and imagination, I place myself side-by-side with my father, Carson, when he was my same age, whether thirty, forty, or fifty years old. Do we share similar features? Were his hair and beard streaked with gray then, as mine are at the half-century mark? I compare our interests, activities, work and family lives. I wonder if, during this season of life, he was thinking many of my same thoughts, perhaps grappling with many of my same fears and regrets.

This father/son comparison helps, in a retroactive sort of way, for me to see life through his eyes, even all these years later. I find that it also helps me to see my relationship with my own children with a fresh perspective. I think, "My Dad was probably thinking the same things about me, and worrying about the same things regarding me, as I do with my own son and daughter." Wordsworth wrote, "The Child is the father of the Man," which is true, but the father is very often the future image of the son as well.

I wonder if Isaac's mind ever drifted down this same stream. For instance, at the beginning of this momentous chapter, Isaac is at least one hundred years old, probably older. To us, of course, centenarians are way over the hill, but even in those ancient days of extensive lifespans, hundred-year-olds were no spring chickens. Isaac himself says it bluntly, "I am old" (Gen. 27:2). Yet, when Isaac's father, Abraham, was one hundred years old, he was bouncing baby Isaac on his knee (Gen. 21:5). Isaac is virtually blind at this point but his father, Abraham, appeared to be in relatively vigorous health. From the age of one hundred to one hundred seventy five, Abraham had to face the debacle with Hagar and Ishmael, dealt diplomatically with Abimelech and Phicol, nearly sacrificed Isaac, mourned the death of Sarah, arranged for the choosing of Isaac's wife, married a second time to Keturah, and fathered many more children with her and his concubines (Gen. 21:8-25:10). Isaac will end up with a lifespan five years longer than his father—he will die at one hundred eighty years old—but it appears he spent his last few decades in relative inactivity. Between the mention of his displeasure at Esau's choice of wives (Gen. 28:8) and his reunion with Jacob and subsequent death (35:27-29), not a single action of Isaac is recorded for posterity. Compared to his father, Abraham, and to his son, Jacob, the patriarch Isaac is the most normal, mundane, and (dare I say it?) boring of the patriarchs.

And yet, what an incredibly important player he is in God's long-range plan of salvation—a player who, in a divinely humorous sort of way, has little clue of what's going on half the time! Isaac, Mr. Laughter, is indeed a sort of God-given joke (in a non-pejorative sense). His birth to old parents was comedic, a source of good-natured laughter, as we have seen (Gen. 21:6). Later, he's completely oblivious to the fact that he's lugging up the mountain the very wood on which he is about to be sacrificed (Gen. 22:6). Parroting his father's earlier foolish actions, Isaac claims Rebekah is his sister (26:7), but gets caught publicly "caressing" (in flagrante delicto?) his supposed "sister" and so is found to be a liar (26:8).[1] There's some cringe-worthy humor for you. As we shall see in this chapter, Isaac acts like he might be at death's door but, wrong once again, his ticker keeps on ticking for several more decades. What's more, he gets deceived by

---

[1] There is a play on words in the Hebrew. The same root, *tzachaq*, forms both the name "Isaac" and the verb for "caressing" (NASB), "laughing" (ESV), or "sporting with" (KJV). Robert Alter translates it as "playing with." Isaac with "isaacing" his wife, which, whether sexual intercourse or mere foreplay, was sufficient evidence for Abimelech to realize Isaac and Rebekah were spouses not siblings.

his younger son when he leans too heavily upon his senses of smell and touch, when his sense of hearing told him, in no uncertain terms, this was not Esau but Jacob (27:22).

Poor Isaac. It's not that he's a fool. He's not unintelligent or unaware. Rather, he is simply an ordinary specimen of humanity, caught up in a story much bigger than himself, a story that he is incapable of fully understanding. He embodies our common foibles and flaws, the very imperfections through which God is busily and faithfully at work to bring about his will for all of us.

For that reason, I thank God for Isaac. Like that patriarch, our lives and perceptions can frequently be compared to that proverbial group of blind men, each of whom did not know what an elephant was or what it looked like, but who were asked to touch the animal and draw a conclusion based on their experience. You know the legend. The blind man who touched the trunk said the elephant was like a big snake. The one who touched his leg said the elephant was like a tree trunk. The one who touched his tail said he was like a rope. And the one who touched his side said that the elephant was like a wall. Each of the men were right and each of them were wrong. They were incapable of seeing the big picture, the total reality. Limited in knowledge, limited by sensory deprivation, limited by lack of experience, each of the men tried his best to grasp the complete truth, to get it right, but each one came up short.

Our lives often feel like we're shuffling around some immense and mysterious body, touching this, touching that, attempting to wrap our minds around what we experience, what we feel, so that we can finally say, "This is 'the elephant,'" as it were, "This is what life is all about!" When we're young, we get our hands on a career and think, "Ah, this will bring me fulfillment!" only later to realize we've just touched the "tail of the elephant." In our 30's and 40's, we get our hands on a big achievement, that trophy we thought would finally bring us fulfillment, only to realize later that we've just touched the "leg of the elephant." Somewhere along the way, we probably fall in love and think, "Yes, this person will complete me," then, as time goes on and the relationship is strained by life's burdens, it dawns on us that we have only grasped the "trunk of the elephant." Welcome to human life. We all go through this. So much of our existence is thinking, "This 'thing' is what life is all about," only to discover we're wrong.

Isaac was hampered by mortality, beset by weakness, easily deceived by his inability to see what was really going on. In that way, Isaac is our "patron saint." His life also is a beautiful reminder that the Lord's will for us—and our place in his grand plan of salvation—is unhampered by our weakness, confusion, and long list of stupid decisions. We are experts at getting things wrong and misaligning priorities. We look for fulfillment in all the wrong places. Like buffoons, we wave the elephant's tail and proclaim we've found "the answer" to humanity's quest. And our Father just shakes his head, walks over, grabs us by the shoulders, and guides us away from our error and into a broader understanding of his will for our lives.

As you follow Jesus, do not expect your personal weaknesses and unwelcome character traits to disappear. They will not. Do not expect to get everything right all the time. You will not. Do not expect, as a disciple, that life will be a little easier for you than for unbelievers. Most likely, it will be more difficult, for the world is an unwelcome place for citizens of the kingdom of God.

Here is what you can expect: the constant presence of Jesus in your ordinary, predictable, mostly mundane, often confused life. The life of discipleship is human life suffused with the unseen presence of Jesus, using you as his hands and feet and mouth to spread his love and truth among fellow sinners. Much of the time, if not most of the time, you will be utterly unaware that he is doing this. You'll think, "I am just doing my job," but that job will be Christ's workplace. You'll think, "I'm just taking care of my children," but that parenting will be the means by which Jesus raises your children to fear, love, and trust in him. You'll think, "I'm just offering a word of encouragement or extending forgiveness to someone who has wronged me," but those words of mercy and grace will be pregnant with the Spirit's power.

We will all fail along the way, sometimes catastrophically, often in ways that hurt many other people. We will do selfish, dumb things like Isaac lying about his wife. And, like him, we will get caught in our lies, our cheating, our backstabbing, our petty little crusades of revenge or malice. Usually what will happen is that dark forces of hell will slither into our heads and hearts to whisper, "God hates you now. You're a lost cause. You are beyond hope." But they lie, they always lie. Falsehood is the only language spoken in hell. Our Father will shut them down and shut them up. He loves you. He will draw you back to him. On this side of the grave, no human is a lost cause. And far from "beyond hope," we have hope in Jesus that is beyond measurement. In ways we will likely never realize, the Lord of redemption can create something good and beautiful out of the junkyard of our spoiled pasts.

To be a disciple of Jesus is not to have everything figured out, but often to feel like old, blind Isaac, doing what we can to pass on a blessings to others, blissfully unaware that the Lord is using us in ways we don't even realize to continue writing the story of his kingdom's spread in this world.

DISCUSSION QUESTIONS

1. How was Isaac's life very different from that of his father, Abraham? Do you compare where you are at this stage in life with where your parents were at the same age? Does this help to provide perspective?

2. What are some examples of Isaac being an ordinary specimen of humanity in which he embodies our common foibles and flaws? How is he just like we are today?

3. Give some examples of how we too are like the proverbial blind men who are asked to identity what the elephant is. How does our limited perspective actually free us as disciples of Christ? How does not having everything figured out leave room for divine work?

4. Discuss how Jesus uses us as his hands and feet and mouths to spread his love and truth among fellow sinners.

CHAPTER 6

The Maternal Plan of Deception

> Now Rebekah was listening when Isaac spoke to his son Esau.
>
> Genesis 27:5

We're told, "First impressions are everything," but you don't need much experience with humanity to know that's not true. Sure, first impressions are important, but we know virtually nothing about a person based on first impressions. We see what they want us to see. And what they want us to see is almost invariably their "best foot forward" side. First impressions are fraction impressions.

Rebekah is a parade example of this. What are our first impressions of her? She is very attractive, hospitable, and hardworking (Gen. 24:15-20). All good qualities, of course. This is how she is described when Abraham's servant met her on his quest to pick out a bride for Isaac. We are not told her age, but, given the cultural traditions of the time, she was probably in her teens. Isaac was forty years old when they married. Also, Rebekah was Isaac's second cousin. To moderns, of course, a forty-year-old wedding a teenager—and a relative at that!—is scandalous, but that's because we are, well, moderns. What bothers us, most people of most ages would find quite commonplace. We are, what one author calls, the W.E.I.R.D. ones.[1]

---

[1] Joseph Henrich, *The WEIRDest People in the World: How the West Became Psychologically Peculiar and Particularly Prosperous* (New York: Farrar,

As the narrative unfolds, Rebekah's personality fills out more and more. She marries Isaac and is a comfort to him (Gen. 24:67). After two decades of waiting, she finally conceives the twins who give her such a painful pregnancy that she consults God to find out what's wrong (25:21-23). Later, she and her husband both make the far-too-common parental mistake of favoring one child over another: Isaac loves Esau the hunter while Jacob is Rebekah's chosen son (25:28). Then, while she and her family are living in Gerar during a famine, she—willingly or begrudgingly—plays along with Isaac's ruse about her being his sister (26:1-11).

Finally, we learn that the two Hittite wives of Esau "made life bitter" for both Rebekah and her husband (26:25). Rebekah is so disgusted by these daughters-in-law that she will later say, "I loathe my life because of the Hittite women" (27:46). Esau's marriage is the last mentioned fact before the dramatic birthright scene of Genesis 27. This strongly suggests that Rebekah's antipathy to Esau's marital choices at least partially influenced her deceitful mission to cheat him out of his inheritance. As if to say, "No son of mine who isn't even smart enough to marry decent women should be the heir!"

Yes, our first impression of Rebekah is that she is "very attractive in appearance" (Gen. 24:16), but she, like all of us, has an ugly streak.

As the scene opens in Genesis 27, Isaac instructs Esau to grab his bow, bag some game, whip up his favorite dish, and bring him a plate so Isaac can bless him (27:1-4). Don't miss one small but significant detail in the following verses: "Now Rebekah was listening when Isaac spoke to *his son* Esau. So when Esau went to the field to hunt for game and bring it, Rebekah said to *her son* Jacob...." (27:5-6). Esau is "his son" while Jacob is "her son." What we learned in 25:28 regarding playing favorites has come into full flower.

Rebekah's devious plan of beatitude theft is basically this: the Esaufication of Jacob, that is, the transformation of the younger into the older. She is either a quick thinker or, having long anticipated this day, has premeditated everything. Because Esau is a hairy man but Jacob smooth-skinned, Rebekah makes gloves out of the skins of hairy goats and wraps goat skins, scarf-like, around

---

Straus and Giroux, 2020). W.E.I.R.D. is an acronym for Western, Educated, Industrialized, Rich, and Democratic.

his neck. Heel becomes Hairy. That would take care of the sense of touch.

Next, Rebekah picked out some outdoorsy clothing from Esau's closet and vested Jacob with these. That would take care of the sense of smell. She also threw on her apron and went to work in the kitchen, preparing Isaac's favorite meal of goat. That would take care of his sense of taste. (Although, one can't help but wonder if Isaac's sense of taste was all that keen. Would he not be able to tell the difference between goat meat and wild game?). Isaac was either altogether blind or, as the Hebrew suggests, "his eyes were too dim to see," so his sense of sight was a non-issue. Touch, smell, taste, and sight—all those sensory bases were covered. The only one of the five senses that Rebekah could not control was Isaac's hearing, which, as we shall see in the next chapter, almost derailed her whole plan.

Perhaps some will argue that Rebekah's plan of attack is entirely—or at least mostly—justified. During her pregnancy, God had told her that "the older shall serve the younger" (25:23). That prophesy must have prompted her preparations. She is "helping God out." As we noted in Chapter 2, however, the Hebrew of that phrase is ambiguous. It could be translated "the older shall serve the younger" or "the older, the younger shall serve." We wonder, too, did Rebekah ever tell Isaac about this word from God? One would think she did, but then again, if so, we are never informed.

We are left with this conclusion: we can't blame Isaac for going against God's word in planning to bless Esau, nor can we excuse Rebekah by claiming she was only out to do God's will. In fact, the narrative seems to suggest something much less theological and much more blandly, banally, predictably human: both parents were simply playing favorites. Both parents just wanted what they wanted. As our favorite "prayer" goes: *My* will be done." Isaac, for his part, at least had tradition on his side.

If I'm correct in my interpretation, this puts us in an uncomfortable quandary. We have a story of competing self-interests. We have a strong undercurrent of family division. We definitely have unscrupulous, purposefully deceptive actions planned by the mother and embraced by the son. It's all rather seedy and underhanded and back-alleyish. Nasty, selfish, and gross. Here we have all the makings of a future train wreck of biblical proportions.

And, here, smackdab in the middle of this mess—this mess, remember, which is God's holy and chosen people—we have the Lord driving up, stepping out, and surveying the scene to make sure that, whatever these silly humans do, his good and gracious will most certainly shall be done.

I once pastored a small congregation, in a small town, full of a few families with deep secrets, old resentments, and a few fresh wounds. By the time I had been there two years, I was privy to most of the sordid details of the prior fifty years. An author could have wrung a dozen novels out of the spats and feuds and adulteries and general mayhem that flowed through that little community. But I had grown up in a town just like it, so I knew it was not unique. Our little church, fat with sinners, was no different than any other church in that town, state, country, or world. Show me a church and I'll show you a hotbed of hypocrisy, self-interest, mini-political parties, the jockeying for power, the flexing of holiness, and all manner of unscrupulous activities. In other words, show me a church and I'll show you a truckload of sinners, pastored by a sinner himself, usually tottering on the brink of implosion.

And yet there, Sunday after Sunday, in the middle of that congregation of disciples, the Lord drives up, walks into the church, and gets to work doing what he does best: forgiving, cleansing, disciplining, helping, loving, and—through it all—making sure his good and gracious will is done.

There are Isaacs, Rebekahs, Jacobs, and Esaus in every church, along with a smattering of Ahabs and Jezebels. Sometimes, if you're fortunate, you'll get a Jonathon or Ruth or Barnabas as well. One thing you will never get in the church, however, is a non-sinner. Even the best of them will make a mess of their lives at times. Most of us become quite professional at performing poorly in the life of faith. Our walk with God is a limp.

What we learn from the Scriptures, however, is that our gracious Lord Jesus does not walk away from either self-created or other-created disasters. He comes marching in without a moment's hesitation, his scarred hands laboring to restore and rekindle hope. We may not see him at work in the big picture—we probably won't— but he will be there, using his word to break stony hearts, to mend cracked souls, to push forward his kingdom, and to love his people by giving them his holiness and righteousness.

First impressions of humans are not everything. But our first impression of God in the Bible is that he likes to make good things, indeed, very good things, happen for his people. And unlike other first impressions, that one tells the whole truth and nothing but the truth. That is precisely the kind of God we have in Jesus Christ.

DISCUSSION QUESTIONS

1. What are the differences between first impressions and later impressions? Give some examples. After you review Genesis 24 and 27, talk about how our later impressions of Rebekah do not align well with our first impressions of her.

2. If Rebekah's motivation for the deception was because she believed that God wanted Jacob to receive the blessings of the firstborn, why did she contrive such a complicated plan? What were the particulars of her plan? How might the events of Genesis 26:34-35 have influenced her?

3. How is God's will done in the middle of this messy situation? What are other biblical examples where the Lord makes the best out of a bad, complicated, or horrible situation?

4. What kinds of congregational messes does the Lord still use to work good? Discuss how this is characteristic of how God chooses to work. What does this tell us about the Christ whom we follow as disciples?

CHAPTER 7

The First Recorded Instance
of Identity Theft

Isaac said, "Are you really my son Esau?" Jacob answered, "I am."

Genesis 27:24

There have always been readers and teachers of the Old Testament who approach these writings with one overarching question: How does this text show us how to live? We might call this a Moral Hermeneutic. In this interpretive scheme, questions of right and wrong, the imitation of good examples and the avoidance of bad ones, is the primary lens through which the Scriptures are studied and applied. Naturally, those who espouse such an approach tend to treat the heroes and heroines of the OT as role models of virtue. If you attended Sunday School as a child, as I did, you were probably spoon-fed a steady diet of such lessons, high on sugary moralism, low on theological protein, with an occasional reference to Jesus tossed in.

People who follow a moralizing approach, however, run into major problems when it comes to Jacob. As one of the three patriarchs, he can hardly be skipped over. And as the father of the nation of Israel, one would certainly assume he was a spiritual hero. Holding Jacob up as a role model of virtue, however, is akin to pointing to the town drunk as an positive exemplar of sobriety. And none of the stories about him is less virtuous than when he, dish in hand, dressed in his brother's clothes, disguised under goat hair, enters his father's tent to lie to his face, take the Lord's name in vain, and burglarize the blessing of the firstborn.

When his mother had proposed this hustle, his only hesitancy had been that, if he were found out, he would "seem to be mocking [his father] and bring a curse upon [himself] and not a blessing" (Gen. 27:12). Getting caught and suffering the consequences were evidently his only concerns. But, as it turned out, Jacob had little to fear because he played his part with thespian finesse.

After the initial greeting between son and father, during which Isaac asks, "Who are you, my son?" Jacob launches into his lying spree, "I am Esau your firstborn. I have done as you told me; now sit up and eat of my game, that your soul may bless me" (Gen. 27:18-19). Notice how Jacob, not content merely to use his brother's name, adds, "Your firstborn." In fact, up to this point in the narrative, Esau has not been called "firstborn," only "older son" (27:1). Jacob, by adding the title of primogeniture, is doubling down on the deception and underscoring why he is there. He's not just there as Esau but specifically as Esau *the firstborn*. This would be like a perpetrator of identity theft stealing someone's ID and their birth certificate. We also learn, via Jacob's invitation for his father to "sit up," not only that Isaac is old and blind, but he seems to be lying down as well, as if bedridden. Our already cloudy opinion of Jacob only darkens.

Whatever weaknesses from which Isaac suffered, however, his ears and brain were in tip-top shape. He was no dummy. Something was off. First of all, he's skeptical about the speed with which "Esau" made this happen. This is Guinness Book of World Records hunting stuff. To his father's query, "How is it that you have found it so quickly, my son?" Jacob replies, "Because the LORD your God granted me success" (Gen. 27:20). If there are "lies" and "damned lies," then this falls into the latter category. If you are ever searching for a parade biblical example of what it means to take the Lord's name in vain, look no further than when Jacob gilded his dung of duplicity with the Lord's gold of success.

As the rest of the scene unfolds, it becomes obvious that Isaac is struggling with a sort of sensory dissonance. He touches Jacob's goat-skin-covered hands and feels Esau's hands. He eats of Rebekah's meal and tastes Esau's cooking. He sniffs what Jacob is wearing and smells Esau's clothing. Jacob's only major handicap is in his mouth.

Isaac says, "The voice is Jacob's voice, but the hands are the hands of Esau" (27:22). Finally, however, touch, taste, and smell win out over the sense of hearing. Isaac makes the decision. He pronounces the blessing. He invokes divine benefits related to creation, mastery over other nations, Jacob's lordship over his brothers, and makes his son one toward whom both blessings and curses will rebound to the speaker (27:27-29). And because a blessing cannot be unblessed, the words sink into Jacob, regardless of his deceit.

The baby who tried to pull his older brother back into the womb has finally pulled ahead of him.

When I drove a truck in the oil and gas fields near Pampa, Texas, I worked on the night shift for a couple of years with a guy named Robert. A group of five or six of us would get to work around 6 PM and each would receive a list of gas wells which we were to service that night. There was no real oversight. All the managers worked during the day. Ordinarily, as long as we didn't get in a huge hurry and worked safely, it would take us most of the night to finish our list. Not Robert. He barreled down those dirt country roads like a NASCAR driver. When most of us still had a couple of wells to service, and three more hours to work, Robert was parking his truck for the night. He left our yard about 2 AM. His logbook, however, told a different story. According to his logs, which determined the hours for which he got paid, Robert was hard at work until 5 AM every day. It was, of course, an easy deception to pull off. He simply manipulated the hours he logged to reflect a normal working speed. What makes the story interesting is that when he was eventually caught, with the skill of a courtroom lawyer, Robert argued his case. In his eyes, his theft of income—and that's what it was—was completely justifiable.

Martin Luther once wrote that sin "does not want sin to be sin...It wants to be righteousness."[1] Robert wasn't about to admit, with blunt honesty, "I wanted more money so I devised an easy way to lie on my logbooks." No, he wanted his theft to be righteous. This, of course, is the material of Humanity 101. Show me a sinner and I'll show you, a thousand times per day, how that sinner will rarely, if ever, say to himself or herself, "I am about to do something wrong. I know it's wrong. But I will do it anyway. I don't care." No, we will make up excuses;

---

[1] *Luther's Works*, American Edition (AE) 1:179.

justify our actions; blame others; claim we are living according to our own rules (but notice, they are still "rules"); or, if all else fails, play the "it's not nearly as wrong as what he's doing" game. What we will not do is treat our sin as sin. Rather, we want it to be righteousness. And this starts when we are very young. Every parent, for instance, knows that already as toddlers, children are their own lawyers, zealously defending their innocence, even when caught red-handed.

We see this same my-sin-is-righteousness in Jacob. He thinks that, no matter what, his actions are justifiable. One can't but wonder if Jacob doesn't actually believe that what he said to his father is true, "Because the LORD your God granted me success" (Gen. 27:20). And, to be sure, on the one hand, Jacob is right even as he's wrong. It was the will of the Lord, all along, for Jacob, not Esau, to carry on the promise. In that sense, yes, God did grant Jacob success. Simultaneously, how Jacob did this was not divinely willed but diabolically wrought. To co-opt the words of Jacob's future son, Joseph, "What Jacob intended for evil, God intended for good" (cf. Gen. 50:20). While the patriarch was falling all over himself to justify himself and his actions, the Lord's righteous plan was also falling into place.

One of my sainted professors, Kenneth Korby, once quipped in class, "The only time a liar tells the truth is when he says, 'I'm a liar.'" That's a good place for all of us to start. To say, "I'm a liar. I'm a cheat. I'm a gossiper. I'm an ingrate. I'm a hater. I'm a sinner. I'm a Jacob." The reason these words almost have to be wrenched out of our mouths is because we are unmasked by them. They reveal truths about us that we would like forever to be hidden. In our day, being "real" and "just who you are" and "vulnerable" are popular. But do not be fooled. This is just humanity's latest tactic. We substitute one self-created mask for another. Embracing the truth about ourselves—the cold, hard, naked, damning truth that we are lost and alone and without hope when left to our own devices—that will never be trending on Twitter.

Yet, for the followers of Jesus, that is the way forward. We confess not only that we are sinners in thought, word, and deed, but that even our best and holiest works are in need of forgiveness—perhaps even more in need of forgiveness—because we rely on them to shore up our salvation, to make God happy with us. As if all this were not bad enough, we are constantly making excuses for ourselves, gilding our own worst deeds with the Lord's holy name.

And how does our Lord respond to our confession? Not with a to-do list whereby we can win back his favor. Not with a scowl and wagging finger, warning us never to do it again...or else. Not by sitting across the room from us, arms crossed, lip upturned, as if disgusted by our very presence. No, a thousand times, no. Like the prodigal's father, he's so ready to love and forgive us that he interrupts our confession. He throws his arms around us, kisses us, and calls for a party in our name. "It is time to celebrate my child!" he says. "It is time to throw a party of absolution."

Perhaps some of those standing around will say, "But, Lord, we just did that last week—the thousandth time he came crawling back home from a distant country." And our Lord will say, "So what? I don't care if he comes home every day of his life. Then we will celebrate every day of his life, for this my son was dead and is alive again. He was lost and is found."

To follow the path of discipleship is to embrace honesty, to confess the worst about ourselves, over and over, and to hear from Jesus, also over and over, "I love you. I forgive you. Follow me."

All of us are like Jacob in this sense, because we are clothed in the garments of our older brother, Jesus, by which we receive the blessing of the Firstborn from our heavenly Father.

Discussion Questions

1. Why is a moralizing approach to the Old Testament so popular? What is a better way to read and interpret the Old Testament?
2. Review Genesis 27:1-29. Analyze the conversation between Isaac and Jacob. Why is Isaac skeptical? How often does Jacob lie? Is it ever permissible to lie?
3. Discuss and give examples of this statement by Martin Luther: "Sin does not want sin to be sin...It wants to be righteousness."
4. What is the value of confession? Why are we so stubborn about wanting to confess our wrongdoing?
5. When we do confess, how does the Lord respond? Read Psalm 32:5 and 1 John 1:8-10.

CHAPTER 8
Seventy-Year Old's in Midlife Crisis

Esau said, "Is he not rightly named Jacob?"

Genesis 27:36

When we picture the events of Genesis 27 in our minds, most of us see Jacob and Esau as relatively young men. Two brothers in their 20's or maybe 30's. They were just beginning their adult lives, each in his own way ready to take on the world. But the popular images from children's Bible Story books and even famous paintings have misled us regarding the age of these twins. They were not young men.

To do the math, we have to skip forward and work our way backwards. When Jacob found out that Joseph was still alive, he moved down to Egypt to join him. At that time, Jacob was one-hundred-thirty years old (Gen. 47:9) and Joseph was thirty-nine (Gen. 41:46; 45:6, 11). This means that Jacob was about ninety-one years old when Joseph was born. Where and when was Joseph born? In Haran, around the fourteenth year of Jacob's time with Laban, that is, fourteen years after his deception of Isaac and resultant exile (Gen. 30:25; 31:41).

Therefore, when Jacob deceived his father, aroused Esau's wrath, and fled from home, he was about seventy-seven years old.

"Seventy-seven!" I can hear some of you exclaiming. "I had no idea he was that old." Well, yes, but let's also do a little comparative math. Because Jacob lived to be one-hundred-forty-seven years old, he was about halfway through his life at this time (Gen. 47:28). Using today's life expectancy as a model, we might say Jacob and Esau were, at the beginning of their fraternal feud, like a couple of modern forty-year-olds. By the standards of those days, they were neither young nor old. These brothers were, quite literally, entering a midlife crisis.

When Esau grabbed his bow and headed out to hunt, he must have thought that this was going to be one of the best days of his life. He would receive the blessing of the firstborn. He would take over leadership of the family. He would be set for life. Since Isaac had informed his older son that he planned to bless him, we can assume the father had never been informed that Esau had earlier sold his birthright to Jacob. Or perhaps it happened so long ago that it seemed not to matter anymore. Either way, Esau supposed he was all in the clear now. After over seven decades of waiting, Hairy would beat Heel for good.

While Esau was out hunting game, the other brother was at home, bagging the blessing. Hardly had he pulled off this deceit before Esau showed up (Gen. 27:30). After Jacob's initial greeting of his father, Isaac had asked, "Who are you, my son?" but to Esau's similar greeting, he responds, "Who are you?" (27:18, 32). There is no "my son." The blind father is bewildered. When Esau says, "I am your son, your firstborn, Esau," Isaac "trembled [*charad*] very violently" (27:32-33). The Hebrew verb *charad* carries the connotation of panic, fright, or even horror at receiving bad news (e.g., Gen. 42:28; 1 Sam. 14:15; 1 Kings 1:49). Here, the verb is doubled with the addition of "very," communicating something like "seized with a very great trembling" (R. Alter). Isaac fears the worst. Although he asks, "Who was it then [that I blessed]," the old father must have known. Who else would it be? His younger son, Rebekah's favorite, had tricked him. Suddenly, as if resigning himself to this unforeseen reality, Isaac adds, "Yes, and he shall be blessed," (27:33). There was no ritual for unblessing Jacob. What was done, was done.

Whatever you may think of Esau, I find it difficult not to have compassion on him at this moment. Yes, he sold his birthright. Yes, that was wrong. We can all agree on that. But if you've ever been near the pinnacle of joy, thinking that life is finally going to fall into place for you, and had someone strip that happiness away from you, then you have felt the same knife enter your back as was plunged into Esau's. The emotions and words that flooded through this older brother—and that have flooded through many of us, me included—are a toxic mixture of shock, fury, bitterness, confusion, numbness, and an irrational desire to strike out, to hurt the one who hurt you.

When I was a young boy, one of the lessons my father taught me was never to rush up to a wounded animal, even if it's a dear and beloved pet. The family dog, as sweet and cuddly as it might ordinarily be, in its pain and shock and confusion, might turn its teeth on you. Something like that can happen to people, too. In fact, it happens with sad predictability. In Esau's case, like that wounded animal, he first "cried out with an exceedingly great and bitter cry" (27:34). Then he verbally lashed out about his brother, "Is he not rightly named Jacob [*Ya'aqov*]? For he has cheated [*aqav*]¹ me these two times. He took away my birthright, and behold, now he has taken away my blessing" (27:36). In the aftermath, "Esau hated Jacob because of the blessing with which his father had blessed him, and Esau said to himself, 'The days of mourning for my father are approaching; then I will kill my brother Jacob'" (27:41). From a painful shock, to bitter words, to a brooding and murderous hatred, Esau, hurting and wounded, bared his teeth and salivated for revenge.

There are many pursuits in life that promise a prize but produce a poison. These passions tell us, "It will all be worth it," but once we have achieved our goal, our satisfaction is fleeting. There is none of the lasting, ecstatic thrill we thought we'd have. A drain seems to have opened at the bottom of our souls. And soon we are empty, baffled by the arid desert sands that blow in the void of our lives. Revenge, my friends, is such a pursuit.

When we have been seriously wronged, revenge can rapidly advance through the ranks of our desires to sit unchallenged on the throne of our hearts. This seething and rancid god, full of acidic hate, reigned within me for years. The homage he demanded were the liturgies of fantasy, whereby I plotted how to get even. The sacrifice he required was a life of positivity, hope, and joy, all to be slaughtered and bled out on the altar of reprisal. And the salvation that this false

---

¹ The Hebrew name of Jacob, Ya'aqov, means "heel," but the related verb, *aqav*, which Esau uses here, means "trip up, trick, cheat, supplant." The wordplay in Hebrew would be something like, "Is he not rightly named Jacob, for he has jacobed me these two times?"

deity held out was that, once revenge was achieved, once my enemy felt my pain, once my vigilante justice was accomplished, then I would feel better. I would heal. I could finally move on. Revenge would be my redemption.

Sheerly by the grace of God, my addiction to revenge remained internalized and was never acted out. But I have been a sojourner in that land where joy goes to die and demons clad in the soiled garments of stolen dreams sing siren songs to woo the wounded to their soul's demise. Do not go there, my fellow Esaus. Do not go there. It is hell on earth.

"If anyone slaps you on the right cheek, turn to him the other also," Jesus famously said (Matt. 5:39). It takes no effort, no rationality, no wisdom, not even any humanity, to strike back. Strike a wild animal and it will strike you back. Nothing is more inherent in the beast than to kill you before you kill it. But to turn the other cheek, to deal in patience and wisdom, to ponder consequences and to cultivate peace, that is being human.

The life of a disciple of Jesus is an odd existence. On the one hand, because it is so otherworldly, so non-conformist to the widely accepted maxims of ordinary life, it is difficult. It is never easy to go against the cultural flow. On occasion, it means being labeled the enemy. In the worse cases, it means being martyred. On the other hand, being a Christian does not entail being unhuman or subhuman or transhuman *but being precisely the humans that God created us to be.* In that way, nothing is more truly natural than being a disciple of Jesus. To say "Be a Christian" is to mean "Be a human being recreated to bear the image of God in Christ and so fully to be the person that our Creator wants us to be."

For that reason, not seeking revenge, not returning evil for evil, while difficult inasmuch as we are sinners, is also radically fulfilling inasmuch as we are the children of a merciful and forgiving God. It seems both wrong and right simultaneously. Our "Esau nature," if you will, wants that pound of Jacob's flesh. But we also know, because the Spirit of God lives within us, that to take that pound of flesh is to heap onto our hearts a ton of guilt and shame and regret.

We will see, in a later chapter, that Esau himself eventually arrived at the same place where I, and many others, have arrived: on the other side of the shadows, in the land of the light of forgiveness.

To journey there sometimes takes days, sometimes years. However long the trek, we are all borne by the Spirit of our Lord, who cried, "Father, forgive them" from his cross of death. Not, "Father, incinerate them!" or "Father, make them pay!" but "Father, do not hold this sin against them."

St. Ambrose wrote, "No one heals himself by wounding another." Rather, we are all healed—wounder and wounded alike—in the crucifixion scars of our forgiving Lord.

Discussion Questions

1. Read Genesis 27:30-41. How did Jacob's deception affect both Isaac and Esau? What characterized their respective responses?

2. Give examples of modern situations, either from your own life or the lives of others, in which someone might feel like Esau and want to seek revenge. What motivates this desire? Deep down, what are we seeking in revenge: justice? punishment? balm to our wounded egos? something else?

3. Read Romans 12:17-21. How does Paul say we should treat our enemies? How is this similar to Jesus' words in Matthew 5:38-48? Compare this to Matthew 5:9 and Luke 23:34.

4. Discuss these statements: "Being a Christian does not entail being unhuman or subhuman or transhuman *but being precisely the humans that God created us to be.* In that way, nothing is more truly natural than being a disciple of Jesus. To say 'Be a Christian' is to mean 'Be a human being recreated to bear the image of God in Christ and so fully to be the person that our Creator wants us to be.'"

Part 2

The Exile:
The Growth of Jacob's
Dysfunctional Family

CHAPTER 9

A Staff in His Hand and
a Word in His Pocket

Thus Isaac sent Jacob away.

Genesis 28:5

Our lives are often demarcated by departures. At the age of nineteen, my Ford pickup loaded with all my worldly possessions, I grinned as I waved Goodbye to my mom and dad and began the long drive to college in Austin, TX. At the age of thirty-six, when my marriage was in the throes of impending divorce, my lips quavered as I waved Goodbye to my young daughter and son as we watched each other through the dirty back window of the departing car. At the age of fifty, I waved Goodbye first to my son, as we dropped him off at the Naval Academy, and second to my daughter, as she drove away to start a full-time job in Utah. Three departures, one full of hope, one full of tragedy, one full of promise. At each one, I was the same man and yet a different man, ever molded in new and painful and often surprising ways by the hands of my heavenly Father.

It is time for Jacob to wave Goodbye as well, though his departure is neither full of hope, tragedy, nor promise, but potential bloodshed. Should he remain, there will likely be a rerun of Genesis 4, when an older brother murders a younger brother. After Jacob took the blessing from his brother, Esau hated him and said to himself, "The days of mourning for my father are approaching; then I will kill my brother Jacob" (Gen. 27:41). When Rebekah was told about Esau's grudge (did she really think Esau would just shrug this off?), she who had devised the deception now devised the departure. Using the exact same words as before, she says to her favorite son, "Obey my voice" (27:8, 43). Then she lays out the plan, "Arise, flee to Laban my brother in Haran and stay with him a while, until your brother's fury turns away—until your brother's anger turns away from you, and he forgets what you have done to him. Then I will send and bring you from there. Why should I be bereft of you both in one day?" (27:43-45).

Do not miss three significant details in this maternal speech. First, she says to "stay with him a while." In Hebrew, "a while" is literally "a few days." The same expression will be used later when "Jacob served seven years for Rachel, and they seemed to him but *a few days* because of the love he had for her" (Gen. 29:20). What Rebekah assumed would be "a few days," however, ended up being twenty years! Since only Isaac is mentioned after Jacob returned (35:37), it is likely that Rebekah died sometime during her son's two-decade absence—one of the unforeseen consequences of her actions. Second, she tells Jacob to remain in Haran until Esau "forgets what you have done to him." Really—what "you" have done? Why not "what *we* have done"? This was Rebekah's scheme, after all. Yes, Jacob willingly obeyed her, but it seems rather disingenuous to speak as if this were all his brainchild. Third, she promises, "I will send and bring you from there," but, of course, that never happens, probably because her death prevented it. Either way, the fact that no messenger ever arrived from Rebekah to tell him it was safe to return home likely fueled the fear that he still had for Esau. The lack of a message from mom, saying, "Esau has cooled down," could only be interpreted to mean, "Esau is still hot with anger."

This mother-to-son Goodbye is followed by a father-to-son Goodbye. If Rebekah is worried about keeping Jacob alive, Isaac is concerned about keeping Jacob from marrying outside the extended family. He instructs him to wed one of the daughters of Uncle Laban, then he repeats and expands upon the blessing that he had spoken beforehand.

> "God Almighty bless you and make you fruitful and multiply you, that you may become a company of peoples. May he give the blessing of Abraham to you and to your offspring with you, that you may take

possession of the land of your sojournings that God gave to Abraham!"
(Gen. 28:3-4)

Here are echoes of the words spoken to Adam and Eve ("be fruitful
and multiply" Gen. 1:28) and the promises to Abraham concerning
offspring and land (Gen. 12:1-3; 13:14-17). Unworthy and deceptive
as he is, Jacob has been mercifully given the grand promise that will
be passed down from him to Judah, from Judah to David, and will
finally come to live and grow inside Mary's womb.

With only this word in his pocket[1] and a staff in his hand
(Gen. 32:10), Jacob leaves behind everything he has known for the
uncertainty—and the adventure—of a life in exile.[2]

We know, of course, what awaits Jacob in Haran. Marriage to
two sisters. Intense rivalry between those sisters. The births of eleven
sons and at least one daughter (the twelfth son will be born post-
exile). Hard, and often unrewarding, work as a shepherd. A Scrooge
uncle for a boss. And, through it all, the divine hand, taking this messy
and sin-packed situation, and guiding it toward his desired outcome.
This microcosm of a nation—the nation of Israel, the nation he will
one day call out of Egypt, the nation that will keep alive the promise
of the messianic seed—*this nation has its genesis in exile*. With one
exception, the father of every tribe in Israel was born outside the
promised land.

God put Jacob in exile because it's often there where the Lord
does his most defining work in our lives. And by "defining work" I
mean the kind of work that we are probably not going to enjoy. What
we might find pleasurable is a monthly visit from Jesus, who stops by
our home to have a cup of coffee with us, makes sure we're holding
up okay, then drives on down the road to check on other disciples.
In other words, the kind of relationship where Jesus respects our

---

[1] I have borrowed the image of "a word in his pocket" from Martin
Franzmann in his fine little collection of sermons entitled *Ha! Ha! Among the
Trumpets: Sermons by Martin Franzmann* (St. Louis: Concordia Publishing
House, 1994), where he speaks of Jesus sending the nobleman home in John
4:16-54 "with only a word in his pocket," 105.

[2] A helpful summary of the connections between Jacob's exile and Israel's
later exile/exodus can be found in David Daube's classic study, *The Exodus
Pattern in the Bible* (Eugene, Oregon: Wipf & Stock, 2020), 62-72.

boundaries. He lets "you do you." But here's the thing: Jesus doesn't want you to do you, to define who you are, to follow your own paths, to be the person you want to be. That is very American; it is also very satanic. It is precisely that kind of egocentric attitude that the forces of hell are all about. That is what Jesus is keen on shattering into nothingness. And the ideal place to do that is exile.

I don't know what your exile will look like. To outsiders, it might not look like an exile at all. You still get out of the same bed, in the same house, every morning. You still go to work. You are still married. You still go to your kid's soccer practice. That's what others see. But your heart and soul and mind? They're in Haran. They're confused and wandering and homeless. Maybe you begin to struggle with questions about God. Maybe you fight some serious demons of despair or loneliness. Maybe you suffer from what the Egyptian monks called acedia or the "noonday demon," a kind of stupor or apathy of the soul. Or perhaps your exile is more obvious. It follows on the heels of a divorce, the death of a loved one, a battle with cancer, wrestling with addiction, or a stint in prison.

During that exile, I can almost guarantee that you will be thinking that God is doing "A" when he's really doing "Z." You will think he's far away when he's closer to you than ever before. You will think he's an uncaring bastard of a deity when he's watching over you with a paternal heart of love. You will think he is out to kill you when he's… well, actually, there you will be right. He is out to kill you by poking holes in your ego, torching your idols, shredding your narcissism, and emptying as much of you out of you as he can, in order to fill that void with himself. This is the kind of defining work that God does in exile.

Christ is always doing this work in his disciples. It's his life's labor. It's just that this labor of love intensifies and sharpens during those exilic seasons, when the poignancy of our lack of control is more patently recognizable. When we are forced, by dent of circumstances, to confess our own ungodness. To stare into the void of our mortality. Then and there, outside the walls of comfort, in the howling wilderness, we see that all we have and all we really need is Jesus. We cannot lean on our ethical achievements. We can't buttress ourselves by appeal to how well we have our lives organized. No, in the swirl of confusion, in the fever of anxiety, in the sheer terror of fallen and frail humanity, we cry out from the vortex of our exile:

Lord have mercy!

Christ have mercy!

Lord have mercy!

And he does, always and abundantly. He had mercy before we cried out. We prayed for what he had already given, and will always give. He knew that every cell of our body, every drop of our blood, is in need of mercy. He just needed us to know that. And there's no better place for that to happen than in exile.

Being a disciple of Jesus means a life where we will have our exiles. But take heart: the Lord we follow has already gone into exile himself and come back again. Getting out of the grave, and getting us out of the grave, healed and alive and back home, is precisely what he lives for.

Discussion Questions

1. What are some significant, milestone "Goodbyes" that you have experienced? What gave you hope, or caused you fear, as you moved forward into an unknown future?
2. Read Genesis 27:42-28:5. In what way does Rebekah seek to be a "fixer" or "controller"? As further background, discuss how Genesis 27:46 enlightens us regarding her attitude toward Esau and his growing family.
3. Jacob goes into exile with only a "word in his pocket." Read Genesis 28:3-4. What is the content of that "word"? How would this sustain Jacob? What word(s) does Christ put in your pocket?
4. Discuss the variety of exiles that we experience. What was God doing with Jacob in his exile? What is the Lord doing in our own? What main truth is he teaching us during those times of trial and tribulation?

CHAPTER 10

Alone, Unsuspecting, and Asleep

Jacob lay down in that place to sleep.

Genesis 28:11

A journey of hundreds of miles, on foot, stretched before Jacob. The typical reticence of biblical narrative to provide details leaves us curious, asking unanswerable questions. How long did this trip from home to Haran take? What dangers or adventures did Jacob face? What kinds of people did he meet on the road? What were his thoughts, regrets, fears, hopes? All we know about this hike into the unknown, however, is what transpired during a single night. But what a night it was! Jacob sees a ladder or stairway stretching from the soil to the stars. He watches angelic beings go heavenward and earthward upon it. His eyes behold Yahweh himself, standing beside him, and his ears soak in a divine speech chock-full of promises.

All of those dazzling, momentous happenings are highly significant, worthy of our deeper reflection upon them. And reflect upon them we will. But before we do, before we shift to the majors, let's meditate upon the minors. Let's focus upon some smaller details, some explicit, some implicit, but all important and instructive moments for us to consider.

To begin, this is the first time that we see Jacob when he is alone. So far, we've seen his interactions with his brother; with his mother; and with his father. But we have not observed him alone, until now. Twenty years hence, we will see him alone again, once more with God, though in that future event, he will not be dreaming but fighting (Gen. 32:24). This first event happens when Jacob is leaving for exile, the latter when he's coming home. These two lone encounters with the Lord shape Jacob in fundamental ways, as we shall see.

Second, this theophany or God-appearance catches Jacob off-guard. He was not seeking God. He was not on a religious quest or a sacred pilgrimage to a holy site, fervently praying for a visionary tete-a-tete with the deity. He was just a man on the run, bone-tired, and camping under the stars on what he assumed was an ordinary plot of ground. In other words, Jacob was not looking for God when God came looking for him.

Third—and, to me, most interestingly—this event happens when Jacob is catching some Z's. We are, by now, well aware of what Jacob is capable of when his eyes are wide open. He can lie, cheat, deceive, and get his way like an old pro. When awake, Jacob can do Jacob exceptionally well. The Lord chooses to visit him, however, when the man is asleep, passive, receptive, when the only thing his mouth can do is snore.

Jacob, therefore, is alone, unsuspecting, and asleep. I think there's wisdom to be gleaned from each of these. Using Jacob is a mirror of ourselves, let's think about them.

Have you watched the reality television series, "Alone"? In the show, contestants are dropped off in remote wilderness areas to see how long they can survive in isolation. Each is allowed to pack in ten items. Each is a skilled survivalist. The dangers are real. Wolves have prowled in their camps and one man was charged by a grizzly. Some have seriously injured themselves. A few had to be medically evacuated because, having lost so much weight, they were in danger of organ failure. Time and again, however, what drives contestants to tap out are not predators, cold, or hunger, but one simple fact: they can't handle being alone any longer.

I suspect every one of us understands that fact in a deep and visceral way. "All of humanity's problems," Blaise Paschal famously wrote, "stem from man's inability to sit quietly in a room alone."[1] Of course, this is why we amuse ourselves to death, as Neil Postman

---

[1] This is the quotation that is frequently cited. Another is this: "I have often said that the sole cause of man's unhappiness is that he does not know how to

would say. Or, as Reed Hastings, the CEO of Netflix, once said of his company's purpose, "Fundamentally we're about eliminating loneliness and boredom."[2] But, of course, that is all a lie. Phones, tablets, and televisions eliminate loneliness or boredom like methamphetamines eliminate the desire for drugs! They exacerbate the very problem they claim to solve.

Being alone, for most of us, is difficult, if not painful. But we do need time alone, undistracted, in the silence of our thoughts, because without it we will likely never know ourselves. And knowing ourselves—our deepest fears, longings, struggles, identities, loves—is not optional for someone who also wants to know God. Whom does Christ love? You. Okay, who exactly are you? What kind of person are you? What are your longings? What wicked shadows skulk through the darker corridors of your soul? Why won't you ever talk about "that thing" with anyone? What are you afraid of, and why? What do you want out of life? What do you really want from God? We could go on and on with the questions. Here's the point though: if you never ask them, if instead you keep snorting another social media line, or "binging" (notice the verb we use) Netflix, or doing almost anything to avoid sitting quietly in a room alone, you will live your life largely unaware of the you who is living it.

Practice being alone. Think. Pray. Remember. Listen. Ponder. Two of the most impactful experiences that Jacob experienced occurred when he was all alone. Both were terrifying in their own way, but both were also life-changing.

To follow up on that, however, also realize that this is not entirely up to you. You are not master or manipulator of those seasons when the Lord will pay you a visit to teach you a thing or two about both him and yourself. In Jacob's case, he didn't pitch a tent beside a temple and sweat himself into a visionary experience. Rather, he was just tired. He lay down. He dozed off. And God showed up. He wasn't looking for the Lord when the Lord came looking for him.

---

stay quietly in his room," from *Pensées* §136, trans. by A. J. Krailsheimer (New York: Penguin Books, 1995), 37.

[2] Cady Lang, "Netflix's CEO Says Entertainment Pills Could Make Movies and TV Obsolete," *Time*, October 25, 2016, https://time.com/4544291/netflix-ceo-pills/

Let's also remember that these divine visitations are not always pleasant experiences. Nor will they necessarily take on the visionary quality of Jacob's. They may look like a tumor on a CT scan. An email about your termination of employment. Or a phone call at 3 AM that begins with, "I am so sorry I have to tell you this, but...." And suddenly, in an instant, everything changes. The floor falls from beneath you. In the days, weeks, and months to come, following Jesus feels like a cruel joke. You're not following anyone. You're chained to despair. You're sinking in a swirling sea of chaos. The glowing eyes of monstrous uncertainties blink at you from the darkness. Rather than seeing a ladder from earth to heaven, it seems there's an escalator from hell to earth, with demons showing up in legions on your doorstep.

This is ordinary. These things happen to the people of God in our fractured world. So, when these events do happen, when you feel beyond overwhelmed, know that the Lord Jesus is near, right at the door. He is wading into this darkness, eyes only for you. Christ has come because you cannot come to him. He is following you, not the other way around—following you into the vortex of pain and loss and fear and anger. He does so unblinkingly. Without hesitation. Since Jesus, "for the joy that was set before him endured the cross," do not for a moment imagine that he grimaces or flinches or weighs his options before entering your pain and loss and the crucible of your own suffering (Heb. 12:2). He's all in, all for you, all for the joy of loving and saving you. You will learn much about yourself, but more importantly, you will learn much about the magnanimity of the Lord's heart. With greater clarity, you will realize that apart from him, you have no hope. But in him, hope is an inexpressible gift that enables us all to face the future, which is already enfolded within the resurrection of Christ.

Finally, that God opted to visit Jacob in a vision while he was asleep, incapable of doing anything but listening and seeing and receiving, is a perfect picture of the essence of discipleship. God gives, we receive. Those four words encapsulate our lives as followers of Jesus.

Question: "What do you have that you did not receive?" (1 Cor. 4:7).
Answer: Nothing.
Question: Of what then can you boast?
Answer: Nothing.

All we have is a gift from God. The Father created us, giving us eyes and ears and hearts and brains. He cares for our bodies by clothing and feeding us. He protects us from dangers. He gives us family and friends. Why? Because he delights to give, to nurture, to love us. The Son has redeemed us by his birth, passion, and resurrection, so that he might bring us into his kingdom. Why? Because he joyfully desired to save us and make us his brothers and sisters. The Spirit has called us to Christ, given us repentance and faith, baptized us into the church, forgives us, and promises to raise our bodies on the last day. Why? Because he has mercy upon us, loves us, and wants nothing but the best for us.

God gives us all these things, and we receive them from him as gifts. Yes, of course, as disciples, we pray to our Father, meditate upon his Word, live by the Spirit, serve our neighbors in sacrificial love. In many ways, we are active. But even our activity is God's work through us. To borrow the language of Isaiah: "You have indeed done for us all our works" (26:12). Or, as Paul will say, "I worked harder than any of them, though it was not I, but the grace of God that is with me" (1 Cor. 15:10). That phrase, "though it was not I, but the grace of God" could be applied across our lives.

- I served my spouse and children, though it was not I, but the grace of God.
- I have followed Jesus as his disciple, though it was not I, but the grace of God.
- I have studied the Scriptures, though it was not I, but the grace of God.
- I have labored in my vocation, though it was not I, but the grace of God.
- I have repented, confessed, believed, though it was not I, but the grace of God.

Jacob was asleep when the Lord visited him with promises of great blessing. God gave, Jacob received. He had nothing of which to boast, for all he had was a gift from God. So it is with all of us as followers of Jesus. Rather than boasting, we simply say: Glory be to you alone, O Lord.

DISCUSSION QUESTIONS

1. What is the longest period of time when you have been utterly alone? What are the challenges, pitfalls, and blessings that can come from being alone? What can we learn from Jacob's time of being alone?

2. How is it helpful to remember that Jacob was not looking for God when God came looking for him? What are some occasions when the Lord might show up in an unexpected way in our lives? Think of the examples of Abraham (Gen. 18:1-15); Zacchaeus (Luke 19:1-10); and Paul (Acts 9:1-19). How does Christ's visit to Paul exemplify the fact that these divine visitations are not always pleasant experiences?

3. How do these four words—God gives, we receive—encapsulate our lives as followers of Jesus? Apply this to your life and your vocations. How does the grace of Christ shape every part of our lives as disciples?

CHAPTER 11

Stairway to Heaven

And, behold, the LORD stood beside him.

Genesis 28:12 (NJPS)

If there is a single image that we associate with Jacob's nocturnal vision from Yahweh in Genesis 28:10-22, it is the famous "ladder," "stairway," or "ramp" that stretches from earth to heaven. All three of those words are possible translations of *sullam*, the Hebrew noun used here for this "angelic interstate." While our fascination with the *sullam* is understandable—and we will spend some time talking about it—it can also distract us from the primary message of the vision. The main focus of this account is not the angels, the stairway, or the stone pillar, but God and his Word. He appears. He speaks. He promises.

First, let's sketch out what happens. At sundown, Jacob "happened upon [*paga*] a particular place [*maqom*]" (Gen. 28:11 NASB). The Hebrew verb *paga* stresses the randomness of the campsite. It wasn't on Jacob's "List of Places to Visit." He just "happened upon" it. The word *maqom* has the definite article attached to it, so it is not "a" place but "the" place. In other words, God knew what he was doing; Jacob did not. The Lord providentially led his servant to this specific site, which Jacob subsequently named Bethel, a location which will loom large in the rest of biblical history.[1] While asleep,

---

[1] Bethel had already been visited by Jacob's grandfather, Abraham (Gen. 12:8; 13:3-4). The ark of the covenant was there for a time (Judg. 20:26-27). After the split of the northern kingdom from the southern kingdom, Jeroboam set up

with a stone near (not under)[2] his head, Jacob has a dream vision in which he sees the messengers of God going up and down the stairway. Because of this, Jacob, once awake, says, "This is none other than the house of God, and this is the gate of heaven" (Gen. 28:17). The idea that such "gates of heaven" existed was widespread in the ancient Near East. Here was the portal between the celestial and terrestrial. In the morning, Jacob takes the stone at his head, sets it up as a pillar, anoints it, and names the place Beth-El, that is, "House of El" or "House of God."

Sandwiched between all these events, however, is the main drama of the night: the theophany of Yahweh to Jacob. If you search Google for artistic depictions of this event, almost all of them will show some divine figure standing in heaven at the top of the stairway or ladder. There is Yahweh, way up high, head in the clouds, looking far down below on his sleeping servant. These paintings follow the lead of many translations, which say "above [the stairway] stood the LORD (NIV); "the LORD stood above it" (KJV; ESV); or "the LORD was standing above it" (NASB). But the Hebrew prepositional phrase *alayv* could just as accurately be translated "beside him," that is, beside Jacob (NEB; NAB; NJPS; CSB), not "above it." This rendering also accords better with Jacob saying, "the LORD is present in this place" (28:16). He was not up in heaven, calling down. God descended to Jacob, to where he was, and there spoke to him. "Beside him" accents the nearness of God. He was the opposite of aloof.

Since we are well aware of Jacob's inglorious past, especially his recent escapades, we would reasonably assume that he is about to receive a divine tongue lashing. After all, he does deserve it. We know his selfish deeds. And God knows them, too. The Lord God Almighty is about to pound a string of Woes! into this weasel of a

---

his idolatrous calves in Dan and Bethel (1 Kings 12:28-29). Both Hosea (10:15) and Amos (3:14) explicitly preached against the idolatry practiced in Bethel. The place that originated as the gateway to heaven devolved into the gateway of hellish idolatry.

[2]   The stone did not serve as a pillow but likely a protection for his head. The exact Hebrew phrase for "at his head" describes the placement of Saul's spear in the ground "at his head" (1 Sam. 26:11, 16) and the cake laid "at the head" of Elijah (1 Kings 19:6). See also 1 Sam. 19:13, 16 where the pillow of goat's hair is "at the head" of the image.

man. It is more than a little disconcerting, therefore, when nothing but love and grace and promise come pouring from the lips of the Lord into the ears of Jacob.

> "I am the LORD, the God of your father Abraham and the God of Isaac: the ground on which you are lying I will assign to you and to your offspring. Your descendants shall be as the dust of the earth; you shall spread out to the west and to the east, to the north and to the south. All the families of the earth shall bless themselves by you and your descendants. Remember, I am with you: I will protect you wherever you go and will bring you back to this land. I will not leave you until I have done what I have promised you." (Genesis 28:13-15)

See all those "I's"? I am the LORD. I will assign to you. I am with you. I will protect you. I will not leave you. I have done. I have promised. It appears as if the Lord has nothing but good to say to Jacob. He passes on to him the gift of land and the promise of a cosmopolitan blessing which involves "all the families of the earth." Why would the Lord act this way? Where is the God of justice?

With some regularity, people caricature God in the OT. The picture him as a mean, bloodthirsty, sadistic tyrant who gets off on steamrolling sinners with plagues and other nastiness. Even if they don't go to those extremes, they still depict him as a God of wrath, who is then juxtaposed with the God of love in the NT. This is theological hogwash, of course, a false dichotomy utterly untrue to the witness of both the OT and NT. But that doesn't stop people from thinking this way.

So, I have a suggestion: the next time you encounter this caricature or false dichotomy, recollect how God treated Jacob. Here is a fellow who justly deserved heaven's rebuke. He had earned nothing but the payment of punitive damages. Yet when the Lord God descended and stood within boot-stomping distance of Jacob, what did he do? He spoke words of promise. He showed nothing but mercy. Jacob was a loser who won. A liar forgiven. A runaway redeemed.

This episode has always reminded me of that other wayward disciple, the prodigal son. He returns home, fully expecting to have to earn his way back into his father's favor. He'll volunteer to be a servant. He'll demonstrate his remorse. He'll show everyone, especially his dad, that he's learned his lesson. But no sooner has the son begun his rehearsed confession when the father interrupts him by saying to his servants, "Bring quickly the best robe, and put it on him, and put a ring on his hand, and shoes on his feet. And bring the fattened calf and kill it, and let us eat and celebrate. For this my son was dead, and is alive again; he was lost, and is found" (Luke 15:22-24). Where is the justice in that? Where is the punishment? Where is the grim-faced, prove-me-you're-really-sorry, fire and brimstone father? There is none of that. Only the scandalous, shocking absolution, with a keg and a BBQ to boot.

As it was with the prodigal, so it was with Jacob. And so it is with every one of us who stumble and fumble our way down the discipleship road. Every moment of every day, we live and follow Jesus exclusively by mercy. "He does not deal with us according to our sins, nor repay us according to our iniquities" (Ps. 103:10). If he did, we'd all be dead. "For as high as the heavens are above the earth, so great is his steadfast love toward those who fear him; as far as the east is from the west, so far does he remove our transgressions from us. As a father shows compassion to his children, so the LORD shows compassion to those who fear him" (103:11-13). Write those words somewhere in gold and read them every day.

What happens at the foot of the stairway is this: Jacob does not get what he justly deserves but receives what the Lord mercifully gives. How fitting it is, therefore, that Jesus, our Lord of mercy, the very one who stood by Jacob those long centuries before, once alluded to that incident. He told Nathanael, "Truly, truly, I say to you, you will see heaven opened, and the angels of God ascending and descending on the Son of Man" (John 1:51).

There are a couple of different ways that we can understand these words, both of which lead us to the same destination.

The most common interpretation is that Jesus is identifying himself with the stairway that connects earth to heaven. The Son of Man joins God to humanity. In his body, God comes down to us and we ascend to God. He is the union of divinity and humanity. That is certainly all true and infinitely comforting.

The other possible interpretation understands Jesus to be echo-ing a widespread, first century, Jewish tradition that said the image of a man's face was engraved on the throne of God.[3] This face was the face of Jacob. The angels ascended and descended *on Jacob*, that is, they came down to him to compare his actual face with the image they had seen on the divine throne. Jesus, playing off this tradition, is saying, "Nice try, but they've got it all wrong. The angels of God will be ascending and descending on *me!*" That is, Christ's image, his face, his person is connected with the throne of God, for he is the one who sits on that throne alongside his Father.

As such, to see the face of Jesus is to see the face of the one who rules all creation, who is Lord over his church, the teacher of disciples, priest of sinners, redeemer of the lost, shepherd of the wayward, and judge of the living and the dead. As he once dealt with Jacob, so he will deal with us: in mercy. Do we deserve it? No, of course not. But that is the point!

I thank God that he didn't choose a rule-following, t-crossing and i-dotting, cream of the moral crop, most-likely-never-to-do-anything-shameful man to be the patriarch of the OT people of God. He chose Jacob. He chose a disciple with a shady past, a troubling future, a dysfunction family, and a heart drunk on ego to be his #1 guy.

Christ wanted it to be patently clear that being his follower is not about climbing a ladder of spiritual success but being greeted by mercy at the bottom of the ladder by the Lord who climbs down to us.

Discussion Questions

1. The events in Genesis 28 happened in Bethel. What does Bethel mean in Hebrew? How does this location feature in the rest of the biblical story? Read Gen. 12:8; 13:3-4; Judg. 20:26-27; 1 Kings 12:28-29; Hosea 10:15; and Amos 3:14. Discuss how places originally associated with God's holiness can become corrupted over time.

2. Read Genesis 28:10-22. What are some of the specific promises that God speaks to Jacob? How do these align with some of the same promises spoken to Abraham

---

[3] This tradition is represented, for instance, in Targum Ps-Jonathan and Targum Neofiti I, as well as in the later rabbinic commentary, Genesis Rabbah 68:12.

and Isaac? Why is it so necessary for us to hear, over and over, the promises of God?

3. Talk about what difference it makes if we see God standing "above the ladder" or "beside Jacob." Do you think of Christ as far off, near, or sometimes both? What does he promise in Matthew 28:18-20?

4. Discuss what mercy is and how God shows us mercy (see Ps. 51:1; Eph. 2:4-8; Luke 18:13). Did Jacob deserve mercy, or do we deserve it? How does this incident contradict the caricature of God in the OT as mean and hardhearted?

5. Read John 1:43-51. Talk about what it means for Jesus to be the one on whom angels ascend and descend. What does it mean for us as disciples that Christ is at the bottom of the ladder with us?

CHAPTER 12

The Vegetable Side of Marriage

And in the morning, behold, it was Leah!

Genesis 29:25

"It is not good that the man should be alone" (Gen. 2:18). This is the first "not good" of the Bible, made all the more remarkable by its contrast with the six "goods" and one "very good" of the creation account. It means that Adam, even before sin, was not in a *perfectly* good situation. His self was insufficient. He needed another person, one outside him, distinct from him yet matched to him, bone of his bones and flesh of his flesh. The fact that the Lord built the woman not from trees or water or soil but from the body of the man resulted in an innate, divinely designed magnetism by which man is drawn to woman and woman to man. This attraction is simultaneously biological and theological. From the awkward flirtations of middle schoolers to the wedding bells of brides and grooms today, we perpetually witness the ongoing impact of Genesis 2 in our lives.

Of course, there is another, darker side, as well. We perpetually witness the ongoing impact of the following chapter, Genesis 3, on humanity, including in the areas of marital and sexual relations. In fact, for most of us, that is where sin's blades cut most deeply, leaving lifelong scars, some of which never fully heal. All abstract talk of evil becomes painfully concrete when you walk in on your husband in bed with the woman you thought was your best friend. Now you've been gut-punched by wickedness in a whole new way. The brokenness of the world becomes very tangible when you check your wife into rehab. And we could easily fill the next hundred pages with nothing but real life examples of emotional abuse, physical abuse, sexual infidelity, gaslighting, weaponizing children, and passive-aggressive spousal revenge techniques that transmogrify some marriages—and I'm talking about the marriages of Christians too—into houses of horror.

Marriage is a truly amazing, wonderful gift of God. And *for that very reason*, it has always been, and will remain, in the crosshairs of hell's snipers.

Jacob was about to discover all of this firsthand. When we last left him, he was waking up from his dream vision, in awe over what he had experienced (28:16-19). Having made a vow to return to this location and to give a tithe to the Lord of all he had received, Jacob continued his journey to Haran (28:20-29:1). His arrival there echoes, in many ways, what happened a generation or two before when his grandfather's servant made this same journey to choose a wife for Jacob's father, Isaac (Gen. 24). That servant found Rebekah at a well, watering livestock, as Jacob now finds his own future bride, Rachel, watering her sheep at the well (Gen. 29:10). Both of these seemingly random events are, of course, divinely designed encounters. Behind the scenes, God is matchmaking, bringing man and woman together. As we shall soon see, however, Isaac and Rebekah's marriage was far more drama-free than would be their son's.

In a highly charged scene at their first encounter, Jacob "kissed Rachel and wept aloud" (Gen. 29:11). This sounds extremely weird to us. Even given cultural differences, I'm guessing it was awkward to Rachel as well. There are extremely few biblical instances of men kissing women, especially those they have just met! That being said, it is also a welcome, fresh view of Jacob. Here he is behaving in an uncalculating, vulnerable, "real deal" sort of way. There is no scheming, no trickery. Gratitude spontaneously erupts from within him. His journey is over. He is safe. He has found his extended family. And, as if all that were not enough, here is a beautiful woman with whom he seems instantly to fall head over heels in love.

In a mere twenty-two verses, we speed through the next seven years of Jacob's life (Gen. 29:11-23). He meets Laban, his mother's brother, who welcomes him with open arms. (As we shall see, after this positive first meeting, Jacob and Laban's relationship will go downhill precipitously.) The two men come to an agreement that Jacob will labor seven years to earn Rachel's hand in marriage. In one of the more moving passages of the Bible, we read that these years "seemed to [Jacob] but a few days because of the love he had for her" (29:20). Here is exemplary devotion. Jacob is no longer looking out just for himself, but working long and hard for another. The narrative, at this stage, seems to be building within us a respect, even a fondness, for Jacob.

Finally, the seven years having passed, the wedding day arrives. And yet, for the alert reader, behind the festive atmosphere, something ominous is brewing. Earlier, we were told about another daughter, Leah, the older sister of Rachel. Very rarely are biblical characters introduced willy-nilly, just to fill space on the page. We already have our Adam-character and Eve-character, so we wonder: how will Leah fit into this story? Soon we find out. Either because of the darkness of the wedding tent, the heavy veil of the bride, or the inebriation of the groom[1]—probably a combination of all three—when Jacob takes his bride to bed that night, he is wholly unaware that the woman to whom he makes love is not the woman whom he has loved the last seven years.

With gripping rhetorical brevity, this following verse says it all, "And in the morning, behold, it was Leah!" (Gen. 29:25). Laban had brought her to Jacob the night before (29:23). With words dripping with irony, the man who had deceived his father to cheat his older brother, now that he himself has been tricked into marrying the older sister, protests, "Why then have you deceived me?" (Gen. 29:25). Oh, Jacob, how the tables have turned. The deceiver has been deceived. He who pretended to be Esau sleeps with the woman pretending to Rachel. One Jewish legend expresses it this way: All night, Jacob kept calling her "Rachel," to which Leah kept answering "Yes." In the morning, when an angry Jacob called Leah a liar, she responded,

---

[1] Laban "made a feast" (Gen. 29:22). The Hebrew word *mishteh*, commonly translated "feast," is formed from the verb "to drink." There was certainly food but this was also drinking banquet. As early as the first century, Josephus explains that Jacob did not realize the deception because he was "in drink and in the dark" (*Antiquities* 1.19.7 [§301]).

"Was it not just this way that your father called out to you, 'Esau' and you answered him, 'Yes.'"[2]

In the aftermath of this shocking morning-after scene, Jacob reads the riot act to Laban, Laban flimsily justifies his deception, and both parties agree that Jacob will marry Rachel in a few days, then work an additional seven years for this second wife (Gen. 29:25-29).

Adam's first recorded words after seeing Eve are these: "This at last is bone of my bones and flesh of my flesh. She shall be called Woman because she was taken out of Man" (Gen. 2:23). What a contrast there is between Jacob's first recorded words after seeing his "Eve": "What is this you have done to me?"[3]

I think it's safe to assume that none of us, on the morning after our wedding, had quite the same shock as Jacob did. We didn't hunt down our new in-laws, pound on their door, and demand to know, "What is this you have done to me?" But for most of us, if not all of us, there does come a day or year, hopefully long after our wedding, when we ask, "What is this you have done to me?" Perhaps we ask it of our spouse. Perhaps we yell it toward heaven. Or perhaps—indeed, more than likely—we ask it of ourselves.

During marital seasons of frustration or disappointment or sheer boredom, if as Christians we were to pose that question to God, "What is this you have done to me?" perhaps his response might be something like this: "I have given you a co-sinner with whom to live, so that together, in this university of marriage, you might study and learn what a life of sacrificial love is like." That will never make it on a Hallmark card, but it is very realistic. You see, in those times when husbands and wives are on cloud nine, enjoying one another's company, relishing the gifts of stability and love and sex and friendship, there is no need to explain the Why of marriage to them. It's obvious. Just like there's no need to explain why chocolate cake is a delicious dessert. Words are unnecessary. You just know. But marriage is more than chocolate cake; there are also vegetables involved. And some of

---

[2]   A paraphrase of Genesis Rabbah 70:19.

[3]   It is telling that Jacob's words in Hebrew for "What is this you have done to me?" echo verbatim Pharaoh's words to Abram after he discovers that the patriarch deceived him regarding Sarai, "What is this you have done to me? Why did you not tell me that she was your wife?" (Gen. 12:18).

them, while they might be healthy for us, might also make us want to spit them out upon tasting them.

Welcome to the vegetable side of marriage.

The Lord was not blindsided by Adam and Eve's rebellion after their union as husband and wife. He knew very well what was looming on the horizon. He realized that these two creatures, once they were embroiled in sin, would need each other in a different, far more critical, way. We all come into this world with a shared birth defect, inherited from Adam and Eve. You won't find it in a medical textbook, but it's a sickness written into humanity's history. The Latin name is *incurvatus in se*, which means, "curved in on oneself." If you want a rapid review of what *incurvatus in se* looks like, try to make toddlers do anything they don't want to do. While this is not a learned behavior, it certainly can become a practiced, highly skilled behavior, damaging both to ourselves and others. Once we belong to Christ, the Spirit's lifelong operation within us might be summarized as repeatedly uncurving us to curve us outward toward others.

Marriage is an ideal workshop for the Spirit's uncurving labor, that we might be disciples characterized not by egotism but by "otherism." Marriage necessitates sacrifice; my will not always being done; sharing; looking out for the interests of another; fidelity; telling the truth; letting another person see my faults and bad habits and stupid mistakes; forgiving and being forgiven; in many and various ways, dying to self that the Spirit might raise us up anew in the image of Jesus.

In short, marriage is a God-given school of discipleship. Yes, it has its highs. And, yes, it has its lows. It is in the valleys that we might cry out, "What is this that you have done to me?" And let me tell you: it is fully OK to ask that question. The psalms are full of "Whys" and "Whats" and "How longs," all directed to God, all uncensored by our Father, who welcomes all laments. On the other side of lament, however, let us remember Jesus never said, "Take up your champagne and flowers and follow me." He bids us heft our crosses. As we bear them, the Spirit will never leave us, but will be laboring within us— perhaps in ways we will never fully understand—to wound and heal, to kill and enliven, to form us into the image of our crucified and resurrected Lord.

We will have ample opportunity to talk more about Jacob's marriages, and our own, in the following chapters. But for now, let's conclude with this final (and hopefully encouraging) thought: had it not been for the patriarch's unplanned marriage to Leah, Judah would not have been born. And had Judah not been born, there would have been no tribe of Judah. And had there been no tribe of Judah, there would have been no Boaz or Jesse or David or a young virgin in Nazareth named Mary, in whose womb grew the hope of our world.

"What is this that you have done to me?" an angry and disappointed Jacob demanded. Oh, if only he had known the good that our Father would one day bring from his marriage, he would have kissed Leah and wept aloud for joy.

Discussion Questions

1. Review Genesis 2, especially the creation of man and woman. Why was it not good for the man to be alone? Why did God create marriage?

2. Read Genesis 29:1-30. Talk about Laban's character, the descriptions of Rachel and Leah, and the love of Jacob. Do we see a new side of Jacob in this account? Are we given any clues as to what Rachel and Leah thought of this bride-switch?

3. What do you think of this statement? God says, "I have given you a co-sinner with whom to live, so that together, in this university of marriage, you might study and learn what a life of sacrificial love is like." Do you agree or disagree? Why?

4. What does *incurvatus in se* mean and how does it manifest itself in marriage? Give examples. How is marriage a God-given school of discipleship?

CHAPTER 13

The Sisters Who Built the House of Israel

> "May the LORD make the woman, who is coming into your house, like Rachel and Leah, who together built up the house of Israel."
>
> Ruth 4:11

The deeper we go into the Old Testament story, the more scowling and brow-wrinkling we are likely to engage in. This holy book is riddled with gross unholiness. We've got brothers murdering brothers, deceiving others, and making a few bucks by selling one into chains. We've got the sailor Noah, inebriated on the floor of his tent, wearing nothing but his birthday suit, cursing his grandson when he sobers up. We've got two of the three patriarchs saying of their wives, "Oh, this beautiful woman? Yeah, she's my sister." Abraham even gets rich off the lie. And that's only the beginning. Later, a son will have sex with the mother of his half-brothers. A daughter-in-law will dress up as a prostitute, with the express goal to be hired and impregnated by a "John" who's the father to her two dead husbands. And wait until the books of Judges, Samuel, and Kings, where familial, fraternal, and sexual craziness runs rampant.

Welcome to the highly dysfunctional biblical family.

For modern Christians, perhaps even more disconcerting than the stories themselves is the fact that sometimes we search in vain for an explicit condemnation of the actions—actions that we find, if not abominable, at least unethical. The Lord never expressly says that it was wrong for Abraham to lie about Sarah being his sister, nor is there a negative word said about him having concubines (Gen. 12:10-20; 25:6). The practice of polygamy is not prohibited. Indeed, in the situation of levirate marriage, it is expected that a brother, even if he already has a wife, will also marry his dead brother's widow to father children with her so as to carry on the legacy of his deceased brother (Deut. 25:5-10). In later biblical history, the Lord will even say to David, "[I gave] your master's wives into your arms and gave you the house of Israel and of Judah. And if this were too little, I would add to you as much more" (2 Sam. 12:8).

What are we, the disciples of Jesus, to make of these soap-opera-ish episodes? As we think about our own marriages, children, and families, what can we learn from these ancient accounts? To begin to answer those questions, let's ponder the next phase in the life of Jacob that centers on his growing number of (co-)wives and children (Gen. 29:30-30:24).

As we learned in the last chapter, the patriarch, thanks to his sly father-in-law, is now husband not to one but two wives. It doesn't take a prophet or marriage counselor to know this will not end well. Nor did it begin well. Right away, we are told that Jacob "loved Rachel more than Leah" (29:30) and that "the LORD saw that Leah was hated" (29:31).[1] We might assume, given Jacob's obvious fondness for good-looking Rachel, that he and she enjoyed romantic pillow talk every night. They did not. However rocky Jacob and Leah's marriage was, he certainly did not shy away from Leah's bed, at least during the first few years. She had four successive sons with him. The names of these sons, however, betray an ongoing bitterness. This couple's "love-making" must have been more like formalized baby-making. Leah named the boys Reuben, Simeon, Levi, and Judah. The names of the first three are Hebrew puns which convey the same dismal message: "maybe this son will make my husband love me." She names

---

[1] The Hebrew verb for "hate" (*sane*) probably carries here the connotation of "unloved" or "unchosen." As Nahum Sarna comments on this passage, "Hebrew *senu'ah* ['hated'] is paired with *'ahuvah* ['loved'] in Deuteronomy 21:15 in a similar context of the relationship of a husband to his co-wives. The term has sociolegal implications in addition to its emotional dimension. It expresses not 'hated' as opposed to 'beloved' so much as a relative degree of preference." *Genesis*. The JPS Torah Commentary (Philadelphia: The Jewish Publication Society, 1989), 206.

her firstborn, Reuben, saying, "Because the LORD has looked upon my affliction; for now my husband will love me" (29:32). Of the next son, Simeon, she says, "Because the LORD has heard that I am hated, he has given me this son also" (29:33). Levi is so named because "Now this time my husband will be attached to me, because I have borne him three sons" (29:34). Picture a modern mother naming her son, "Just," saying, "If my husband would 'just' love me." That's the message these three names convey. Only her fourth-born, Judah, receives an optimistic name, for Leah says, "This time I will praise the LORD" (29:35).

We read, too, that the initial heated romance of Jacob and Rachel began to chill over time. While her sister bore son after son, "Rachel was barren" (29:30). In time, the green-eyed monster of jealousy roared. "When Rachel saw that she bore Jacob no children, she envied her sister. She said to Jacob, 'Give me children [Hebrew: *banim* (sons)], or I shall die!'" (30:1). And how does Jacob respond to this outburst? With a reciprocal outburst: "[His] anger was kindled against Rachel, and he said, 'Am I in the place of God, who has withheld from you the fruit of the womb?'" (30:2). Once, long ago, while I was a pastor, I was in the home of a young husband and wife who were embroiled in a screaming match, each in the other's face, hurling accusations at one another. It is that scene that comes to mind when I read of Rachel and Jacob's razored words. She's hurting. He's defensive. They both say stupid, painful things. Indeed, these are Rachel's first recorded words. As is frequently the case with scriptural characters, the first recorded speech tells us much about their character. So it is with Rachel. Her life is iconic of one who, above all else, wants boys or burial. In a sad irony, it will be the birth of her second son, Benjamin, that sends this mom to the grave (Gen. 35:16-20).

Eventually, as the sisters compete for a gold medal in this baby-making competition, each enlists her maidservant to stack the nursery odds in her favor. It's the old Abraham-Sarah-Hagar move, legally and culturally acceptable at the time, in which a wife's servant was her maternity surrogate (Gen. 16:1-3). So, Rachel puts Bilhah into Jacob's bed, and Leah follows suit with Zilpah. Jacob now has a mini-harem, although it also appears that he has boycotted Leah's bed. Leah, in desperation, "hires" her husband for sex one night by bartering with Rachel, who wanted some of Leah's mandrakes (a fruit with aphrodisiac connections). When Jacob gets off work one evening, Leah informs him matter-of-factly, "'You must come in to me, for I have hired you with my son's mandrakes.' So he lay with her that night" (30:16).

By the time we reach a much-needed break in this story of nativity after nativity, here is what we find: Rachel has given birth to one son (Joseph); Leah has six sons and one daughter (Reuben, Simeon, Levi, Judah, Issachar, Zebulun, and Dinah); Bilhah has two sons (Dan and Naphtali); and Zilpah has two sons (Gad and Asher). The man who went into exile as a single guy, years before, now has two wives, two co-wives, eleven sons, and one daughter. With the exception of Benjamin, who will be born upon the family's return from exile, every one of the future patriarchs is now in the picture.

And what exactly is this a picture of? The chosen family of God. The holy community of Yahweh. The "church" of the Old Testament, warts and all.

I asked, "What are we, the disciples of Jesus, to make of all this tangled mess?" There is much to be made of it. We could talk about the rotten fruit that grows from the soil of polygamous marriages. We could talk about bitterness, jealousy, playing favorites, and unhappy marriages where "love" is something people try to earn from their spouse. The story itself could serve as a parable of problematic marriages.

What I would like us to consider, though, is this: no family, however broken, however disfigured, however dysfunctional it might be, is beyond the pale of divine grace and redemption. Generations later, when Boaz prepares to marry Ruth, the people of Bethlehem say, "May the LORD make the woman, who is coming into your house, like Rachel and Leah, who together built up the house of Israel" (Ruth 4:11). These two sisters, rivals for their husband's affection, each sorely dissatisfied in her own way, nonetheless "together built up the house of Israel." In Christian language, we would say they together built up the church. Did they do so perfectly? Of course not. Did they do so with pure motives? Hardly. But did the Lord God of Israel work through and despite their weaknesses and failings—not to mention Jacob's—to create a community in which his promises would eventually spread to the uttermost corners of the world? Yes! Yes, by grace alone, he most certainly did.

Within our communities of faith today, we are all acutely aware of families that have more than a faint reflection of the Jacob-Leah-Bilhah-Zilpah family. If you know my personal story, as I relate in *Night Driving*, I have been very happily married to my wife, Stacy, since 2013. But in my past are two divorces, as in Stacy's is one divorce. Together, we are a family, but a family with scars. At our church on Sunday morning are parents and children who have been hurt by addiction, abortion, incarceration, adultery, and a host of other traumas and evils. Even families with the outward appearance of harmony and stability often nurse deep and secret wounds, masked behind an obligatory smile.

Look carefully at every pew in church and you'll see the stains of tears and blood, and the shards of the shattered dreams of familial bliss.

Yet here we are, precisely where the Lord wants us: in his holy house, submitting ourselves to his easy yoke, that we might be his disciples. Weak and wavering, we follow him. Frightened and faltering, we nonetheless limp after Jesus. And our Lord? He couldn't be more pleased with us. He didn't say, "Come unto me, all you who have your act together, who boast idyllic households, who have dreamboat marriages." No, he said, "Come to me, all who labor and are heavy laden, and I will give you rest" (Matt. 11:28). So we do. Frustrated, like Rachel, we come. Bitter, like Leah, we come. Used, like Bilhah and Zilpah, we come. And, yes, selfish and overwhelmed, like Jacob, we come.

We come to remain in the only place where there is hope for marriage and family and children: at the foot of our Lord's cross and beside his vacant tomb. We bask in his redemptive love. We are forgiven and we forgive. And we believe that, no matter how unworthy we are, we worship a King who does not sit on his throne in vain. He rules. He rules the kingdom of which we are a part. And he rules the entire universe. How he will use us in that kingdom may not be entirely evident to us, but we confess it nonetheless. Casting ourselves on his mercy, we receive his gifts by faith and, by the Spirit's work, endeavor to let his love flow from us to others.

We know that the biblical family, if it is characterized by anything, is characterized as a community where divine mercy reigns supreme.

Discussion Questions

1. Does the dysfunctional nature of so many biblical families bother you? Why or why not?
2. Read Genesis 29:31-35 and 30:1-24. Discuss the marriages and children of Jacob. What fears, challenges, pains, disappointments, joys, and resentments were present in this family? How do we see those things evidenced in modern families and marriages?
3. What are we, the disciples of Jesus, to make of the tangled mess of the "holy" family? What major and minor truths can we learn from this part of Jacob's story?
4. How might we use this part of Jacob's life to give encouragement to spouses, children, or parents who think their family is a "lost cause" or "beyond redemption"? Read Ephesians 5:22-6:4. What instructions does Paul give to disciples about marriage and children?

CHAPTER 14

The Fruitful Winter

> Thus the man increased greatly and had large flocks, female servants and male servants, and camels and donkeys.
>
> Genesis 30:43

Over the years, I have had countless conversations with brothers and sisters in Christ that follow this same basic pattern: "I went through a very dark and difficult time in my life. It hurt. It was stressful. At times it felt like I was living through a nightmare from which I could not awaken. When it was finally over and some time had passed, I realized, in retrospect, that it was during that season of tears and tribulation that the Lord was laboring most intensely in my life. On the one hand, yes, it was the worst of times. But on the other hand, it was the best of times for Christ to shape and bless and move me down the path he wanted me to go."

We might call this spiritual season the Fruitful Winter.

The Fruitful Winter is nothing new in the lives of the people of God. Paul gives classic expression to it in his writings, especially in 2 Corinthians (e.g., 4:8-12; 6:1-10; 12:7-10). What Jesus said to Paul epitomizes this truth: "My grace is sufficient for you, for my power is made perfect in weakness." The Greek verb for "made perfect," *teleo*, is the same verb spoken by Jesus on the cross when he cried out, "*Tetelestai*," that is, "It is finished" or "It has been made perfect." And the Greek noun that Paul uses for "weakness," *astheneia*, is the same word Paul will use in the next chapter when he says that Christ was "crucified in weakness" (2 Cor. 13:4). We might summarize it this way: as the crucifixion death of Jesus, in weakness, made perfect our salvation, so our own weaknesses, trials, and crosses are when the gracious power of God does its perfect work within us. Or, as Paul ironically phrases it: "When I am weak, then I am strong" (12:10).

In Genesis 30, we are in the middle of Jacob's Fruitful Winter. In our next chapter, we will explore in greater detail his tale of woes, complete with setbacks, sufferings, and deprivations. Suffice it to say for now that if Jacob had a Paul-like "thorn in the flesh," that thorn was named Laban, who was Jacob's uncle, father-in-law, boss, and Pharoah-like character, all rolled into one. Laban's name means "white" but he was a man with glowing green dollar signs in his eyes. We first meet him, decades before, when Abraham's servant arrives in Haran to find a wife for Isaac. The servant's camels were laden with rich and elaborate gifts, for Abraham was a man of wealth. The narrator masterfully drops a strong hint about Laban's avaricious and predatory personality. He says that Laban ran out to meet the servant and "as soon as he saw the ring and the bracelets on his sister's arms," he said, "Come in, O blessed of the LORD" (Gen. 24:30-31). He had an eye for things that glittered. It was like Abraham's servant pulled up to Laban's house in a Rolls Royce. Laban knew—and wanted—a pocketful of wealth when he saw it.

At this late point in Laban's life, he has many more wrinkles, but his greediness does not seem to have lost its youthful vigor. Here's how we know. Having served Laban for fourteen years, seven for Leah plus seven more for Rachel, Jacob is itching to get back home, so he asks for permission to leave (Gen. 30:25). His father-in-law, however, is in no hurry to lose Jacob. He knows good and well that the Lord has blessed him with healthy and rapidly growing flocks (cha-ching!) precisely because of Jacob (30:27-30). So, in Laban's mind, his son-in-law is a human cash cow. The two men do a bit of haggling and make a deal—a deal that, on the surface, looks very bad for Jacob. The two men will divide the sheep and goats between them. Laban will retain the white sheep and dark goats, while Jacob will take "every speck-led and spotted sheep and every black lamb" as well as "the spotted and speckled among the goats" (Gen. 30:32). As Jacob continues to take care of Laban's livestock, every newly born non-monochromatic animal will be his.

There are, however, two major problems with this contract. First, no sooner had they made this deal when Laban stabbed Jacob in the back. He "removed the male goats that were striped and spotted, and all the female goats that were speckled and spotted, every one that had white on it, and every lamb that was black, and put them in the charge of his sons. And he set a distance of three days' journey between himself and Jacob" (Gen. 30:35-36). In other words, every animal that should have belonged to Jacob, Laban preemptively absconded with! As Nahum Sarna points out, the second problem is that in "the Near East sheep are generally white and goats are dark brown or black. A minority of sheep may have dark patches, and goats white markings."[1] At best, Jacob might hope to get an occasional lamb or kid that is striped or spotted, but they will be few and far between. As on Jacob's wedding night, so here, it appears that Laban has outfoxed his son-in-law again.

But not so fast. Laban may seem to have stabbed Jacob in the back, but God had Jacob's back. As we read in the next chapter (Gen. 31:8-12), the Lord appeared to Jacob in a dream to give him a breeding stratagem that was as unique and weird as it was effective. Jacob would peel part of the bark from "poplar and almond and plane trees," thus "exposing the white of the sticks" (30:37). These striped and spotted sticks were then placed in the troughs in front of the flocks when the stronger of the animals were mating (30:38-42). The offspring born to them would then mirror the sticks, coming forth striped and spotted. What sounds like magic, however, was anything but. This was the method that the Lord himself prescribed. If God could later use the staff of Moses to bring forth the plagues and to part the Red Sea, then he could certainly use these sticks of Jacob to bring forth non-monochromatic sheep and goats. The Lord has always joined his word of promise to physical objects to bring about good for his people.

What was the result? Over the next six years, "the man increased greatly and had large flocks, female servants and male servants, and camels and donkeys" (30:43; cf. 31:41). In fact, so greatly did Jacob's flocks increase that his cousins, Laban's sons, began to grumble,

---

[1] *Genesis*, The JPS Torah Commentary (Philadelphia: The Jewish Publication Society, 1989), 212.

"Jacob has taken all that was our father's, and from what was our father's he has gained all this wealth" (31:1). Or, as Jacob more accurately states it when speaking to Rachel and Leah, "Thus God has taken away the livestock of your father and given them to me" (31:9).

What the Lord did for Jacob is a key theme in the Old Testament. The storyline goes like this: (1) God's people are in exile; (2) they are oppressed; (3) God enriches them at the expense of their oppressors; (4) and they leave exile with more than they entered with. We see this with Abram and Sarai during their stay in Egypt (Gen. 12:10-20). We see this here with Jacob, who is soon to depart for home (31:17ff). And we observe it yet again when the Israelites leave Egypt with that country's riches in tow (Exod. 3:22; 12:36). In other words, this is the theme of the Fruitful Winter, when Yahweh's power is made perfect in their weakness.

I doubt there is a more difficult truth for us, the disciples of Jesus, to swallow than this one. I readily confess that I loathe being weak. When the Labans in my life take advantage of me, cheat me, lie to me and about me, my first instinct is to crave revenge. My desire is to be in complete control of my life, a step ahead of my competition, have all my ducks in a rows, and be strong and healthy enough to push my agenda toward a successful completion. In other words, I want *my* will to be done—and done in my way, at the time of my choosing, and according to my precise specifications. And, if it's not too much to ask, I'd like a little applause along the way.

In short, I like Fruitful Summers not Fruitful Winters. Don't we all?

But what we like and what our Father knows is best for us are rarely in alignment. The end result of our will always being done would be our undoing, our destruction, both in this life and in eternity. We are like three or four-year-old children whose wills are bent toward those things that satisfy momentarily and disappoint permanently. So, our Father, whose will is to save and bless and refine us, often leads us into a wintery exile, where we learn—usually the hard way—that he is God and we are not.

In this wintery exile, however, we are not just learning our mortality, weakness, and vulnerability but, much more importantly, our Savior's mercy and grace toward us. As the apostle says, "When I am weak, then I am strong" (2 Cor. 12:10). Our weakness opens up a vacuum within us to be filled by the strength of Jesus. We are enrolled in the school of the cross which, by definition, is going to hurt, but is also simultaneously going to show forth the glory of God in our lives. In Jacob's case, without Laban, without exile, without bearing his own cross, the patriarch would never have gained a family and possessions with which to return from exile. God's power was made perfect in Jacob's weakness.

We see, therefore, that for the disciples of Jesus, the cross will always define for us how the Lord is at work in our lives. This doesn't mean that we are always hurting, always overshadowed by the dooms and glooms of life. Rather, it means that discipleship is dying to self, dying to self-will, dying to what we want, by our co-crucifixion with Jesus. We die with him in order to be raised with him to a new life. As Paul says, "Do you not know that all of us who have been baptized into Christ Jesus were baptized into his death? We were buried therefore with him by baptism into death, in order that, just as Christ was raised from the dead by the glory of the Father, we too might walk in newness of life" (Rom. 6:3-4). Our new life is shaped by baptism, in which we both die and rise with Jesus. This once-in-a-lifetime union with him in the Word-soaked water of baptism is the pattern for our entire lives, as daily the Spirit puts to death our rebellious and egocentric natures and raises us to reflect the image of our Lord and King.

In our Fruitful Winter, the Messiah does not abandon us. Quite the opposite. With his own hands and side still bearing the marks of the spear and nails, those stigmata of divine love, he gently shepherds us into our own weakness and his ongoing and merciful strength.

DISCUSSION QUESTIONS

1. Discuss times in life (either your own or others) that could be described as a "Fruitful Winter." Besides Jacob, what are some other biblical examples of individuals who endured such a "winter"?

2. Read Genesis 30:25-43. What is the basic strategy (devised by God [31:4-13]) to increase Jacob's herds and flocks? What are some other examples of the Lord's use of ordinary things, joined to his word, to produce good

for his people? Read Exodus 14:16; Numbers 21:8-9; Judges 7:16-22; Acts 2:38.

3. Read 2 Corinthians 4:8-12; 6:1-10; 12:7-10. Use these passages to discuss this statement: "We are like three or four-year-old children whose wills are bent toward those things that satisfy momentarily and disappoint permanently. So, our Father, whose will is to save and bless and refine us, often leads us into a wintery exile, where we learn—usually the hard way—that he is God and we are not."

4. Read Romans 6:3-4. How do God's actions upon us and for us in baptism shape our lives as disciples?

CHAPTER 15

Pocketing an Idol on the Way to Church

Rachel stole her father's household gods.

Genesis 31:19

In his book, *The Cost of Discipleship*, Dietrich Bonhoeffer famously wrote, "When Christ calls a man, he bids him come and die." Die to what? Bonhoeffer lists martyrdom; dying to our affections and lusts; dying to our own will; and dying to our attachments in this world. All of this is true. To "bear the cross" as a disciple of Jesus can mean one thing and one thing only: that cross is there to kill you. An uncrucified disciple is a contradiction in terms.

When those words of Bonhoeffer were first quoted to me, I was a university student, a young believer. And I grabbed hold of the words. My heart was on fire for Jesus. I was ready to sacrifice my all for him and his kingdom. Show me a cross, O Lord, and I'll bare my hands and feet for the nails. I would work. I would suffer. If necessary, I would even bleed. The one thing I would never do is turn my back on my Savior. And I could not fathom how other people, supposedly Christians, did so on a regular basis. They were self-indulgent, worldly, vain, lustful, and greedy. Some were drunks. Others did drugs or slept around. But I, thank God, had died and was fully committed to Jesus. I was a real Christian.

As you might suspect, I was also a raging hypocrite. I had just as well been praying the Pharisee's prayer, "God, I thank you that I am not like other men…" (Luke 18:11). It was concealed from me then, but at that young age I was already nursing within my breast a dragon of spiritual arrogance that one day would rear its ugly head to devour me and all my precious spiritual trophies.

One of the many truths that I had yet to comprehend, on a deep visceral level, was that the dying to which Christ called me—the dying of which Bonhoeffer actually wrote—was not a once-in-a-lifetime event; it was a *daily, recurring, non-stop* death to self. It wasn't as if one day Jesus made me a disciple, all my weaknesses and temptations and predilections to evil fell away like scales from my heart, and I became a radically new person adorned with a virginal soul. No, I was still prone to self-destructive thoughts and vain whims. I still acted stupidly, egocentrically, judgmentally. And, at the root of all this was the factory within my heart that still churned out false gods, false trusts, false religiosities, 24/7.

I was going to church all the time, but I pocketed plenty of idols along the way.

Pocketing idols, it seems, is a fairly consistent biblical theme. As we shall see shortly, Rachel did it when she and her family left Haran (Gen. 31:19). When the Israelites left Egypt, Moses warned them to stop worshiping goat demons (Lev. 17:7). Much later, Ezekiel says the Israelites did not "forsake the idols of Egypt" (Ezek. 20:8). Long after their entry into Canaan, when Joshua is an old man, he tells the Israelites, "Put away the gods that your fathers served beyond the River and in Egypt, and serve the LORD" (Josh. 24:14). In the New Testament, the old Canaanite gods and goddesses had morphed into Roman or Greek deities—or went under the title of possessions or power or sex—but their reality and influence remained unchanged.

What else remained unchanged is that one of the many ongoing deaths that we, as disciples, must endure is perpetually dying to our fear, love, and trust in something more than our one true heavenly Father.[1]

Genesis 31 documents the tumultuous events surrounding the undercover flight of Jacob and his family from Laban. This was "Jacob's exodus," a foreshadowing of Israel's future exit from Egypt. As we discussed in the last chapter, Laban was a supremely unsavory character, a kind of mini-Pharaoh who harassed and plagued the

---

[1] I am alluding to Martin Luther's explanation of the First Commandment in his *Small Catechism*, "We should fear, love, and trust in God above all things."

patriarch and his family for twenty years. In the traditional Jewish Passover liturgy, Laban is even said to have been worse than Pharaoh![2] His rap sheet is impressively long: he deceived Jacob on his wedding night with the sister-swap; forced him to work seven more years for the woman he loved; cheated Jacob and changed his wages ten times (31:7); basically sold his daughters to Jacob and devoured any money that would have been theirs (31:15); like a rustler, stole the sheep and goats that were rightfully the patriarch's (30:35-36); and, to top it all off, would have sent Jacob away empty-handed had not God intervened (31:42). After two decades of such abuse, Jacob and his wives agreed that enough was enough. The Lord, too, affirmed Jacob's desire, saying to him, "Return to the land of your fathers and to your kindred, and I will be with you" (31:3). That was divine music to Jacob's ears. So, seizing the opportunity provided by Laban's absence during the time of sheep shearing, the patriarch and his entourage of wives, co-wives, children, servants, flocks, camels, and donkeys surreptitiously began their long journey homeward (31:17-21).

Right in the middle of this narrative, however, the author drops these ominous words, "Rachel stole her father's household gods" (31:19). Reading these words is like finding a hair in that tasty bowl of soup you're eating. It's nasty. It's disgusting. And it's all too real. The Hebrew word for these "household gods" is *t'rafim*. They were probably figurines that represented the deities who looked out for the well-being of Laban's household, akin to the later *penantes* in Roman homes. Why Rachel stole these, we are not told. Maybe she thought they would watch over her and her family on this long journey. Maybe she thought that by taking them away from her father, these gods would now be with her instead of him.[3] Whatever her reasons, by

---

[2] By a complicated and highly creative interpretation, Deuteronomy 26:5 is understood to mean "an Aramean sought to destroy my ancestor," that is, Laban the Aramean sought to do this. See Jeffrey H. Tigay's discussion in *Deuteronomy*, The JPS Torah Commentary (Philadelphia: The Jewish Publication Society, 1996), 240.

[3] The traditional rabbinic interpretation spins this in a positive direction: Rachel was intending to free her father of his attachment to idolatry (*Genesis Rabbah* 74:5). Martin Luther, in his lectures on Genesis, argues that Rachel stole the gods for monetary reasons, because that was all that was left of her inheritance (American Edition [AE] 6:25-35).

this woeful action, Rachel, the matriarch of Israel, foreshadowed her own family's future problem of pocketing idols on their way to the promised land.

There is more to the story of these *t'rafim*, of course, and we will get to that in the next chapter, complete with the darkly humorous account of a menstruating woman sitting on kidnapped gods. For now, however, let's simply pause and ruminate on Rachel's actions and their implications for our lives.

It wasn't as if Rachel were ignorant of the true God. Nor had she kicked him to the religious curb in favor of some sexier popular deities in the neighborhood of Haran. When Joseph was born, for instance, Rachel exclaimed, "May the LORD add to me another son!" (Gen. 30:24). She knew the LORD, that is, Yahweh. She believed in and prayed to Yahweh. Rachel simply wanted "Yahweh *and t'rafim*." The technical term for this is syncretism, but we can think of it as Yahweh And-ism.[4] Yahweh and Baal. Yahweh and Asherah. Yahweh and Power or Money or Popularity or Family or Work or Ego or fill-in-the-blank. The particular god that follows the "and" really doesn't matter. They all communicate the same diabolical lie: Yahweh alone doesn't quite measure up. He needs another god to lend him a hand. He is an insufficient deity with insufficient power that he displays in insufficient ways. He is not enough.

I wish I could say that, given enough time and spiritual maturation, we move past Yahweh And-ism. We outgrow this juvenile syncretism and, with souls wedded to our Lord, we are able to concentrate on purging other areas of our lives where peccadilloes, those "minor sins," still lurk. But that is never the case with any disciple, whether we are ten or one hundred years old. The *t'rafim* of Rachel, rather than ceasing to woo our hearts, simply change their tunes and alter their forms.

What is so sinister and dangerous about *t'rafim* is that, unlike Rachel's figurines, ours are very often, in and of themselves, good. We trust in Christ and Family. We are devoted to Christ and our Political Party. What is most important to us is Christ and our Nation, our

---

[4] C. S. Lewis gives classical expression to this in *The Screwtape Letters*, where Screwtape advises Wormwood to keep his patient focuses on "Christianity And." (New York: Macmillan Publishing, 1961), 115.

Job, our Success, our Body, our Stuff. There is nothing wrong or evil about any of these, in isolation. And that is why, of course, they are ideal masks behind which the *t'rafim* can hide. Paul is hinting at the same when he says that "even Satan disguises himself as an angel of light" (2 Cor. 11:14). He wraps himself in the mantle of that which is good and wholesome so as, slowly and deliberately, to beckon us into the embrace of night.

For this reason, our Lord often uses the Greek verb *prosecho* in the Gospels, such as: "Beware of men" (Matt. 10:17); "pay attention to yourselves" (Luke 17:3); "watch yourselves" (21:34). Or, Jesus will use the verb *gregoreo*: "stay awake" (Matt. 24:42) and "watch therefore" (25:13). In other words, "Check your pockets for idols." They will always be there. And for this reason, too, the life of discipleship is lifelong repentance—or, in the words of Bonhoeffer, coming to Christ and dying. Dying to synergism. Dying to Yahweh And-ism.

Therefore, a helpful question for us to ask ourselves is this: which *t'rafim* are in my pocket today, this week, this year? What has grabbed hold of my heart? When I am lost in thought, what captivates my mind? What do I worry most about? Chances are, the answers to those questions are our own *t'rafim*.

With that answer on your mind, and the confession of that sin upon our lips, we are ready to die once more. But a sweet death it is, for death to self is simply life in Jesus. Our daily, ongoing contrition and repentance is the Spirit's way of emptying our pockets of idols and filling our hearts with forgiveness, salvation, peace, life, and freedom in the Messiah.

Discussion Questions

1. Talk about the various meanings of "idol" in our society, everything from "pop idol" to "American Idol," to simply an "idol." What do all of these suggest? What definition might you use to encompass all these usages?
2. Read Genesis 31:1-21. Why did Rachel steal her father's gods? What might have been her motivations?
3. Discuss "Yahweh And-ism," or what C. S. Lewis called "Christianity And." What are we most prone to put after that "and"? Why is idolatry so pervasive and dangerous?

4. Read 1 Corinthians 10:1-14. What does Paul want us to learn—positively and negatively— from the history of Israel? In particular, what does he say about idolatry?

5. Talk about this statement and what it means for us as disciples: "Our daily, ongoing contrition and repentance is the Spirit's way of emptying our pockets of idols and filling our hearts with forgiveness, salvation, peace, life, and freedom in the Messiah."

CHAPTER 16

Peaceful Goodbyes to the Labans
in Our Lives

"Come now, let us make a covenant, you and I. And let
it be a witness between you and me."

Genesis 31:44

Fifteen years ago, I sat across from a man who was gravely disappointed in me. And he had every right to be so. He was the president of the seminary where, for the last five years, I had taught. During that time, I had been unfaithful to my wife. My sin dealt a fatal blow to my marriage—and with my marriage, my job and career and so much more. At the time of our meeting, the ripple effects of my actions were only beginning. Things would get much worse before they got better. Rumors would fly. The truth leak out. A whole community would soon feel the impact of my stupid and selfish actions.

That afternoon, as I sat in the president's office, I knew this would be our parting of ways. He and I would probably never see each other again (we have not). The looming question was this: how would we say Goodbye? In silence? In anger? In bitter disappointment?

We said Goodbye with him forgiving me. I confessed to him what I had done. No excuses. No blame-shifting. Just a full, gut-wrenching outpouring of my sin and shame. And he, who had always been a pastoral and grandfatherly figure to me, pronounced over me the absolution I so desperately wanted and needed. To this day, I don't know that I have ever felt more empty and more full at the same time.

After a short conversation in which he offered me some sage advice, we rose and shook hands. I drove away from a campus to which I will never return, and from a man who, on this side of eternity, I will probably never again see face to face. Given the circumstances, we said Goodbye in the best possible manner: with a peaceful acknowledgment that our Lord, who reigns over both of us in mercy, was charting different paths for our lives from that day forward.

I wish I could tell you that all my Goodbyes to former friends and acquaintances have been characterized by such grace. Sadly, they have not. And I shoulder much of the responsibility for those less-than-ideal parting of ways. I do hope, however, that I have learned this much from the errors of my past: that "if possible, so far as it depends on you, live peaceably with all" (Rom. 12:18). If that is not possible, however, at least part in peace and forgiveness, dropping every vestige of bitterness and anger into the fire of our Lord's mercy.

Genesis 31 is about a final parting of ways: the emotionally intense separation of Jacob and Laban. In the end, the men will have their peaceful (or, at least, semi-peaceful) Goodbye, but not at the beginning. Not at all. When these two deceivers stand before each other one last time, you can envision them right in each other's face, spit flying, shaking their fists, letting old grievances rise volcanically to the surface and spew forth the lava of rage.

As we noted in the last chapter, Jacob and his family snuck away while Laban was away shearing his flocks of sheep (Gen. 31:19). If you grew up around wheat farmers, as I did, at harvest time you don't plan on seeing much of the farmer or his crew for days, if not weeks. They seem to work, eat, and sleep in their combines and grain trucks. Shearing time was like harvest time. Laban, his sons, and his servants would have been sweating and shearing, shearing and sweating, from sunup to sundown. For that reason, word of Jacob's exodus didn't reach Laban until the third day, so, although in hot pursuit, it took him and his men a full week to catch up with them (31:22-23).

I picture Laban, on these seven days, cursing Jacob under his breath, daydreaming of revenge, fuming over how much of his own money and property had fallen into his son-in-law's lap. To add insult to injury, he likely began this pursuit before all the sheep were sheared. Now he would be way behind when he finally returned from this chase. He was incensed. In fact, given the warning that God gives to Laban, and the way Laban later speaks to Jacob, this man's fury was potentially murderous. The Lord warned him in a dream, "Watch yourself, lest you speak to Jacob either good or evil!" (Gen. 31:24, R. Alter). And, when relaying this divine word, Laban says to Jacob, "It is in my power to do you harm..." (31:29).

Laban is a mad dog that God has on a short leash.

Twenty years before, Jacob's life had been endangered by his brother. Now, the danger is his father-in-law. His exodus years are thus bookended by a sword hanging over his head. In that way, he is like his namesake, the nation of Israel, during their exodus years in Egypt. The looming threat of famine drove them to Egypt at the beginning, and, at the end, their life was endangered by Pharaoh at the Red Sea. In the case of both the individual and the nation, Jacob/ Israel was saved from death only by the protective care and ferocious love of Yahweh.

When Laban finally confronts Jacob, the old man becomes quite the drama queen. Using virtually the same expression that Jacob had used against him on the morning after his surprise wedding to Leah, Laban now accuses Jacob, "What have you done...?" (Gen. 31:26; 29:25). Laban, the deceiver, has now been deceived, even as Jacob, the deceiver, had earlier been deceived by Laban. It's been a vicious cycle of reprisal and counter-reprisal. Rachel and Leah have already told us that their father cared not one iota for them; he had sold them out and devoured their money, after all (31:15). So, they were fully cooperative in this flight from their unpaternal father. But Laban, in full-blown hypocrite mode, accuses Jacob of driving his daughters away like "captives of the sword" (31:26). He would have us believe that his earnest desire had been to send them off with a party worthy of Mardi Gras, "with mirth and songs, with tambourine and lyre" (31:27). I seriously doubt anyone believed Laban, including Laban himself.

Then, almost in mid-sentence, Laban drops all pretense and levels a serious accusation: "Why did you steal my gods?" And by "you" he points a finger at Jacob alone. The "you" in Hebrew is not y'all, that is, the family of Jacob, but it is the second person masculine singular. The entire scene that follows this accusation would be comedic were it not so serious. Jacob is standing firm on his and his family's innocence. Unbeknownst to Jacob, Rachel is sitting on the very idols that her husband thinks are not there (she's on her period no less, thus ritually unclean and desecrating these idols [Lev. 15:22]). And Laban, like a raging drunk who can't find the remote control, is turning everything upside-down, throwing the cushions off the couch, groping through all the tents. Rachel, with what I can't help but believe is a bit of relief, says basically, "Sorry, Dad, but I can't get up to give you a hug because, well, it's my time of the month, so I'm stuck here perched on my camel saddle."

Finally, Jacob has had enough. In Kenny Rogers' classic song, "Coward of the County," Tommy has "twenty years of crawling... bottled up inside him" when he lets loose on those "Gatlin boys" who have hurt his Becky. Likewise, Jacob has twenty years of anger bottled up inside him—and he lets that anger fly through a flurry of verbal fists. "What is my offense? What is my sin, that you have hotly pursued me?" he begins (Gen. 31:36). Then he launches into a point-by-point exposé of Laban's perfidy in the face of Jacob's own unflinching fidelity (31:37-42). When Jacob is done, all Laban can do is offer a short, lame defense that's as unconvincing as the toddler's oath that he didn't eat the cookies while chocolate is smeared all over his face.

All that being said, however, let's give credit where credit is due. In the end, it is Laban, not Jacob, who sues for peace (Gen. 31:44). Did Laban realize that he would need a dream team of lawyers to defend his indefensible deeds or did he genuinely desire peace? Who knows? It doesn't really matter. What does matter was that, once both men had vented their spleens and cooled down a bit, they did the right thing. They cut a covenant. They agreed to the mutual conditions. They offered a sacrifice and ate the ceremonial meal which sealed the deal (31:44-54). As the sun rose, Laban kissed his daughters and grandchildren Goodbye (31:55). When Jacob first showed up in his life, two decades before, Laban "ran to meet him and embraced him and kissed him and brought him to his house" (29:13). As they now part, there is no kiss. No embrace. But at least there is peace. The animosity has been dealt with. Both men can now move forward, guided, each down a different path, by the same Lord of peace.

I think it's safe to assume that we all have Labans in our past. Perhaps our present, too. Maybe it was a boss with a demeaning and dictatorial attitude. A spouse who came into our lives like a warm April breeze and left like a frigid February storm. Jesus isn't the only one who's experienced a Judas kiss him, after all. And, if we're honest with ourselves, we have probably been a Laban (or a Judas) to somebody else as well. I certainly have, more than once. We hurt and we get hurt. We lie and we are lied to. We're a motley mixture of both Jacob and Laban. Therefore, sometimes, whether due to external circumstances or personal choices, we part ways with others. We say Goodbye. The question is, How?

Above all, with forgiveness. To forgive others is, first, to confess, "I am not God. Forgiveness is not my property to do with as I see fit, when I see fit, and to whom I see fit. God alone owns forgiveness. Our name is not written on the absolution; the name of Christ is." Second, to forgive others is to pray, "God forgive you. God be merciful to you. Jesus be your God as well as mine." The president of the seminary could have given me the cold shoulder of non-forgiveness or the warm embrace of mercy. He chose the latter. And my life was enriched by those words more than he or anyone else could ever fathom. Why not enrich the lives of those to whom we say Goodbye with the same word of forgiveness that the Father, in Christ, has spoken to us? As we pray, "Forgive us our trespasses, as we forgive those who trespass against us."

Let me hasten to clarify that saying Goodbye with forgiveness is not the same as saying, "I really wish you would stay in my life." Not every fellow disciple is a good friend, a healthy influence, a trusted confidant, or even someone we want to be around much. Wise is the advice of Jesus ben Sirach: "Let those who are friendly with you be many, but let your advisers be one in a thousand" (Sirach 6:6 NRSV). Laban may have been a believer, but, let's face it, he also comes across as a huge jerk and pain in the posterior. Had Jacob continued to live with him, both men would probably have eventually come to blows, if not bloodshed. Jacob made the prudent decision, blessed by God, to go a different path and put plenty of distance between himself and his father-in-law. Often, we are wise to do the same with those who, for whatever reason, mix with us like fire and gasoline.

"If possible, so far as it depends on you, live peaceably with all," Paul says (Rom. 12:18). Those words, "so far as it depends on you," mean that we are not responsible for creating peace-loving, forgiving hearts inside other people. Again, we are not God. Lord knows, we cannot even create those kinds of hearts inside ourselves! What we can do is pray, "Create in me a clean heart, O God," (Psalm 51:10). Spark in me a love of peace. Nourish in me a desire to forgive. And rescue me from thinking I am the Savior of others.

In what was possibly the greatest understatement of his ministry, Jesus said, "In this world you will have trouble" (John 13:33 NIV). Trouble with Laban. Trouble with Laban's sons. Trouble with Laban's uncle's third cousin's stepfather's grandchild. On and on it goes. We will have trouble, and most of that trouble will be due to relationships with others. Take heart, friends. We are not called to fix the world. We are not called to fix any and every relationship. When we can, yes, let's do it with humility, love, and self-sacrifice. But when we can't, let us forgive, pray for them, and trust that we are both covered in the mercy of the Son, who, in his strange and mysterious way, not only loves us all, but likes us as well.

Discussion Questions

1. Read Genesis 31:22-55. Why does Laban pursue Jacob and his family? What are his motivations and accusations? Is there any merit to them? Why or why not?
2. What kind of response does Laban receive from Rachel (Gen. 31:35) and Jacob (31:36-42)? What is the essence of Jacob's complaint? Is there any merit to it? Why or why not?
3. Suppose you were the designated peacemaker between Laban and Jacob. What would you have recommended? Have you ever been in a situation where you were trying to bring peace between two groups or two individuals? What were the challenges you faced?
4. Read Romans 12:18; Ephesians 4:32; Matthew 6:12-15; Colossians 3:13. What does it mean to forgive? Does forgiveness mean that we must also maintain a close relationship with the person whom we have forgiven? Discuss specific scenarios where this might (or has) happened.

Part 3

Coming Home: Fighting God and Limping Onward

CHAPTER 17

The Beating of His Hideous Heart

> Then Jacob was greatly afraid and distressed.
>
> Genesis 32:7

In Edgar Allan Poe's gothic short story, *The Tell-Tale Heart*, a madman describes his murder of an old man whose "vulture eye" made his blood run cold. After killing the man, dismembering his corpse, and hiding the body parts beneath the floorboards of the old man's room, the assailant convinced himself that he had gotten away with it. He'd covered all his tracks. The perfect crime. Even when three policemen show up at his door to investigate the report of a scream from the house that night, he greets them "with a light heart," so certain is he that they will discover nothing.[1] In the "wild audacity of [his] perfect triumph," he not only invites the policemen to sit in three chairs inside the room where the crime was committed, but positions his own chair directly "upon the very spot beneath which reposed the corpse of the victim." Wild audacity, indeed.

The tale famously concludes, however, with the perpetrator becoming his own prosecutor. He begins to hear a "low, dull, quick sound—much such a sound as a watch makes when enveloped in cotton." It is the beating of a heart. As its volume increases, the madman, highly agitated, is astonished that the policemen pretend as if they hear nothing. Louder, louder, louder, louder it sounds! Finally, losing

---

[1] All quotations are from *Great American Short Stories*, Introduction and Notes by Jane Smiley (New York: Barnes and Noble, 2012), 81-85.

all self-control, he shrieks at the officers to stop their make-believe. "I admit the deed! –tear up the planks! here, here! –It is the beating of his hideous heart!" But, of course, it was not. The beating of the hideous heart arose from the chest of the guilty man.

His tell-tale heart, unseen and unheard by others, was both inescapable and unforgiving.

In Poe's story, the time span between the crime and its effect upon the murderer is very brief, mere hours. In many, if not most, situations of life, that span is much longer. Weeks, months, years, even decades will crawl by. To others, it may seem as if the skeletons in our closet have turned to dust, which in turn has been blown away by the winds of time. But we will not forget. Open the closet of our minds and there will lie the skeletons, fresh, accusing, their lifeless stares keeping alive the guilt, the shame, the fear. And boom, boom, boom will beat that hideous heart within us.

When last we left Jacob, he had just made peace with one family member, Laban, his father-in-law. No sooner is that wound healed, however, when he is forced to deal with a far more seriously fractured relationship with yet another family member, Esau, his twin brother. From the frying pan into the fire goes our friend, Jacob.

As you will recall, twenty years ago, the last recorded words of Esau were, "I will kill my brother, Jacob" (Gen. 27:41). Now there's a plainspoken man. And it was no empty threat. What Jacob did to Esau would be the modern equivalent of a younger brother taking advantage of his older brother's absence on a hunting trip to commit identity theft against him in order to steal the right to run the family farm, to own all the tractors and other implements, to manage the herds of cattle, to hire and fire the workers, and to inherit the hefty bank account—and to do all of this with no legal penalty, no recourse for the older brother in a court of law, no way to undo the theft. So, *of course* Esau wanted to kill Jacob. He had burglarized Esau's entire future. I daresay most of us, in the same situation, would have been just as murderously angry.

I've always wondered—perhaps you have as well—what Jacob thought of himself in light of his actions. Did he pat himself on the back for pulling this off, for snagging that blessing that he'd been fighting for since, quite literally, the day of his birth (Gen. 25:26)? Or, as the years drug by, did he begin to question the wisdom of what he'd done? In his diatribe against Laban, Jacob had bitterly complained of his life as a shepherd: "There I was: by day the heat consumed me, and the cold by night, and my sleep fled from my eyes" (Gen. 31:40). As he alternately sweated and shivered, did he ever think, "If I hadn't stolen my brother's blessings, how different might my life have been"? On those nights of insomnia, was he also dwelling on his past, ruminating on his brother's anger, and still hearing those chilling words echo in his mind, "I will kill my brother, Jacob"?

A few things we are told about Jacob reveal what was going on in his mind. One, as Jacob nears the land of his birth, his first action is not to find his parents. It's not to locate a new home for his large family. Rather, he seeks the favor of his brother:

> And Jacob sent messengers before him to Esau his brother in the land of Seir, the country of Edom, instructing them, "Thus you shall say to my lord Esau: Thus says your servant Jacob, 'I have sojourned with Laban and stayed until now. I have oxen, donkeys, flocks, male servants, and female servants. I have sent to tell my lord, in order that I may find favor in your sight.'" (Gen. 32:3-5)

In accordance with the style of other near Eastern letters, the Hebrew should probably be translated: "Thus you shall say—'To my lord Esau, thus says your servant Jacob....'" (32:4, R. Alter). Jacob does not begin his brief epistle with "Dear Esau" or "Dear Brother," but by calling Esau "lord" and himself "servant." The great irony is that Jacob, both by prophecy and paternal blessing, was supposed to be "lord" over Esau (Gen. 27:29), yet here the exact opposite obtains. This standard language of a vassal means that Jacob is not feigning equality with Esau. Whether he is sincere, or merely trying to placate his brother, is not our concern. He obviously realizes he has a twenty-year-old, burned-out bridge to repair and he's starting the reconstruction with these obsequious words.

Second, the message from Jacob isn't simply, "Hey, brother, I'm back. Let's grab a beer and hash things out." No, he mentions "oxen, donkeys, flocks, male servants, and female servants" (Gen. 32:5). Jacob is not flashing a bunch of cash in front of his brother to show how well he's done for himself. That might only incite Esau. Rather, as Nahum Sarna notes, he "obliquely hints that he has the wherewithal to pay off his brother, if need be."[2] His goal? "To find favor in [Esau's] sight" (32:5). In other words, as Rashi, the medieval Jewish scholar, points out, Jacob is saying, "I am at peace with you and seek your friendship."[3]

When these messengers return, however, a dark cloud hovers over them: "We came to your brother Esau, and he is coming to meet you, and there are four hundred men with him" (Gen. 32:6). In other parts of Scripture, four hundred men are the typical size of a militia or raiding party (e.g., 1 Sam. 22:2; 25:13; 30:10,17). If you're Jacob, there is only one interpretation you can put on this: Esau is marching to make good on his threat to put you six feet under. If revenge is a dessert best served cold, then Esau's is ice cold; it's been cooling for two long decades. He has dreamed of this day. Finally, it's here. His brother will get what he has coming. The man who stole his future will have his own future stolen from him with the blade of sword.

Jacob's reaction? He "was greatly afraid and distressed" (Gen. 32:7). Oh, I bet he was. The tell-tale heart began its ominous beat.

We will get to both Jacob's prayer and the brothers' reunion soon enough. Right now, let's just sit beside Jacob for a moment and reflect. You see, we are at a distinct advantage: we know what Jacob could not have known. We know that Esau, far from marching with a clenched fist, comes with an open heart. He can't wait to see his brother, hug him, and kiss him as if no bad blood has ever existed between them (Gen. 33:4). Even if we could tell that to Jacob, he'd probably think we were a few fries short of a Happy Meal. Mercy does often sound insane. It's hard to hear the truth, even a welcome truth, over the drumming of that tell-tale heart.

One of the takeaways from this episode is that unconfessed guilt ranks high among the great tragedies of life. David describes how, when he was silent about his sin, his body wasted away, he groaned, his "vitality was drained away as with the fever heat of summer" (Ps. 32:3-4 NASB). In Fyodor Dostoevsky's novel, *Crime and Punishment*, Raskolnikov has murdered two women. After the

---

[2] *Genesis*, The JPS Torah Commentary, 224.

[3] The helpful comments and explanations by the famous medieval Jewish scholar, Rashi, can be found at the website sefaria.org.

crime, he discovers the full physical, psychological, and spiritual hell of unconfessed and unabsolved evil. It is a python that wraps itself around the soul and begins to squeeze. I often wonder if most of our world's horrors—the shattering of families, the acrid bitterness of some marriages, the nightmarish despair that drives some to end their own lives, or even to take the life of another in a fit of rage—I often wonder if those horrors cannot ultimately be traced back to the beating of that hideous heart. It will not stop accusing. It poisons our lives and relationships. And it will not be silenced.

Ah, but it can. "Confess your sins to one another," James says (5:16). Dietrich Bonhoeffer writes, "You are a sinner, a great, desperate sinner; now come, as the sinner you are, to the God who loves you. He wants you as you are; He does not want anything from you, a sacrifice, a work; He wants you alone."[4] "Me," we might object, "this epic failure at life? Me, this adulterer, murderer, thief? Me, this person who can't ever seem to do anything right?" Yes, precisely you. Jesus has no time for perfect people (as if they existed anyway). But he has all eternity for sinners. Indeed, he cries out, "Come to me! Come to me, all you who are weary and heavy laden, all you who are lousy disciples, all you who can't unhear that tell-tale heart."

We come to him in the great gift of true Christian community, where sin has been wholly democratized. When I stand before my pastor, or when I sit with any fellow disciple, and say to them, "I have sinned," we speak their native tongue. A sinner to sinners. And having heard our confession, they say to us, "Friend, you are forgiven. In Christ, you are free. God does not know or remember your sin. It has been buried so deeply in the flesh of Jesus that it will never be seen or heard from again. Mention it to God and he will say, "My child, I have no earthly idea what you're talking about."

It's *that* gone.

And we can never hear this enough. This message of healing grace, of a sin-forgetting God, let its sweet music be the same song we hear day in and day out—in our homes, our churches, our friendships. The more we hear it, the longer we hear it, a phenomenal thing will begin to happen: that tell-tale heart will begin to weaken. What

---

[4] *Life Together*, translated by John W. Doberstein (New York: HarperCollins Publisher, 1954), 132.

once was a boom of guilt will, by and by, become a whimper, a whisper, a wheezing rasp of a dying accusation that finally is silenced for good, so that all we hear is the voice of Jesus saying to each of us, "With you, my beloved child, my treasure, the apple of my eye, with you I am well pleased."

DISCUSSION QUESTIONS

1. Read Genesis 32:1-8. How does Edgar Allan Poe's gothic short story, *The Tell-Tale Heart*, exemplify what is happening during this episode of Jacob's life?
2. Does something you did years ago, even decades ago, still bother you? What are some less-than-helpful ways of dealing with these bad memories? How did Jacob attempt to deal with his?
3. Read Psalm 32:1-5. How does the psalmist describe his pre-confession, pre-forgiveness life? How does he describe his life after confession? Discuss what we can learn from this.
4. Read James 5:16 and John 20:19-23. From whom do we seek forgiveness? How can we make confession and forgiveness more central in our lives as followers of Jesus?

CHAPTER 18

Messy Prayers: (Mis)quoting God's Words Back to Him

"But you said, 'I will surely do you good.'"

Genesis 32:12

Certain prayers stand as signposts along the road of my life. When I was a boy, my father would pray at our kitchen table, thanking the Lord for all the food and asking him to bless it "to the nourishment of our bodies." When I was in the hospital as a teenager, my eyes horribly burned after a firework explosion, my mother's voice relentlessly begged Jesus to heal my eyes (which he did). As a young pastor, every Sunday morning, I knelt before the altar in a silent church and prayed the seven penitential psalms to ready my heart for the day. A decade later, when that heart was in shambles and I was cancerous with rage, I pounded my fist on heaven's door, crying out, "Where the [insert profanity] are you, God, and why are you so intent on making my life a living [insert profanity] hell!" And, not long ago, as I sat crumpled on the floor of my study, suddenly overwhelmed with emotion at what our Lord has done for me, I prayed through hot tears these simple words, "Thank you, Jesus. Thank you for keeping me from ending my life during those dark years, and for carrying me into the light of hope once more."

In ways that we don't usually realize, prayer documents the ebb and flow of our lives.

I find the variety of prayer in Scripture both fascinating and instructive. There stands the Pharisee, patting himself on the back as he prays, "God, I thank you that I am not like other men, extortioners, unjust, adulterers, or even like this tax collector" (Luke 18:11). That same tax collector simply utters, "God, be merciful to me, a sinner!" (18:13). Abraham bargains with the Lord in his effort to spare Sodom (Gen. 18:23-33), as Moses later will plead with God to spare Israel (Exod. 32:11-13). At the dedication of the temple, Solomon delivers an eloquent, thirty-verse prayer (1 Kings 8:23-53), while blind Bartimaeus blurts out this single petition, a mere five words in Greek: "Jesus, Son of David, have mercy on me!" (Mark 10:47). And he who is the master of prayer, King David, crafted prayers of praise, lament, confession, and thanksgiving in the psalms that bear his name.

One consistent theme, from Genesis onward, is that before we speak to God, he speaks to us. Our petitions are birthed from God's promise. In that way, all prayer is like an echo: we voice back to God his own words, calling upon him to *do what he said he would do* and *be who he promised to be*. This is exemplified in David's famous prayer after the Lord promised to establish his dynastic throne forever (2 Sam. 7:18-29). In the middle of the prayer, the king says, "And now, O LORD God, confirm forever the word that you have spoken concerning your servant and concerning his house, and do as you have spoken" (7:25). Notice what David says: "Confirm forever the word you have spoken" and "Do as you have spoken." A child whose father promised him ice cream earlier in the day will remind him later, "Dad, you promised!" Similarly, the king is saying, "Father, you promised! Now do it. Stick by your word. Do what you have spoken." Earthly fathers might not always like their words being quoted back to them by their children, but our heavenly Father does. He not only wants us to pray, but commands us to pray, to hold his feet to the fire of his word, as it were.

That is precisely what Jacob is about to do at this point in his story. As we learned in the last chapter, his tell-tale heart is beating out of his chest when he hears that Esau, with four hundred men, is beating a path toward him. Jacob, ever the take-control-of-the-situation kind of guy, first "divided the people who were with him, and the flocks and herds and camels, into two camps, thinking, 'If Esau comes to the one camp and attacks it, then the camp that is left will escape'" (32:7). If necessary, he would cut his losses, great though they would be.

Jacob then offers this prayer:

> O God of my father Abraham and God of my father Isaac, O LORD who said to me, "Return to your country and to your kindred, that I may do you good," I am not worthy of the least of all the deeds of steadfast love and all the faithfulness that you have shown to your servant, for with only my staff I crossed this Jordan, and now I have become two camps. Please deliver me from the hand of my brother, from the hand of Esau, for I fear him, that he may come and attack me, the mothers with the children. But you said, "I will surely do you good, and make your offspring as the sand of the sea, which cannot be numbered for multitude." (Gen. 32:9-12)

Let's think our way through Jacob's prayer. As we do, let's also think about the way that we pray, what we ask for, and how we ask for it.

On the surface, this might appear to be a relatively typical, biblical prayer. The Lord is addressed as the God of Abraham and Isaac. Nothing unusual there. Jacob declares his unworthiness of all the Lord's munificence toward him. Again, such humility and self-abasement are familiar from other biblical prayers. The patriarch also builds his petitions on the foundation of God's earlier promises to him. This is in accord with what we discussed earlier about quoting the Lord's words back to him. We might be led, therefore, to give this prayer the score of a B or B+. In other words, it's an average kind of prayer.

Oh, but we would be wrong. This prayer has Jacob's all-too-predictable bargaining and manipulation of facts written all over it. We see this "Jacobing" of prayer in two ways.

The first is humorous. When describing how God's steadfast love and faithfulness is evident in his life, Jacob notes that he left home with only a staff in his hand yet has returned with "two camps" (Gen. 32:10). Yet how did Jacob become twin camps? He himself, right before this prayer, divided his people into two camps! And the purpose of these camps was to minimize his losses to Esau, who—according to Jacob's (wrong) assumption—was out for blood. This would be like me, taking $10,000 and dividing it between two saving accounts, then kneeling to say, "Dear God, I once had only a dollar to my name but now, thanks to you, I have two bank accounts!" As Samuel E. Balentine writes, "Thus Jacob camouflages his own scheming as evidence of God's blessing."[1]

The second "Jacobing" aspect of this prayer is this: when the patriarch quotes God's words back to him, he is misquoting him. First Jacob says, "O LORD who said to me, 'Return to your country and to your kindred, that I may do you good....' (Gen. 32:9). Then, at the end, he adds, "But you said, 'I will surely do you good....'" (32:12). Both times, Jacob claims that God explicitly said these words to him. And both times, Jacob says that the Lord used the causative (Hiphil) form of the verb *yatav*, which means something like, "I will cause good to happen to you." In the second of these, in verse 12, Jacob stretches things still further by claiming that God used an intensified verbal form (infinitive absolute), indicated by the adverb "surely": "*surely* do you good." In the recorded words of the Lord to Jacob, however, he said no such thing.

So, what did God actually say? "I am with you" and "I will be with you." In Bethel, at the beginning of Jacob's exodus, he said, "Behold, *I am with you* and will keep you wherever you go, and will bring you back to this land. For I will not leave you until I have done what I have promised you" (Gen. 28:15; italics mine). Then, at the end of his exodus, as Jacob prepared to return home, the Lord said, "Return to the land of your fathers and to your kindred, and *I will be with you*" (31:3; italics mine). In other words, God promised his presence to Jacob, not a proliferation of material goods.

If we are charitable, we would say Jacob is interpreting or expanding on the divine promise. That is, he understands "I will be with you" to mean "I will [surely] do you good." But given what we know about the "heel" side of Jacob's personality, he appears to be trying to employ his bargaining and manipulative skills on heaven itself. After all, he got what he wanted from his father, his brother, and his father-in-law. So, why stop there? Next stop: Yahweh.

Now here is the part that simultaneously infuriates me and makes me laugh with joy: it worked! Jacob got what he requested.

---

[1] *Prayer in the Hebrew Bible: The Drama of Divine-Human Dialogue* (Minneapolis: Fortress Press, 1993), 68.

Indeed, even more than he could have dreamed of receiving. He prayed, "Deliver me from the hand of my brother" (Gen. 32:11) and the Lord was, like, "Nah, that's too easy." He "who is able to do far more abundantly than all that we ask or think," instead of mere deliverance, gave Jacob delight (Eph. 3:20). He arranged a fraternal reunion complete with hugs, kisses, and tears of joy as Esau embraced Jacob (33:4). What is infuriating about this is that, once more, *this scoundrel of a man got what he did not deserve.* And what makes me laugh with joy, and what ought to make us all laugh with joy, is that We. Are. Jacob. We are that scoundrel. But because the modus operandi of God our Father is not merit but mercy, he is always gifting us with what we do not deserve.

Which disciple of Jesus cannot chuckle at Paul's blunt reminder to the church in Rome, "We do not know what to pray for," (Rom. 8:26). That is indeed the truth. To put a twist on the words of Jesus: in our prayers, we are likely to ask for a serpent but our Father gives us a fish; we pray for a scorpion and he gives us an egg (cf. Luke 11:11-12). As Paul goes on to say in that same chapter of Romans, "He who did not spare his own Son but gave him up for us all, how will he not also with him graciously give us all things?" (8:32). If one day I buy my son or daughter a twenty-million dollar mansion, do you dare to think the next day, at breakfast, I will balk at buying them a cup of coffee? Or, if I donate one of my kidneys to someone who needs a transplant, do you imagine that I will refuse to lend a hand to that same person when they stumble and fall? Of course not. Even so, our Father, who bought salvation for us, who sent his Son to die for us, will certainly do unimaginably more for us than we can ever dream of asking him to do. Our prayers are tiny compared to the vastness of his love.

But should we not, as disciples of Jesus, do what we talked about at the beginning of this chapter: call on our Father to be faithful to his word? To be who he has promised to be? To do what he said he would do? Yes, of course, we should. We "ought always to pray and not lose heart" (Luke 18:1). If we're lonely, let us pray, "God, you promised never to leave me; be here with me now." If we're overwhelmed with guilt, let us pray, "Lord, you promised that you will cast all our sins into the heart of the sea; absolve me and sink my sins into the ocean of your love." May our prayers ever rise from his promises.

So, wasn't Jacob wrong in his manipulative use of prayer? Yes, he certainly was. And, all too often, aren't we all? In the rankest of my gutter prayers, I have cussed out God for not fixing bad situations that I myself created; tried to make tit-for-tat deals with him; twisted facts to suit my needs; and petitioned with impure and selfish motives. All of this was wrong, dead wrong. We can safely say that not one, not a single one, of our prayers has been a pure, spotless, selfless request. Why? Because they've all come from the sewer-hearted, unclean lips of sinners, who can do nothing from utterly holy motives. All the words of our prayers, if they stand alone, are soured by the halitosis of our sinful natures.

But therein is the shocking goodness of our Lord displayed. Even when, like Jacob, we hand a mud pie of prayer to our Father, he accepts it like a real piece of delectable dessert. He does so because all our prayers pass from our mouth into Christ's ear, and out of Christ's mouth to the ear of our Father. Our prayers pass through the purifying mediation of our great high priest.

Our voice in prayer is always the voice of Jesus.

Discussion Questions

1. Do certain prayers serve as signposts in your own life? Perhaps ones you prayed a child or a special prayer at a significant point in your life. What is the most common prayer for you?
2. Read Genesis 32:9-12. Analyze this prayer of Jacob. How does he talk to God? What does he ask for? What do you make of his "alteration" of God's words to him?
3. Read Romans 8:26-39. What does this teach us about prayer? Who is interceding for us? Do we really know what we ought to pray for? Why or why not?
4. Discuss this image: "Even when, like Jacob, we hand a mud pie of prayer to our Father, he accepts it like a real piece of delectable dessert." What is meant by this? How is this a comfort to us as we speak to our heavenly Father?

CHAPTER 19

A Dust-Up with Jesus (Part 1)

A man wrestled with him until the breaking of the day

Genesis 32:24

Scars are like hieroglyphics; their stories are carved onto the pyramid of our flesh. On my right wrist is a scar I've borne for four and a half decades, a lasting reminder of when I sprinted full throttle through a huge store window when I was six years old. My sternum is marked where, about four years ago, skin cancer was cut away (the fruit of too many years of roofing while shirtless). And, like most people, my body is punctuated with multiple other mementos of knife slips, work-related injuries, and childhood blunders.

The present state of our bodies pays a hefty tax to the past. Scars are but one example. Wrestlers often have "cauliflower ear" and the heels of longtime hockey players will exhibit Haglund's deformity. The lungs of chain smokers mirror charcoal pits and the livers of heavy drinkers tell their morbid tales. We might try to ignore or forget or conceal our past, but our bodies will not cooperate in this delusional conspiracy. They tell no lies.

Jacob's limp told the truth as well. This book's title, of course, is derived from the aftereffects of the nocturnal wrestling match which is about to take place in Jacob's life between him and "a man"—a man whom we later learn is God himself (Gen. 32:24-32). This brief narrative, which is so dense that we will divide it into two chapters, is arguably one of the weirdest and the most spectacular occasions in all the Scriptures. Unprecedented and unrepeated, this is mortal combat with the Immortal, earth with heaven, man with God. Finally, when the dust has settled and the sun rises, Jacob has a new name and a story for the ages. He also has that limp that tells no lies. His every halting step is a silent sermon, preaching that his body has been marked by the touch of God.

In the day leading up to that unforgettable night, Jacob sent various groups of servants with animals southward as a series of welcoming parties to present gifts to Esau—a plan of pacification to which we will return (32:13-21). The patriarch, along with his family, remained behind at the Jabbok river, which flows east to west through deep canyons, eventually emptying into the Jordan about 20-25 miles north of the Dead Sea. Across a ford in this river, Jacob escorted his family (Gen. 32:22). Then, for undisclosed reasons, "Jacob was left alone" (Gen. 32:24).

In the broad framework of the patriarch's life, this is almost Bethel 2.0, a kind of replay of the stairway-to-heaven vision, when Yahweh visited Jacob to confirm that he would accompany him to Haran ("Behold, I am with you and will keep you wherever you go, and will bring you back to this land" [Gen. 28:15]). Then, as now, Jacob was flying solo. Then, as now, it is nighttime. As in days to come, Yahweh will be with the people of Israel at the crossing the Red Sea and Jordan River, so now he is with the man soon-to-become Israel at the crossing of the Jabbok on his own exodus homeward. As the rabbis were wont to say, *Ma'aseh avot siman l'vanim*, that is, "the actions of the fathers are a sign for the sons." What the father (Jacob) did set the stage for all of his sons (the nation).

As we soon discover, however, what happens at Jabbok is no mere replica of what happened at Bethel. Then, the Lord stood beside sleeping Jacob and spoke words of comfort and reassurance. Now, "a man wrestled with him until the breaking of the day" (Gen. 32:24). What in the world is going on here? Who is this man? Is he even a man? And why are he and Jacob wrestling?

Let's start with the Hebrew. With the exception of the two occurrences here (vv. 24-25), the verb for "wrestled" (*avaq*) occurs nowhere else in the OT. If the verb is derived from the noun for "dust" (*avaq*), it would suggest the lovely English idiom, "a dust-up." This dust-up, we are told, was with Jacob and "a man." The Hebrew for "a man" (*ish*) is nothing unusual, but the individual in question certainly is.

As the story unfolds, it becomes clear to Jacob (and to us) that we are dealing with no mere mortal. For one, Jacob asked the "man" to bless him, surely an odd request if Jacob reckoned him some random stranger who jumped him in the dark. Second, in the Bible, God is the name-changer. As he'd already done with Jacob's grandfather Abram/ Abraham and grandmother Sarai/Sarah, so he does here with Jacob/ Israel (Gen. 17:5, 15; 32:28). Third, there's the "man's" refusal to disclose his own name, as the Messenger of Yahweh will later do when the father of Samson asks for his name (Gen. 32:29; Judges 13:18). And, finally, when the dust-up was over, "Jacob called the name of the place Peniel, saying, 'For I have seen God face to face, and yet my life has been delivered'" (Gen. 32:30).

The man, therefore, is God who has taken on a temporary human form. As with other such man-and-God encounters, an awareness of the identity of the divine individual only dawns on the mortal gradually (Judges 6:11-24; 13:19-23). Generations later, when the prophet Hosea preached on this story, he said that Jacob "strove with the angel [*malak*]" (12:4). This fits perfectly with multiple other OT stories where the *malak* ("messenger") of Yahweh appears in some visible and/or human form (e.g., Gen. 16:7-13; 22:11-19; Exod. 3:1-6; Judg. 6:11-24; 13:1-23). As I have explained in *The Christ Key*, this messenger is none other than the Son of God.[1]

To use NT language: on the banks of the Jabbok, Jesus wrestled with Jacob.

At no other time in biblical history is such an bizarre event recorded. The Son of God had other interactions with people prior to his incarnation. In Eden, where the Lord walked, we can safely assume that Adam and Eve strolled with him (Gen. 3:8). The Lord ate a meal prepared by Abraham and Sarah (Gen. 18:8). He appeared to and spoke with many individuals, including Hagar, Joshua, Gideon, and others. The closest parallel is perhaps when Lord "met [Moses] and sought to put him to death," though there is no evidence in that encounter that direct physical contact was involved, much less rolling in the dirt and mud for hours on end (Exod. 4:24).

---

[1] Chad Bird, *The Christ Key: Unlocking the Centrality of Christ in the Old Testament* (Irvine, CA: New Reformation Publications, 2021), 21-42.

On this singular occasion, then, the Son of God slipped into a human frame for an overnight stay at the Jabbok, and with biceps and brawn, hands and heft, mingled his breath and sweat with the man who embodied the people of Yahweh. Though he was God, he emptied himself, by taking the form of a human wrestler, manifesting himself in the likeness of men. And being found in human form, he humbled himself by refusing to win the fight, even the fight with Jacob (cf. Phil. 2:6-7). He, being divine, accommodated himself to human limitations. He, being omnipotent, limited his strength that Jacob might have the opportunity to win.

And win Jacob did, but in a strange way, in a way rife with a foreboding of grace. "When the man saw that he did not prevail against Jacob, he touched his hip socket, and Jacob's hip was put out of joint as he wrestled with him" (Gen. 32:25). The Son of God "did not prevail." He would not win this fight. Even after suffering an injury, Jacob was still on top. God was still losing to man. The patriarch stubbornly refused to let him go until his divine opponent blessed him. That act would be, as it were, the final acknowledgement of his own blessed defeat, a trophy to the victor, a benediction to the man who overcame God.

You see, do you not, what is happening on the banks of the Jabbok river? As we, the disciples of Jesus, stand in a circle with wide-eyed wonder around these two wrestlers in the dark, hear their grunts and gasps, spy their sweat drip and muscles strain, to what are we spectators but an ancient proleptic portrayal of the final, climactic fight between God and man on the blood-soiled soil beneath a Roman cross, while the skies above were darkened?

Through the keyhole of Jacob's fight, we gaze into the room of the crucifixion.

The descendants of Jacob will lay hands on the Son of God "who, though he was in the form of God, did not count equality with God a thing to be grasped, but emptied himself, by taking the form of a servant, being born in the likeness of men. And being found in human form, he humbled himself by becoming obedient to the point of death, even death on a cross" (Phil. 2:6-8). He whom Jacob pinned on the ground would be affixed to the fatal tree. And the Son of God, embracing his deadly defeat with a knowing sparkle in his eye that winks of a vacated tomb, will say, "It is finished" (John 19:30). A trophy to humanity. A benediction to all of us Jacobs. It is done. God has lost. We have won.

But, of course, so it had been planned from the foundation of world. Remember what Peter said in his Pentecost sermon? "This Jesus, delivered up according to the definite plan and foreknowledge of God, you crucified and killed by the hands of lawless men" (Acts 2:23). According to God's definite plan. According to God's foreknowledge. The sacrifice of Jesus was not a regrettable wrong turn that required the divine GPS to recalibrate the journey of salvation. The cross was the destination of the journey all along, the journey begun in Genesis. And this defeat? What a divine victory! Jesus, "for the joy that was set before him endured the cross, despising the shame, and is seated at the right hand of the throne of God" (Heb. 12:2). For the joy. His defeat was his delight, for his death is our life.

We follow a Master whose scars are a trophy of that time when humanity, all of us Jacobs, won gold purchased with blood. Down into the dirt Jesus went. Up onto the cross Jesus went. And from him, we receive grace upon grace.

DISCUSSION QUESTIONS

1. Read Genesis 32:22-32. Talk about the significance of several details in this account: Jacob being alone; at a river; being at the end of exile; wrestling; etc.
2. Read Hosea 12:1-4. This "man" with whom Jacob wrestled is also called God and an "angel" (which is more accurately translated as "messenger"). This messenger, commonly called the messenger of Yahweh (e.g., Genesis 16:7-16 and Exodus 3:1-6), is the Son of God. Reflect on the importance of Jacob wrestling with the Son of God.
3. Read Philippians 2:5-11. How do these verses reflect and expand upon what was happening with Jacob and this "man"?
4. In what other ways does this story function as a preview of the cross?

CHAPTER 20

A Dust-Up with Jesus (Part 2)

> The sun rose upon him as he passed Penuel, limping because of his hip.
>
> Genesis 32:31

Only thirty-two students received their diplomas from Shamrock High School in 1988. I was one of them. A small town and small school made for big connections during those formative, growing up years. After our senior year, a few students stayed put, sank roots, and began to raise their sons and daughters in this Texas panhandle town. Most of us relocated to where education and employment took us. By and by, we lost contact as miles and years thinned those once thick bonds. Up until a few years ago, I didn't have a clue where most of my classmates lived and worked.

Then along came Facebook. Friend requests were sent and accepted. Family pictures scrolled through and messages exchanged. One fact immediately obvious was that the last names of most of the girls with whom I had graduated had changed. Robinson was now Scarbrough, Haws was now Stepp. That seemingly simple name change, of course, embodied a larger, more intricate story. A story of falling in love and settling down to share joys and tears, pleasures and struggles, with their husbands. Their new last name was emblematic of two lives—and two stories—that God had woven together into a single narrative.

Like my classmates, Jacob received his own new name. But it was not at a flowered altar flanked by bridesmaids and groomsmen;

it was on the dark and muddy banks of the Jabbok River. Jacob's mysterious combatant renamed him Yisra'el (or, as we write it, Israel). My friend, Chris Hulshof, once told me that when he teaches these Genesis narratives to his university students, he reminds them that with name changes like Abram to Abraham, Sarai to Sarah, and Jacob to Israel, "it becomes impossible to tell your story without telling God's story. 'Hey, I thought your name was Jacob?' 'Well, it was but then something happened...'"[1]

Yes, something did happen. The Lord was certainly making things happen in Jacob's life before this nocturnal battle, but this night was different. Life-altering. Forever thereafter, the stories of God and Jacob were woven into a single narrative. Indeed, Israel, the people of God, became the bride of Yahweh.

With the name change also came something else, something not quite as pleasant. Jacob walked away, newly named, but also newly wounded. He limped. He was injured by the divine touch. If every rose has its thorn, then almost every divine blessing has its wound. Even the blessed one himself still bears the stigmata of crucifixion.

In our last chapter, we talked about Jacob's dust-up with the Son of God, cloaked in human form. As we pick up the story in Genesis 32:27-29, we hear this brief dialogue:

Jesus: "Let me go, for the day has broken."

Jacob: "I will not let you go unless you bless me."

Jesus: "What is your name?"

Jacob: "Jacob."

Jesus: "Your name shall no longer be called Jacob, but Israel, for you have striven with God and with men, and have prevailed."

In Hebrew, the name Yisra'el is formed from two words. There's no shortage of scholarly wrangling over how best to explain the name, but the most straightforward way is to follow the lead of the text itself. The second part, "-el," is the divine title, El, which is the Hebrew equivalent of our English word, "God." The first part, "Yisra-" is a form of the verb *sarah*, which means to "strive" or "contend." This is the verb used when the name is given: "you have striven [*sarah*] with God and with men." Jacob is thus now Yisra'el (=Israel), the

---

[1] Private correspondence.

God-Fighter or God-Contender.[2] We traced the trajectories of this "fighting with God" in the last chapter, all the way to Golgotha.

There is, however, one rather odd fact about this famous name change. After Abram became Abraham, he was never called Abram again. After Sarai became Sarah, she was never called Sarai again. But Jacob breaks that pattern. After he became Israel, he was still called Jacob numerous times. In fact, according to my count, from the moment of his name change to the moment of his death, he was called Jacob about twice as many times as he was called Israel. It seems, therefore, that rather than getting a new name, Jacob received an additional name. He is no longer *just* Jacob but also Israel. He is still a Heel; only now he's also the God-Fighter. What his parents gave him and what God gave him, together both of these realities, both of these names, tell this man's tale.

Hold that thought because we will return to it momentarily. Before we do, let's think about Jacob's wound. During the skirmish, the Son of God, "touched [Jacob's] hip socket, and Jacob's hip was put out of joint as he wrestled with him" (Gen. 32:25). When everything was over, we read this, "The sun rose upon him as he passed Penuel, limping because of his hip. Therefore to this day the people of Israel do not eat the sinew of the thigh that is on the hip socket, because he touched the socket of Jacob's hip on the sinew of the thigh" (32:31-32).

In their culinary practices, the descendants of Jacob kept alive the memory of where God touched man. "We don't eat that part of the animal," a father would say to his son. "Why?" the son would ask. "Well," the father would say, "let me tell you a story." And he would tell him the story of when God and man fought, when God lost and

---

[2] One of the complications regarding this interpretation of the name is that ordinarily when "El" is attached to a person's name, El is the subject, not the object, of the verb that is included in the same name. Thus, Samuel means "El has heard [not 'he hears El']" and Ezekiel means "El strengthens [not 'he strengthens El']." Without the accompanying narrative, if we just saw the name Yisra'el, we would assume it meant, "God fights/strives/contends." Instead, in the explanation in Genesis 32:28, El is the object and Jacob is the subject: Jacob fights/strives/contends with El. Who knows, perhaps in reversing our expectations of the meaning of the name, God is amplifying just how extraordinary this whole scenario is.

man won, and the winner gimped away with a wound that tells an unforgettable tale.

I like to imagine that Jacob never quite recovered from his battle with Jesus. After all, none of us really do. Jacob limped into the future bearing the burdens of his past—burdens that were lightened by the memory of the God who christened him with a victorious name.

Anyone who tells you that becoming a disciple of Jesus will make your life easier is a false teacher, a charlatan, or quite simply a madman. When Christ calls a man or woman to follow him, you can be sure he is calling them into an uncomfortable life—or something even better. No, this does not mean that our lives of faith are a dour and dismal existence where we trudge unsmilingly through this world with a holy hangdog look on our faces. Let us never confuse sadness—nor to mention moroseness—for sanctity. Rather, it means that, in one way or another, we will limp, day by day, with the secret joy of the divinely scarred.

What will that look like? I don't know what it will look like for you. I only know what it looks like for me as well as for others who have told me about their own woundedness. It seems as if our scars, like fingerprints, are unique to each person. Jacob had his limp. I have mine. And you have yours—or soon will.

Each of these scars, limps, and Paul-like thorns in the flesh are incessant reminders that we live every moment of every day solely by the grace of God. Should the Lord withdraw his merciful hand from us, even for a few seconds, we would be as helpless and hopeless as an infant laid in the lair of lion. Because we are so prone to self-delusion, to the prideful presumption that we can get by on our own strength, thank you very much, the Lord Jesus lovingly and wisely weakens us. Or, rather, he places us into situations that act as painful eurekas of our inherent, mortal weaknesses.

The life of discipleship is not about us getting stronger; rather, it's about growing increasingly aware of our weakness and the Lord's strength. Emptied of self, filled with Jesus. The words of John the Baptist are the words of a follower of Christ, "He must increase, but I must decrease" (John 3:30).

Our decreasing, however, is ironically also our own increasing, for it is the glory of God to recreate us, in Christ, as those who bear his name and share his kingdom. Yes, we stumble into the future, like

Jacob, still heels, still sinners, still all-too-often acting and speaking like witless fools, but also as those who bear the name Christian. We are sinners and saints, fools and sages, wretched and forgiven, Jacob and Israel, all blended together into a human cocktail that only God can truly divide.

We are limping with God, however, not from him, to him, or apart from him. With him. And, if our eyes could only see the unseen, we would realize that we are being borne along by hands that still bear the scars of a sacrifice joyfully made for us.

DISCUSSION QUESTIONS

1. This chapter used the example of a woman changing her last name at marriage as a signal that God had woven two lives together. What other examples come to mind of life-altering decisions, relationships, or actions that forever thereafter define us, so that we can't tell "our story" without also telling someone else's?

2. What does the Hebrew name, Yisra'el (=Israel), mean? What message does it convey?

3. Discuss this statement and its implications for our lives as disciples: "Anyone who tells you that becoming a disciple of Jesus will make your life easier is a false teacher, a charlatan, or quite simply a madman." Why is this so?

4. When you think about your own scars or limps, what comes to mind? Talk about how the life of discipleship is not about us getting stronger; rather, it's about growing increasingly aware of our weakness and the Lord's strength.

CHAPTER 21

The Prodigal Brother Returns

Esau ran to meet him and embraced him and fell on his
neck and kissed him, and they wept.

Genesis 33:4

There's a little game of self-delusion we like to play. It's called, "I'll
Never Do That Again." When the convict exits prison, he says, "I'll
never steal again." When the addict, post-rehab, eases back into ordinary life, she says, "I'll never do meth again." We all know the drill.
We've trod this path a thousand times with ten thousand different
oaths. I won't smoke another cigarette. I won't gossip about a friend
again. I won't make three trips back to the dessert table at Thanksgiving.
I won't miss another one of my son's little league games. I just won't.

Until we do. Much of the time anyway. Criminal recidivism, for
instance, is depressingly high. One study found that after state pris-
oners were released, about 83% of them were rearrested within nine
years.[1] Most of us have friends and family who have been through the
revolving door of rehab. And I don't need to rehearse for you how
our own little "never again" promises and resolutions last about as
long as a donut in a kitchen full of teenage boys.

Yes, thanks be to God, sometimes the lessons we learn from our
sins and blunders are so profoundly painful that we never touch that

---

[1] According to a 2018 study by the U. S. Justice Department. https://www.prison
legalnews.org/news/2019/may/3/long-term-recidivism-studies-show-high-arrest
-rates/

proverbial "hot stove" again. Yet even then, the allurement sticks around, does it not? Daydreams woo. Desires whisper. We find ourselves toying with the idea of getting our hand as close as possible to the heat without getting burned. We'll just let it hover an inch or two over the fire, that's all. Such are the dangers with which we flirt. If we experience the most positive, uplifting encounter with God imaginable, or if we experience the most negative, debilitating encounter with sin imaginable, either way, the temporary euphoria or existential dread that trail these events will only keep us on the straight and narrow for the short term. The approach of the human will is always signaled by the sound of rattling chains.

It's a very good thing, therefore, that our hope is built not on us and our own righteousness, but on Christ alone. Even when we are faithless and fickle as shifting sand, he is the unmoving rock of our salvation.

I cannot read the account of Jacob's reunion with Esau without thoughts such as these running through my head. You see, here's how I wish the story *would* have read:

> Now Jacob, limping from his fight with God, his soul filled with wonder at the new name bestowed upon him, lifted his eyes and, behold, his brother, Esau, was drawing near. The brothers ran and embraced each other, weeping with joy. Esau forgave Jacob, Jacob forgave Esau. Each recounted the Lord's gracious dealings with him. Later, when Esau bid his brother join him in Seir, Jacob gladly accepted his invitation. The brothers, once estranged, now reunited, journeyed southward side by side.

But, of course, that never happened. What did happen, while not quite a happy ending, is truer to human nature. In this fraternal reunion, we learn a little more about Esau, a little more about Jacob, and plenty about ourselves.

When last we heard about Jacob's looming encounter with Esau, his tell-tale heart was beating wildly. The most recent intel was that Esau was marching toward him with four hundred warriors. Jacob was "greatly afraid and distressed" (Gen. 32:7). That seems to be a common sense reaction, given the twin's not-so-rosy past. So, Jacob acted swiftly. He divided his livestock and servants into groups. As each one met Esau and his men, they were to say that they belonged to Jacob; that the animals were a present "to my lord Esau"; and to inform him that Jacob was behind them, on his way (32:18). Jacob's motives were clear: "I may appease [Esau] with the present that goes ahead of me, and afterward I shall see his face. Perhaps he will accept me" (32:20). It appears as if the ancients knew as well as we do that "money talks."

All these preemptive plans, however, transpired prior to Jacob's encounter with the Lord. Does it not seem reasonable that, after such a once-in-a-lifetime night, after seeing God face-to-face, after having the Almighty bless him with a new name, that all his anxieties would evaporate? That his inborn Jacob-ness, memorialized in the name "Heel," would be replaced by an unwavering commitment to honesty? That having deceived his brother once, with disastrous consequences for his entire family, that he would never dream of going down that road again? Would he not say to himself, "God is 100% with me. God has richly blessed me. I have nothing to fear. I will be a new man, even as I bear a new name"? Yes, given all the evidence we have, that seems a completely reasonable response.

If there is one thing, however, that sinners will rarely do, it's be reasonable. Morally erratic? Yes. Self-protecting? Oh, yeah. Often absurdly dumb? For sure. But reasonable? No.

So, what happened? Jacob, to his credit, did not treat his wives and children as a human shield, but he "himself went on before them, bowing himself to the ground seven times, until he came near to his brother" (Gen. 33:3). Now, were we eyeballing this whole scene as it was happening live, we might say to ourselves, "Oh, boy, here we go. The moment of truth has arrived! One of two things is about to go down: either Esau will kill his brother or be pacified with his gifts and let him live. Those are really the only two options." But we would be wrong.

In one of the most gripping displays of merciful human love recorded for us in the Scriptures, Esau neither killed his brother nor merely let him live to see another day. Instead, "Esau ran to meet him and embraced him and fell on his neck and kissed him, and they [he?][2]

---

[2] Some scholars have suggested that, in the course of the Hebrew text being copied, the first letter (a *waw*) of the next word ("and-when-he-lifted-up") was

wept" (Gen. 33:4). If this language seems vaguely familiar to you, good! You are hearing echoes of the return of the prodigal son, whose father "saw [his son] and felt compassion, and ran and embraced him and kissed him" (Luke 15:20). The two scenes are so strikingly similar, both in language and theme, that one can make a very strong argument that Jesus had the Esau-Jacob reunion in mind when he told this famous parable.[3] Luke 15 would be what Jewish interpreters call a midrash, an interpretation and expansion, on Genesis 33. If so, then we reach this remarkable conclusion: *Esau is the father-figure in the Parable of the Prodigal Son!* He is the one who sees, who has compassion, who runs, hugs, kisses, and weeps over Jacob the prodigal.

Here is true brotherly compassion. Here is unexpected grace. Here is unearned, undeserved, one-way love.

In fact, this entire emotional scene is so pristine that I wish we could just leave it right there. Slowly walk away smiling. Breathe a sigh of relief. Whisper a prayer of thanks that God softened the heart of Esau over those long years.

But there is more to the story. There is, as the 90's pop song put it, "a black fly in our Chardonnay."

We pick up on a hint of tension in the conversation between Jacob and Esau. The older twin refers to Jacob with the familial "my brother," but Jacob does not reciprocate. He deferentially addresses Esau as "my lord" and himself as "servant." Then, as if trying to outdo himself, he even says that seeing his brother Esau's face is "like seeing the face of God" (33:10). Finally, Esau asks Jacob to journey with him to his home in Seir, even offering to leave some of his people behind to travel with them. Jacob, however, says, "Let my lord pass on ahead

---

accidentally duplicated onto the end of the verbal form "and-they-wept," thus making a plural form of the original singular verb. This is called dittography ("double-writing), a fairly common error in hand-written manuscripts. The result was that the singular, "he [Esau] wept," became the plural, "they [Esau and Jacob] wept." It is an intriguing conjecture because all the verbs leading up to this are singular, with Esau embracing, falling upon Jacob's neck, and kissing him. It would also dovetail with Jacob's other not-so-emotional reactions to Esau as their conversation ensues.

[3] For a book-length treatment of this, see Kenneth Bailey, *Jacob & the Prodigal: How Jesus Retold Israel's Story* (Downers Grove, IL: InterVarsity Press, 2011).

of his servant, and I will lead on slowly, at the pace of the livestock that are ahead of me and at the pace of the children, until I come to my lord in Seir" (33:14).

The narrative continues: "So Esau returned that day on his way to Seir. But Jacob journeyed to Succoth" (33:16). In case you don't know your biblical geography very well, that would be like two brothers reuniting in Kansas. When the older goes southward to Oklahoma, the younger promises, "I'll catch up with you in Oklahoma," then actually heads north to Nebraska.

In other words, Jacob deceived his brother. Again. There are only two recorded conversations between Esau and Jacob: here and in the "lentil soup" exchange from their younger years (Gen. 25:29-34). As Victor Hamilton points out, "On the first occasion… Esau failed to perceive Jacob's capacity for exploitation. On the second occasion he fails to perceive Jacob's hesitancy and lack of excitement about going to Seir. In both cases, Jacob succeeds in deceiving Esau."[4]

Perhaps you think I'm being too hard on Jacob. And perhaps you're right.[5] But by this time in the patriarch's bio, we have a fairly clear track record of his wily ways. Years ago, a counselor friend of my wife would say, "Consistency over time proves change." In Jacob's case, we could say, "Consistency over time proves non-change." He has been consistently deceptive.

In other words, he has been consistently *all too much like we are.* And I don't mean merely in his cunning, underhanded ways. I mean this: having just studied his wrestling match with God, having been wowed by the Lord's favor toward him, and now being blown away by his brother's magnanimous love and forgiveness, we might be excused

---

[4] *The Book of Genesis: Chapters 18-50.* NICOT (Grand Rapids, MI: Eerdmans, 1995), 348.

[5] Martin Luther, with whom I usually agree on matters of biblical interpretation, would certainly think I am being too hard on Jacob. He argues that "we should not suspect Jacob of acting in a hypocritical and guileful manner with his brother, but there is in him a heart that is absolutely open and filled with boundless joy because of the reconciliation that has been brought about." So, why didn't Jacob go to Seir? Luther says, "My answer is that he did not promise that on this journey he wanted to go directly to Seir but told Esau to proceed until he should follow him and come to Seir [at a later date]." I find the Reformer's interpretation a little too extravagantly excusing of Jacob (AE 6:177).

for thinking that we are now dealing with a radically changed man. But we're not. Yes, he certainly does come across as humble (formally anyway). And, yes, he does place himself between Esau and his family. Let's give the man credit where credit is due.

Nevertheless, when it's time to bid his brother adieu, he leaves him with a lie. I suspect, as do most commentators, that Jacob does not quite trust his brother. What if Esau's magnanimity is a masquerade? A pretext for getting him down to Seir so he could redeem that longstanding debt? Jacob decides not to roll the dice. No sooner has his big brother disappeared over the southern horizon than Jacob and his entourage head north to Sukkoth, where he "built himself a house and made booths for his livestock" (33:17).

Sukkoth is a place we all have lived. It's that village of the soul where we go when we stubbornly refuse—or fail—to alter the fundamental reality of who we are. Consistency over time proves our non-change as well. Over the entrance to the gate of Sukkoth are inscribed the unforgettable words of St. Paul, "For I do not understand my own actions. For I do not do what I want, but I do the very thing I hate" (Rom. 7:15).

If you, as a disciple of Jesus, find yourself, five or ten or even fifty years after you started following Jesus, still weak in the same areas of life, still struggling with lust or anger or greed or hatred, then welcome to the Club of Discipleship, commonly known as The Church. No, we are not here to excuse one another. But we are here to introduce ourselves, week after week, with the likes of: "Hi, my name is Chad and I'm a sinner."

"I've struggled with (name-your-weakness). I have good days and bad days. Sometimes I have days from hell, where I think the devil must have me in a chokehold. Other days, I seem to do well. But even then, there's always the nagging temptations, the subtle allurements. If I find myself outwardly abstaining from this or that wrongdoing, all too often that's where my heart dwells or my mind daydreams. What's even more maddening is that when I do well and think I'm making some strong progress, I begin to feel proud of myself and—bam!—all of a sudden now my soul is flexing its muscles of arrogance and self-righteousness. Good God, it's frustrating. It drives me nuts. I can't escape from my own worst enemy—myself."

Welcome to discipleship. Welcome to the Christian life. Welcome to Jacob's life.

And welcome, too, to the Jesus who responds to each of us by saying, "Come to me, all who labor and are heavy laden, and I will give you rest. Take my yoke upon you, and learn from me, for I am gentle and lowly in heart, and you will find rest for your souls. For my yoke is easy, and my burden is light" (Matt. 11:28-30).

One of the things we will learn from our Savior is that he did not call us to become witnesses to a complete life transformation in which we are now better than other people. Rather, he called us into a living relationship with himself and the Father through the power of the Spirit in which our true identities are now completely secure in Jesus.

Even when we fail? Yes.

Even when we sin that same sin again? Yes.

Will he continue to call us to repentance? Yes.

Will he continue to discipline us as a father does his child? Also, yes.

Every disciple of Jesus wishes for freedom from sin in this life. But we are *in this life*; thus, we are still at war with ourselves, at war with the sinful nature that doesn't tuck its tail between its legs and flee when we become Christians. It declares war.

But Jesus has won and, in him, we too have won. In fact, in him, we are more than conquerors. We are beloved. And Christ's consistent grace over time proves that he is never going to change from being the Friend and Forgiver of Sinners.

Discussion Questions

1. Why is it so difficult for us to keep resolutions, to avoid repeating mistakes? If we've touched that "hot stove" once, why do we keep our hand close to it at other times?

2. Read or review Genesis 32:13-21 and 33:1-17. Why does Jacob send gifts for Esau ahead of him? What are the possible scenarios that could happen when these two brothers reunite?

3. Compare the tearful reunion of Esau and Jacob with the father's reunion with his son in Luke 15:20-24. What details are the same? How might this OT story have

served as the background of the parable? How does this encounter alter your view of Esau?

4. Talk about the speech and behavior of Jacob when he meets Esau. How does he react, both before, during, and after this encounter? Why does he go north after he had agreed to go south to meet up with his brother? Discuss how we are like Jacob. Give specific examples.

5. Talk about the ramifications of this statement for our discipleship and Christ's grace: "If you, as a disciple of Jesus, find yourself, five or ten or even fifty years after you started following Jesus, still weak in the same areas of life, still struggling with lust or anger or greed or hatred, then welcome to the Club of Discipleship, commonly known as The Church."

CHAPTER 22

Damn the Consequences

"Should he treat our sister like a prostitute?"

Genesis 34:31

When last we left Jacob, he was heading north while Esau trekked south. To our knowledge, the brothers never crossed paths again, except for the burial of their aged father, Isaac, years later (Gen. 35:29). After their reunion and swift parting of ways, Jacob settled near the city of Shechem, where he erected an altar (33:20). By doing so, he was walking in the footsteps of his grandfather, Abraham, whose first stop in Canaan was also at Shechem, and where he too built an altar (12:6-7).

Obviously, Jacob planned to sink deep roots here, because he purchased some real estate "from the sons of Hamor, Shechem's father...for a hundred pieces of money" (lit. "*kesitahs*" [33:19]).[1] At this time, Joseph was very young, likely not yet a teenager. He would die in Egypt at the age of one hundred and ten years, be embalmed, and his bones would eventually be borne out of Egypt and interred on this same plot of ground where he had played as a child (Josh. 24:32). It was also near here, by the way, where Jesus would have his famous conversation with the Samaritan woman, who would say to him, "Are

---

[1] The translation "pieces of money" (ESV) is a modernizing interpretation rather than a translation. Coinage would not be in use in the ancient Near East for another millennium or so. The Hebrew word *kesitahs* could refer to certain measurements of silver or gold, or to livestock (e.g., "a hundred lambs").

you greater than our father Jacob? He gave us the well and drank from it himself, as did his sons and his livestock" (John 4:12).

We can probably assume that Jacob, taking stock of his current situation in life, surmised that he could live out the remainder of his days in relative tranquility. After all, his twenty-year exile was over. That gnawing fear of his twin's fury had dissipated. His older sons could do the heavy lifting of overseeing the flocks and herds. Maybe, just maybe, the topsy-turvy misadventures in his life were all in the rearview mirror. Finally, all would be well in his world.

But if you know the rough outlines of Jacob's life, you're shaking your head. No, all would not be well. As we shall see in the coming chapters, everything was about to get worse—worse than anything he had yet experienced. And as we read about what happens, we are left wondering if Jacob himself has gotten worse, or if he's just a master at making bad situations worse by repeatedly making foolish decisions involving his children.

Case in point: Dinah.

If you have forgotten who Dinah is, you have a good excuse. After all, we only met her once, in a single verse, several chapters ago: "Afterward [Leah] bore a daughter and called her name Dinah" (30:21). That's it. One brief birth announcement. As is characteristic of the Bible, often characters who will feature largely in a future narrative are introduced earlier, almost as an aside. One of the fascinating ways that the narrator tells Dinah's story is through her connections with other family members. She is called "the daughter of Leah" (34:1); "the daughter of Jacob" (34:3); and the "sister" of her brothers (34:13). These family ties are important because, as we shall see, by the end of Genesis 34 we are left scratching our heads as to why Jacob, her father, was so astonishingly passive through her horrific ordeal. Was it because she was the daughter of Leah, the unloved wife? And we will also see (and condone? condemn? remain ambiguous about?) how, rather than Dinah's father, it will be her brothers who redress the wrong done to her.

But we're getting ahead of ourselves. What exactly happened to this girl?

One day, Dinah, Leah's daughter, "went out to see [ra'ah] the women [lit. 'daughters'] of the land" (34:1). One daughter went out to see other daughters. The verb ra'ah is best translated as "see" (and not "visit" [NIV and NASB]) because this same verb is repeated, for rhetorical purposes, when Shechem "sees" her in the next verse (34:2).

Who is Shechem? We mentioned him already, for it was his father, Hamor, the "prince of the land," who sold land to Jacob (33:19; 34:2). These two dads, therefore, already had some business dealings together. Shechem "saw" Dinah, but he did far more than lay eyes on the young woman; he laid hands on her. "He seized her and lay with her and humiliated her" (34:2). The English is horrific enough, but the Hebrew is even more brutal: he did not lay "with" her (as many translations render it) but "lay her." The verb, *anah*, translated here as "humiliate," can also be rendered "afflict, mistreat, or abuse." In short, Shechem raped Dinah. *Anah* is also the verb used to describe how Amnon sexually "violated" his half-sister, Tamar (2 Sam. 13:12, 14, 22), while their father, David, was king.

These two male assailants, Shechem and Amnon, had opposite post-rape reactions. Amnon, who had been infatuated with Tamar, after he violated her, "hated her with very great hatred, so that the hatred with which he hated her was greater than the love with which he had loved her" (2 Sam. 13:15). We read of Shechem, on the other hand, that "his soul was drawn to Dinah the daughter of Jacob. He loved the young woman and spoke tenderly to her" (34:3). If such language makes you sick to your stomach, you're not alone. A rapist who afterward "loves" and "speaks tenderly" to his victim has all the makings of a horror film. Finally, as if the attack, the rape, and the psychotically chilling emotional reaction were not already sufficiently shocking, Shechem then asks his father, Hamor, to go through the formal negotiations with the girl's family so he can marry her.

At this juncture in the narrative, let's pay careful attention to the two different reactions of Dinah's family: the reactions of her father and her brothers. First, the father: "Now Jacob heard that [Shechem] had defiled his daughter Dinah. *But* his sons were with his livestock in the field, *so* Jacob held his peace until they came" (34:5; italics added). Here is an obvious example of how translation involves interpretation. The italicized words, "but" and "so," are the simple Hebrew conjunction *waw* (or *vav*), often translated "and." Now read the verse again, as Robert Alter has (more literally) translated it, "And Jacob had heard that he had defiled Dinah his daughter, *and* his sons were with his livestock in the field, *and* Jacob held his peace till they came" (italics added). The ESV (and most translations) render it in such a way as to give the impression that Jacob was simply holding back, eager to act, just restraining himself until his sons arrived so that together, father and sons, they could redress this defiling of Dinah. As we shall see, however, Jacob kept right on "holding his peace" or "being silent," until the very end of this dark story, when the only ones he rebukes are his sons.

But what about the brothers? How did they react? Quite differently: "The sons of Jacob had come in from the field as soon as they heard of it, and the men were indignant and very angry, because he had done an outrageous thing in Israel by lying with Jacob's daughter, for such a thing must not be done" (34:7). Indignant. Very angry. Isn't this the natural, anticipated reaction of family members to such a malicious and violent crime? Yet no such reaction from Jacob is forthcoming, or even hinted at, ever. The Hebrew word, *nevalah* ("outrageous thing"), is often used to describe a deed—sometimes sexual—so shockingly scurrilous that the nation must respond to it (e.g., Judges 20:10). It cannot be overlooked but must be dealt with decisively.

We are now left with two questions: how will this *nevalah*, this "outrageous thing," be dealt with? And by whom?

As the narratives progresses, we eavesdrop on two conversations. In one, Hamor and Shechem try to wheel and deal with the brothers of Dinah (Jacob, once more, is present but mute—odd for a man so loquacious in previous chapters). They offer to give or do anything to obtain Dinah as Shechem's wife. Not a syllable is said about her rape, but much less an admission of guilt. It's all just business as usual. The basic proposal is that the Shechemite citizens and Jacob's family live together amicably, trade fairly, and intermarry freely. It seems that the sons of Jacob have learned a thing or two from their father over the years, for in their response to this proposal they act with *mirmah* ("deceit")—the same word Isaac uses when he tells Esau that Jacob came "deceitfully" and took away his blessing (Gen. 27:35). The brothers agree to the terms on one condition: that all the males of the city be circumcised. No minor demand!

We then shift to the second conversation: that between the father-son duo of Hamor and Shechem and the men of their city. This "insider" conversation, however, has a very different tone. Nothing is said of Dinah. The father and son repeat part of the proposal but sweeten the pot with greed, saying to their fellow townsmen, "Will not their livestock, their property and all their beasts be ours?" (34:23). So, it appears as if Jacob's sons were not the only ones speaking deceitfully. The Shechemites obviously plan to take advantage of the family of Jacob. Won over by the argument, the males of the city were circumcised en masse.

Three days later, they all were dead.

Simeon and Levi, the two oldest sons of Jacob and—this is important—the full brothers of Dinah, took advantage of the incapacitated state of these recently circumcised men. The brothers "took their swords and came against the city while it felt secure and killed all the males. They killed Hamor and his son Shechem with the sword" (34:25-26). Soon thereafter, the remaining brothers "came upon the slain and plundered the city, because they had defiled their sister. They took their flocks and their herds, their donkeys, and whatever was in the city and in the field. All their wealth, all their little ones and their wives, all that was in the houses, they captured and plundered" (34:27-29).

In the middle of all this mayhem, the biggest bombshell in this story is dropped: after Simeon and Levi slew all these men, they "took Dinah out of Shechem's house [!] and went away" (34:26). Yes, you read that right. The biblical author, a masterful narrator, withheld this crucial detail until this moment. All the while Hamor and Shechem were bargaining for Dinah's hand in marriage, they were holding her hostage![2] Rape. Kidnapping. Lies. Greed. The evils pile up. This revelation about Dinah's whereabouts causes us to reread the story, to reassess what we think about all the characters and their actions.

How did Jacob react to what his sons did? Was he, Dr. Deceit himself, proud of his sons' wily ways? Hardly. He castigated Simeon and Levi, "You have brought trouble on me by making me stink to the inhabitants of the land, the Canaanites and the Perizzites. My

---

[2] I am indebted to Meir Sternberg for this insight. See his excellent literary analysis of this chapter in *The Poetics of Biblical Narrative: Ideological Literature and the Drama of Reading* (Bloomington: Indiana University Press, 1985), 445-481.

numbers are few, and if they gather themselves against me and attack me, I shall be destroyed, both I and my household" (34:20). In a mere sixteen Hebrew words, Jacob manages to say "I" or "me" or "my" eight times. In a shocking display of selfish myopia, the patriarch's vision extends not much beyond his own personal interests.

The last word in the chapter—and what a word it is—is placed in the mouth of the brothers: "Should he treat our sister like a prostitute?" (34:31). Note that they say "our sister" not "your daughter." Once again family associations are pivotal in this story. And who is the "he"? There are two possibilities: Jacob or Shechem. The latter obviously treated Dinah as an object to be bought and sold. But grammatically and thematically, Jacob could be the intended antecedent of "he." If so, the brothers, disgusted by their father's silent acquiescence during Dinah's rape and kidnapping, not to mention Jacob's selfish reprimand after they took action to rescue her, said to each other, "Should [our father] treat our sister like a prostitute?"

As Sternberg notes, the response of the brothers to Jacob amounts to, "Damn the consequences."[3]

Sometimes when we read a Bible story, the theological takeaway from it is relatively obvious. At other times, we might be left saying to ourselves, "Lord have mercy. This is such a horrific episode, I don't know what to make of it." That is my overarching reaction to Genesis 34. A woman is raped. Her father is mute and passive. Two brothers exact revenge upon the perpetrator and his father, yes, but also murder countless other men in cold blood. Their other brothers, like drunk Vikings, plunder the village and enslave the inhabitants. It's like we're reading a chapter from a dystopic novel like *Clockwork Orange* or one of Cormac McCarthy's apocalyptic stories that describes the ugly underside of humanity.

And maybe, just maybe, that is one of the takeaways from this account. Often in our lives, we find ourselves caught in the middle of a modern Genesis 34 nightmare. We look around and see plenty of confusion, guilt, destruction, family turmoil, brutalized victims, vigilante justice, and bloodshed, and very little of God. Indeed, it seems as if the Lord has left the building. He's nowhere to be found. In fact, notice that, in Genesis 34, God is never mentioned.

---

[3] *The Poetics of Biblical Narrative*, 474.

Will the Lord bring some light out of this midnight story? Yes, he will, a brilliant light. In time, Jacob will curse the anger and wrath of Simeon and Levi and not speak over them any farewell blessing (Gen. 49:5-7). But he will bestow upon Judah a lavish benediction in which his tribe will be the one from whom the Messiah will come (Gen. 49:8-12). Had Genesis 34 not happened, the Old Testament would have been a very different narrative, with no mention of a lion from the tribe of Judah, no King David from Bethlehem, and no focus upon "a man whose name was Joseph, of the house of David" (Luke 1:27). Ages after this story in which everyone except Dinah was implicated in wrongdoing, a right-doing Lord would raise up a young woman to bear the Savior of the world.

But, at the time, Dinah did not know this. Neither did Jacob. Neither did the brothers. And in our own Genesis 34's, most of the time, we too don't know how the Lord will cause "all things [to] work together for good" (Rom. 8:28). Instead, as those who live by faith—faith in a good and gracious Father, a loving Savior, and a comforting Spirit—we trust that he is good. And rather than seeking answers to all our questions, we seek instead to live in the light of Christ's cross, where good reigns eternal amidst the dark and evil chaos of the world he came to save.

Discussion Questions

1. Read all of Genesis 34. Take a few minutes to talk about the motives and actions of the major characters: Dinah, Jacob, the brothers, Shechem, Hamor, the townsmen.
2. Talk about what happened to Dinah. Besides the horror of the rape itself, what other crimes were committed against her?
3. What is your overall impression of how Jacob handled this situation? Was he trying to keep the peace, avoid violence, avoid dealing with the situation, something else? What details in this story support your thoughts?
4. What is your overall impression of how the brothers handled this situation? Was their form of "justice" legitimate? Why or why not? What did they think of their father's reaction?

5. As we live through or see "Genesis 34's" in our own lives or culture, what can we, as disciples, learn from this statement: "Rather than seeking answers to all our questions, we seek instead to live in the light of Christ's cross, where good reigns eternal amidst the dark and evil chaos of the world he came to save"?

CHAPTER 23

Deuteronomized Discipleship

"Let us arise and go up to Bethel."

Genesis 35:3

The names of some biblical books make sense; others, not so much. The name "Joshua," for example, fits with the overall content of that book, since it primarily recounts the actions of Israel under the leadership of that man. The books 1-2 Samuel, however, would have been more appropriately titled 1-2 David, since he, not the prophet (who dies in 1 Sam. 25:1 anyway), is the main guy.

The English names of some of the Torah books might not make much sense, either, at least at first glance. Leviticus? What does that name even mean? Numbers? Is that a book about biblical math? One fact to bear in mind is that our English titles of biblical books are not from the Hebrew but from the Greek translation known as the Septuagint (commonly abbreviated "LXX").[1] The Hebrew names come from a word at or near the opening of each of the five books. For instance, the book we call Genesis is, in Hebrew, known as *B'reshit*

---

[1] In Roman numerals, LXX is "seventy." This reflects an ancient tradition, recorded in the *Letter of Aristeas* (3rd-2nd c. BC), that seventy(-two) Jewish scholars in Alexandria, Egypt, labored separately on a translation of the Hebrew Torah into Greek. According to the legend, when they reconvened and compared translations, they were all miraculously the same. The Greek spelling of many Hebrew names—spellings which were later accepted or refined by the Latin Vulgate—greatly influenced the spelling of these same names in English Bibles.

("in the beginning," from Gen. 1:1) and the book we call Leviticus is, in Hebrew, known as *Vayikra* ("and he called," from Lev. 1:1). The fifth and final book of the Torah is called, in Hebrew, *Devarim* ("words"), from the opening: "These are the words...." In English, of course, we know it as Deuteronomy.

I've entitled this chapter, Deuteronomized Discipleship, because when this name turns into a verb, it serves as a useful image of one key characteristic of discipleship: repetition.

The name "Deuteronomy" comes from Deut. 17:18, "And when [the king] sits on the throne of his kingdom, he shall write for himself in a book a copy [*mishneh*] of this law." The Hebrew for the phrase, "*mishneh* ['copy, double, second'] of this law [*Torah*]" was rendered into Greek as *deuteronomion touto* ("this second law"). *Deuteronomion* thus drifted into English as Deuteronomy. And, generally speaking,[2] this is a good name for the book as a whole because what Moses undertakes in this series of sermons is a "seconding" or repetition of the Torah that was given, forty years earlier, at Sinai. We read in the opening section of the book, "Moses began to explain [*ba'ar*] this law [Torah]" (1:5). To *ba'ar* is to "explain, elucidate, make very clear." And what better way to do that than to "deuteronomize" the teachings of Yahweh, that is, to say them a second time, repeat them, go over them again, echo what was said before.

By deuteronomized discipleship, therefore, I mean that we are learning the age-old wisdom of listening a second time (then a third and fourth and fifth time) to words that really matter, to the words that fall from the Lord's own lips. As an example of this deuteronomizing, let's take a look at what happened in Jacob's life after the calamitous events we covered in the previous chapter.

Compared to Genesis 34, in which the Lord is silent, in Genesis 35 he stands at the microphone quite often. As the chapter opens, he summons Jacob back to Bethel, where he had addressed him decades before in the "stairway to heaven" episode: "Arise, go

---

[2] I say "generally speaking" because, as is often pointed out in commentaries in Deuteronomy and introductions to the OT, the Greek *deuteronomion touto* is not a completely accurate translation of the Hebrew. It was not a "second law" but a "copy" of the Torah that was to be written by the king.

up to Bethel and dwell there. Make an altar there to the God who appeared to you when you fled from your brother Esau" (35:1). This may be the Lord's gentle method of reminding Jacob of the (partially unfulfilled) vow he made 20+ years earlier, "If God will be with me and will keep me in this way that I go, and will give me bread to eat and clothing to wear, so that I come again to my father's house in peace, then the LORD shall be my God, and this stone, which I have set up for a pillar, shall be God's house. And of all that you give me I will give a full tenth to you" (28:20-22).[3] The Lord had certainly gone above and beyond what Jacob had requested. The patriarch ordered a bologna sandwich and God brought out a filet mignon and a bottle of vintage wine, to boot. Not content merely to be with Jacob, guard him, and keep his belly full and body clothed, he enriched him extravagantly, made him relatively powerful, and graced him with an incredible extra name.

So the Lord, clearing his throat, says, "Now, Jacob, about *your* part in this vow...."

In Jacob's eyes, God's timing was superb. His sons had just massacred the entire male population of Shechem, so he was probably more than happy to take an extended leave of absence from that place, lest any of Shechem's allies were eager for revenge. Before they hit the road, however, some religious housekeeping was in order. They needed a thorough idol-cleansing. Either their newly acquired slaves from Shechem were clutching Canaanite deities or family members like Rachel were still harboring household gods from Mesopotamia (Gen. 31:19). Or both. Either way, these idols, along with earrings decorated with figures of gods and goddesses, were piled together and Jacob "hid them under the terebinth tree

---

[3] What about this tithe or "full tenth"? Did Jacob ever pay it? Brian Neil Peterson has argued that "the author presents Jacob as having fulfilled his vow of paying tithes to God, which he promised at Bethel, by giving Esau an extravagant gift when he returned to Canaan. While the reader is not told if this was a tenth, based upon the number of animals Jacob gave to Esau (580 total), it seems logical that in light of his many years in Haran, and God's blessing on Jacob's flocks (Genesis 31), that Jacob could easily have had flocks that numbered into the thousands." See his essay, "Jacob's Tithe: Did Jacob Keep His Vow to God?" in *JETS* 63.2 (2020): 255–65.

that was near Shechem" (35:4). Nahum Sarna suggests that this odd burying place might have been intended "to neutralize veneration of the terebinth" tree.[4] With that done, along with ceremonial cleansings and bodily washings, the entourage began the pilgrimage to Bethel. As they journeyed, a "terror from God" fell upon all the cities they passed (35:5), thus proving Jacob's earlier fears unfounded (34:30).

At Bethel, a whole series of "seconding" or "repetitions" commences. To kick things off, Jacob was here pre-exile, as now he is here post-exile. Next, notice how verses 1 and 7 virtually parrot one another:

Do This (35:1)	Done (35:7)
God said to Jacob, "Arise, go up to Bethel and dwell there. Make an altar there to the God who appeared to you when you fled from your brother Esau."	"[Jacob went to Bethel and] there he built an altar and called the place El-bethel, because there God had revealed himself to him when he fled from his brother.

After this, the Lord appears to Jacob "again" (35:9). Of course, the "again" hearkens back to the dream vision of Jacob in Genesis 28, when he saw the stairway and angels. The repetitions or "deuteronomizing" are growing.

Finally, when Yahweh begins to speak—more specifically, to "bless" Jacob (35:9)—we overhear multiple echoes from previous verses, some from earlier in Jacob's life and some all the way back from Abraham's day:

Genesis 35:10-12	Parallel Verses
And God said to him, "Your name is Jacob; no longer shall your name be called Jacob, but Israel shall be your name." So he called his name Israel.	Then he said, "Your name shall no longer be called Jacob, but Israel, for you have striven with God and with men, and have prevailed" (32:28).

---

[4] *Genesis*, The JPS Torah Commentary, 240.

Genesis 35:10-12	Parallel Verses
And God said to him, "I am God Almighty: be fruitful and multiply. A nation and a company of nations shall come from you, and kings shall come from your own body.	[Isaac said to Jacob,] "God Almighty bless you and make you fruitful and multiply you, that you may become a company of peoples" (28:3). [God said to Abraham,] "I will make you exceedingly fruitful, and I will make you into nations, and kings shall come from you" (17:6). [God said to Abraham concerning Sarah,] "I will bless her, and moreover, I will give you a son by her. I will bless her, and she shall become nations; kings of peoples shall come from her" (17:16).
The land that I gave to Abraham and Isaac I will give to you, and I will give the land to your offspring after you."	[Isaac said to Jacob,] "May he give the blessing of Abraham to you and to your offspring with you, that you may take possession of the land of your sojournings that God gave to Abraham!" (28:4). [God said to Abraham,] "And I will give to you and to your offspring after you the land of your sojournings, all the land of Canaan, for an everlasting possession, and I will be their God" (17:8).

Bethel has become a broken record of the positive variety. The same lines, the same song, keeps playing on repeat: "I am your God... You shall be called Israel...I will make you fruitful... I will give you this land...Kings shall come from you." At Bethel, the Lord "deuteronomizes" Jacob. He sits him down, looks him in the eyes, and says, "Now I'm going to say the same thing again to make sure your ears fully drink in these words."

Sometimes, repetition is the mother of faith.

When God finished speaking and "went up from [Jacob]" (35:13), the patriarch put an exclamation point on the repetitive encounter by one more doubling: as he had set up a stone pillar, anointed it, and renamed the location Bethel in Theophany #1 (28:18-22), so he does with Theophany #2: "And Jacob set up a pillar in the place where he had spoken with him, a pillar of stone. He poured out a drink offering on it and poured oil on it. So Jacob called the name of the place where God had spoken with him Bethel" (35:14-15). This whole section is therefore replete with occasions of déjà vu.

A little over thirty years ago, when I was a young university student in Austin, Texas, my roommate and good friend, Rick Cody, bought me a Bible. After three decades of use, and one rebinding, it's still the Bible I read and study today. It's been with me all over the United States, twice to Siberia, at use in classrooms, pulpits, and truck cabs. The pages are marked with highlights, notes, scribbles, and a few coffee stains. Shortly after Rick gave it to me, I copied a lengthy quote on the inside cover from Martin Luther's Large Catechism, part of which is this:

> Even though you know the Word perfectly and have already mastered everything, still you are daily under the dominion of the devil, who neither day nor night relaxes his effort to steal up on your unawares and to kindle in your heart unbelief and wicked thoughts against all these commandments. Therefore you must continually keep God's word in your heart, on your lips, and in your ears. Where the heart stands idle and the word is not heard, the devil breaks in and does his damage before we realize it. On the other hand, when we seriously ponder the Word, hear it, and put it to use, such is its power that it never departs without fruit.[5]

His word enters our ears, reverberates within our hearts, and exits our mouth again as meditation, prayer, instruction, and praise. And we can never get enough of it for, as Luther goes on to say, "it always awakens new understanding, new pleasure, and a new spirit

---

[5] *The Book of Concord: The Confessions of the Evangelical Lutheran Church*, translated and edited by Theodore G. Tappert (Philadelphia: Fortress Press, 1959), 378-379.

of devotion, and it constantly cleanses the heart and its meditations." Why? "For these words are not idle or dead, but effective and living."[6]

Of course, Martin Luther was hardly saying anything novel. Ages before, the Lord through Moses said to his people, "And these words that I command you today shall be on your heart. You shall teach them diligently to your children, and shall talk of them when you sit in your house, and when you walk by the way, and when you lie down, and when you rise. You shall bind them as a sign on your hand, and they shall be as frontlets between your eyes. You shall write them on the doorposts of your house and on your gates" (Deuteronomy 6:6-9). Hearing them only once will not do! Sitting and walking. At breakfast and dinner. Entering or exiting our homes. At all times and in all places, there is nothing better to hear than the Lord speaking.

Why? The reason is simple: our Father likes to talk to us, his children. In his Scriptures, he tells us who he is, what he has done for us, and the kind of life that will lead to true human flourishing. And his words are not mere information or historical data; they are words pregnant with life for they are the Spirit's words, who is "the Lord and giver of life" (Nicene Creed).

Just as he did with Jacob, so the Lord does with us: he repeats himself. He disciples us by deuteronomizing, by saying his words a second time, repeating them, going over them again, echoing what was said before. He calls us to our own Bethel, to the House of God, to the assembly of believers, where we hear his word read, preached, prayed, and sung. He never tires of saying, "I am your Father...I am your Savior....I forgive you...I love you...I will never leave you...I will bless you over and over."

For us as individuals, as families, and as churches, it is both easy and tempting to glut our souls on the processed, fast-food verbiage of a world that's always eager to welcome us to its table of lies. So our Lord never ceases to call us back to his own table, laden with life-giving promises, with the meat of hope, the bread of faith, the wine of wisdom.

Oh, taste and see that the Lord, and his word, are good—time and time and time again.

---

[6] *The Book of Concord*, 379.

Discussion Questions

1. What are some everyday examples that testify to the truth of the maxim, "Repetition is the mother of learning"? What have you had to memorize? Do you still remember things you learned as a child?

2. Read Genesis 35:1-15. Go through the parallels with earlier biblical texts that are listed in this chapter. What is the overall message that God is communicating? Why does the Lord say it again, and again?

3. Read Deuteronomy 6:6-9, Psalm 1:2, and portions of Psalm 119, such as vv. 105-112. How would you summarize the overall message of these verses regarding the Word of God?

4. How can we incorporate more meditation, study, and reflection upon God's Word into our lives? What is the ongoing message that the Word communicates to us?

CHAPTER 24

Cradles and Graves

So Rachel died, and she was buried on the way to Ephrath.

Genesis 35:19

I follow an Instagram account called "They Didn't Die." Each entry displays a real obituary in which, instead of saying an individual "died," a euphemism is used. For instance, Rene didn't die but "left for a great fishing trip in the eternal waters." Or Tony, a mechanic, "walked out to the garage one last time." Still others have bizarre descriptions of life's end, such as "all her breath leaked out." Some are humorous—not to mention theologically dubious—such as when Marcelle "yelled BINGO one last time" and "won a trip to heaven." However creative, strange, or darkly comical each of the entries are, what they share in common is the avoidance of the "D" word. They didn't die.

But, of course, they did die, every one of them. We can whisper a thousand circumlocutions—the Bible itself can speak euphemistically of someone "lying down with the fathers" (Gen. 47:30)—but in the end the singular fact of D.E.A.T.H., spoken or unspoken, is the loudest voice in the room. There's no microphone quite as deafening as the grave.

In Genesis 35, we hear three loud declarations from that microphone of mortality: the deaths of Deborah, Rachel, and Isaac. Intermixed with these notices of life's omega is the announcement of a little boy's alpha moment in this world: Benjamin is born. Three suns set and one sun rises. How do these stories fill out more of Jacob's story? And how do they speak to our own lives—lives which also are punctuated with cradles and graves?

The first death mentioned in Genesis 35 is puzzling. Seemingly out of the blue, in between Jacob's altar-building at Bethel and God's appearance to him, this obituary is dropped into the text: "And Deborah, Rebekah's nurse, died, and she was buried under an oak below Bethel. So he called its name Allon-bacuth [which in Hebrew means 'oak of weeping']" (Gen. 35:8). Why insert this death notice here? And considering that not even the deaths of the matriarchs Rebekah and Leah are recorded, why does a servant's death merit mention?

Truth be told, no one is sure why. Nahum Sarna suggests that Deborah, who came from Mesopotamia decades before with Rebekah, had been "a living symbol of that [Mesopotamian] connection."[1] Just as Jacob "hid" the foreign gods "under the terebinth tree that was near Shechem" (35:4), so now he "buries" the foreign servant "under an oak below Bethel" (35:8). These two events signal, as Sarna explains, that Jacob's links with the land of exile are "finally and decisively severed."[2] Victor Hamilton suggests a slightly more positive reason: that just as the Jacob cycle of narratives began with the birth of two people (Esau and Jacob), so now this closing unit in the Jacob cycle will end with the deaths of two people, namely, Deborah and Rachel.[3] Births and deaths thus bookend this major part of Jacob's story.

Whatever the reason for Deborah's mention, isn't this one more example of the Bible's tendency to throw light on those otherwise darkened by virtual anonymity? When we are first told of Deborah's existence, not even her name is provided; she is simply a "nurse" (Gen. 24:59). Now, in this second and final mention, we learn her name, are informed of her death, and hear of the sorrow which accompanied her departure from this life, so much so that her grave is named "the oak of weeping" (35:8). Here is a heartwarming example of how the Scriptures help us to remember the easily forgotten.

The second death is that of Jacob's beloved Rachel. Several chapters ago, we remarked that Rachel's first recorded words were all

---

[1] *Genesis*, The JPS Torah Commentary, 241.
[2] *Genesis*, The JPS Torah Commentary, 241.
[3] *The Book of Genesis: Chapters 18-50*, 379.

about children and death. She said to Jacob, "Give me children [literally 'sons'], or I shall die!" (30:1). When the Lord did finally open her womb and she bore a son, she named him Yoseph ("Joseph") punning off the Hebrew verb *yasaph*, which means to "add" or "increase." For she said, "May the LORD add [*yoseph*] to me another son!" (30:24). Now, when the Lord does "add" that second son, her first recorded words rebound with dark irony, for as she bears this son, she dies. "When her labor was at its hardest, the midwife said to her, 'Do not fear, for you have another son.' And as her soul was departing (for she was dying), she called his name Ben-oni; but his father called him Benjamin" (35:18). The name "Ben-oni" could mean "son of my vigor," or, more likely, "son of my sorrow." Either way, Jacob obviously did not like the name because, despite his wife's dying words, he changed the boy's name to Benjamin, which means "son of the right hand" or "son of the south."[4] Because both Joseph and Benjamin were the sons of his favorite wife, they too are his favorite children. And, as we shall soon see, playing favorites will result in some long and disastrous consequences for the entire family.

Rachel's death adds another "marker" to Jacob's life. He first saw her after he left Bethel and arrived in Haran (Gen. 29:9-10). Now, having left Haran and arrived back in Bethel, Jacob sees Rachel no more. Her grave will thenceforth forever be associated with exile. Generations later, Jeremiah will portray Rachel weeping for her children, as the northern tribes (many of whom were direct descendants of Joseph) were carried off into exile by the Assyrians in 722 BC (Jer. 31:15). Matthew will echo this lament as he, quoting Jeremiah, applies the weeping and mourning of Rachel to the death of the "Holy Innocents" of Bethlehem, who were murdered at mad Herod's behest (Matt. 1:16-18). Rachel thereby becomes everlastingly iconic of exile and the lamentation of the suffering.

The third and final obituary concerns old Isaac (Gen. 35:28-29). Some point after his return, Jacob visited his father at Hebron (his mother, presumably, had died while Jacob was in exile). This reunion of father and son likely happened much earlier than where it is

---

[4] In the OT, orientation is always facing east, so the Hebrew word for "right" [*yamin*] is also the word for "south," as the word for "left" [*s'mol*] also means "north".

recorded in the narrative. Events in the Bible are not always presented chronologically, a tendency the rabbis noted by the catchphrase *Ein mukdam u'meuchar baTorah* (lit. "there is neither early nor late in the Torah"), that is, no necessary chronological sequence. The patriarch, who decades before thought he might be near death (cf. 27:2), lived much longer than he expected, making it to 180 years. He "breathed his last, and he died and was gathered to his people, old and full of days" (35:29). In a rather touching fraternal "Amen" to their dad's life, the two brothers, Esau and Jacob, once bitter rivals, now formally reconciled, together buried their father in peace.

This one birth and these three deaths are, for Jacob, all symbolic of realities greater than the individuals themselves. With Isaac dead, Jacob is now *the* patriarch in Genesis. He received the baton of blessing, passed to him by Isaac, which he will eventually place in the hand of his fourth-born, Judah. The promise of the Seed in Genesis 3:15, once carried forward by Abraham, then Isaac, is now borne into the future by Jacob. With [his] beloved wife, Rachel, now dead, Jacob seems to transfer his affections to Rachel's sons, Joseph and Benjamin. And as his preference for Rachel over Leah led to spousal rivalries, so now his preference for Rachel's two sons will erupt in sibling rivalries. Deborah's death, while presumably not as consequential for Jacob, does mark the end of the family's Mesopotamian connections. In line with that, Benjamin, the only one of the dozen sons born in Canaan, embodies *the new*. New land. New beginnings. Benjamin is the post-exilic posterchild of the Bible. In that way, this late-born son is like unto his NT counterpart, Saul, from the tribe of Benjamin, who also was "one untimely born" (1 Cor. 15:8; Rom. 11:1).

From the world's perspective, Christians have things completely backwards when it comes to birth and death. The world, of course, lives by what its eyes see and not what its ears hear from God's word. So what does the world see in the newborn? A near perfect specimen of humanity, purity, the beginning of life. What do Christians see? We see a beautiful gift of God, to be sure, as well as the beginning of earthly life, but we see the unseen: we see an infant just as much in need of salvation as a toddler, teenager, or octogenarian. Our eyes could never tell us this, but the Scriptures affirm that this baby, conceived by two sinners, has inherited the same sinful nature as his or her parents, passed down all the way from Adam. So David says of himself—and all of us—"Behold, I was brought forth in iniquity, and in sin did my mother conceive me" (Ps. 51:5). Children do not, at some unspecified moment in their lives, transition from spiritual neutrals to positively sinful. A child's beginning of earthly life is therefore also the beginning of his or her need of Christ's heavenly life, his purity, his perfection, his family name. So, they are baptized into the family name, the "name of the Father and of the Son and of the Holy Spirit" (Matt. 28:19).

Because of our baptism into the living, life-giving body of Jesus, the Christian view of death is also radically different from that of the world. *Disciples of Jesus die long before they die.* Paul expresses it this way: "Do you not know that all of us who have been baptized into Christ Jesus were baptized into his death? We were buried therefore with him by baptism into death, in order that, just as Christ was raised from the dead by the glory of the Father, we too might walk in newness of life" (Rom. 6:3-4). In Greek the phrase "buried...with him" is one word, *synthapto*, which we might translate "co-buried." Paul only uses it twice: here and Col. 2:12, "...having been buried with Christ in baptism." Both times, therefore, the apostle says specifically that baptism is how we are *synthapto* or co-buried with Jesus. In this same section of Romans, Paul will also say we are *sustauroō* ("co-crucified") with Jesus and *suzaō* ("co-live") with him (6:6, 8). By baptism, therefore, we enter fully into Jesus; we are co-crucified, co-buried, and co-resurrected. The end result is that we [are] "dead to sin and alive to God in Christ Jesus" (6:11).

Baptism is therefore our major death, major burial, and major funeral in life. It is "major" in two ways. One, by baptism the Father deals with all our major problems: sin, death, shame, guilt, alienation, condemnation. Two, baptism gives us no minor gift but the major gifts of new life, new peace, new hope, all in Jesus our Lord. We are "dead to sin" for we have been crucified with Christ in baptism so that it is no longer we who live but Christ who lives in us (Gal. 2:20; Rom. 6:11).

Our physical death, therefore, which seems like The End to the world, is simply a minor portal through which we leave this visible world to be with Christ in Paradise, where we will await "the resurrection of the dead and the life of the world to come" (Nicene Creed). We die bodily, yes, but it's only a minor death. The major death we already experienced, long before, in the Christ-soaked grave of baptism. We close our eyes in this minor death and open them to see Jesus, smiling at us, summoning us into his presence.

For this reason, the NT often refers to the physical death of disciples as "sleep" (e.g., Matt. 27:52; John 11:11; 1 Cor. 15:20). Our bodies are, as it were, slumbering in the grave, awaiting the trumpet blast on the Last Day, when Jesus will awaken, resurrect, and glorify our bodies to live in the new heavens and new earth. As an affirmation of this hope, Christians have long called the burial place of their dead a "cemetery," which in Greek is *koimeterion*, formed from the verb *koimaō* ("to sleep"). Cemeteries are "sleeping places." The very name is a confession that Jesus is not done with the bodies that are buried in this sacred soil. Resurrection awaits.

As disciples of a Rabbi whose early followers were said to have "turned the world upside down" (Acts 17:6), our confession will almost always be diametrically opposed to that of the world. For us, the cradle holds a baby in need of the life of Jesus, and the grave holds a child of God who is fully in the life of Jesus. We are more alive after death than before. And in between the cradle and the grave, our "goal in life" (to adopt that language) is to lose our life! "Whoever finds his life will lose it, and whoever loses his life for [Christ's] sake will find it" (Matt. 10:39). We lose our lives by plummeting into the waters of baptism, where we are united to the life of Jesus. And we continue losing our lives as daily, by contrition and repentance, we drown our sinful natures so that our new nature in Christ might rise to live in the presence of our Father as holy, righteous, and forgiven.[5]

Perhaps that Instagram account is half-right, at least with regard to Christians. With a knowing wink of resurrection hope, we can say of every child of God who has passed from this life into the presence of Jesus: They Didn't Die.

---

[5] See Martin Luther's explanation to what baptism indicates in the Fourth Question of his *Small Catechism* section on Baptism.

DISCUSSION QUESTIONS

1. What are some euphemisms we use for death? Why do we use them? Talk about humanity's fascination with death, as well as its fear of death.

2. Read Genesis 35:16-29. Who are the three people who die in this chapter and which baby is born? Talk about the significance of all four of them in relation to Jacob's life.

3. Read Ps. 51:5, John 3:6, Rom. 5:12, and Eph. 2:3. How is the Christian view of birth different from the view of the world? What do our children need from Christ?

4. Read Romans 6:1-11. What are the "co-" words that are used in these verses? Talk about this statement in relation to these verses: "Baptism is therefore our major death, major burial, and major funeral in life."

5. How are we, therefore, as disciples, to think about birth and death? How does baptism give shape to our life as followers of Jesus?

Part 4

Growing Old: Colorful Coats and Saying Goodbye

Chapter 25

The Coat of Many Jealousies

Now Israel loved Joseph more than any other of his sons.

Genesis 37:3

For several decades, Tim Keller has been preaching the gospel in New York City. The congregation that he and his family began in 1989, Redeemer Presbyterian Church, has expanded to multiple campuses around the city. Keller's influence, international in scope, led *Christianity Today* to call him "a pioneer of the new urban Christians."[1]

Yet had it not been for a fascinating series of unpredictable events, Tim Keller might never have ended up in New York City.

As Keller himself tells the story, one particular seminary professor encouraged him to go into the Presbyterian ministry. This professor, who was a visiting teacher from Great Britain, almost didn't make it to Keller's school that semester because he couldn't get his visa to travel to the United States. However, someone from the State Department greased the wheels to get the application process moving along. That happened only because the seminary had a student at the time with family connections to the White House. These connections were only possible because the previous president had been forced to resign amidst the Watergate scandal. And that scandal broke only because a security guard spied an unlatched door and investigated. As Keller writes, "If that door had been latched, and the scandal had

---

[1] https://www.christianitytoday.com/ct/2006/may/1.36.html

not happened, and the changes in government had not occurred, I never would have sat under that professor."[2]

One unlatched door initiated a string of events that culminated in untold thousands of people in New York City hearing the saving message of Jesus Christ from the preaching of Tim Keller. After he tells this story, Keller asks his listeners, "Are you glad Redeemer Church is here?" When they say, "Yes," he responds, "Then Watergate happened for you."[3]

This modern story of our Lord's gracious providence is a fitting introduction to an ancient story of divine providence: Joseph in Egypt. To echo Keller's example, we might have asked generations of Israelites, "Are you glad the exodus happened?" When they said, "Yes," we could have told them, "Then the betrayal of Joseph happened for you." If Jacob had not given his chosen son that (in)famous tunic; if this misguided paternal favoritism had not fed the jealous ire of his brothers; if one of them, Judah, had not suggested they sell this too-big-for-his-britches dreamer to traders bound for Egypt; if Joseph had not been shackled, tempted, framed, incarcerated, forgotten, and eventually exalted to be Vice Pharaoh; and if Jacob and his family, due to Joseph's God-given ability to interpret mysterious dreams, had not wound up in Egypt to escape death by starvation; then the exodus, the crossing of the Red Sea, and all the divine gifts of redemption would not have happened.

In the coming chapters, we will have plenty of time to muse upon several details of divine providence that are woven throughout Genesis 37-50. Since we're all about the life of Jacob in this book, however, we will hold fast to that focus in this final section, tempting though it be to dive headfirst into the deep and rich pool of the "Joseph Story." That story, however, deserves its own book-length treatment.[4]

---

[2] *Encounters with Jesus: Unexpected Answers to Life's Biggest Questions* (Penguin Books: New York City, 2013), 184-185.

[3] *Encounters with Jesus*, 185.

[4] For a deep dive into the Joseph story, from a scholarly perspective, see Jeffrey Pulse's recent book *Figuring Resurrection: Joseph as a Death & Resurrection Figure in the Old Testament & Second Temple Judaism*, Studies in Scripture & Biblical Theology (Bellingham, WA: Lexham Press, 2021).

For now, let's put the narrative in park for just a moment and get our bearings. In our previous two chapters, we discussed various details related to Genesis 35: the disposal of idols, the pilgrimage to Bethel, the Lord's speech to Jacob, the deaths of Deborah and Rachel and Isaac, and the birth of Benjamin. That chapter, as a whole, is a sort of "drawer of miscellany," with lots of stuff thrown in, much of which serves to put the closing touch on earlier parts of Jacob's life. The next chapter, Genesis 36, is not about Jacob at all but delineates the descendants of his twin brother, Esau. By its placement between Genesis 35 (the end of the "Jacob Story") and Genesis 37 (the beginning of the "Joseph Story"), Genesis 36 acts as a kind of genealogical interlude.

When we step over the threshold into this last major section of Genesis, chapters 37-50, Jacob is about 108 years old. He will die at the age of 147 (Gen. 47:28). Using today's average life expectancy as a metric, Jacob is the equivalent of a modern man in his late 50's. He has twelve sons and one daughter; one living wife (Leah) and one dead wife (Rachel); and as far as we know, his co-wives, Bilhah and Zilpah, are also still with him.

Where do all the sons stand vis-à-vis their father? After the bloody events in Genesis 34, when Simeon and Levi killed the men of Shechem, those two sons—the second-born and third-born—were on Jacob's blacklist. And his firstborn, Reuben, had secured his *dis*inheritance when he "went and lay with Bilhah his father's concubine. And Israel heard of it" (35:22).[5] That means Jacob's fourth-born son, Judah, is next in line to receive the paternal blessing. Judah, however, has one major mark against him: his maternal pedigree. He is the offspring of the unloved wife, Leah, so despite his place in the succession of possible heirs, he is not Daddy's Favorite. That pride of

---

[5] It is probably best to understand Reuben's sexual actions as (1) an attempt to secure his place as the rightful family leader or (2) to supplant his father of his leadership. In the ancient world, to engage in intercourse with the concubine of a king or leader was to say, "I am now in charge." This is why David's son, Absalom, during his coup, slept publicly with his father's concubines (2 Sam. 16:20-23) and likely why David's other son, Adonijah, coyly requested that his father's erstwhile bed-warmer, Abishag (1 Kings 1:1-3), become his wife (1 Kings 2:13-25). These actions, while sexual in nature, are more about politics and power than lust.

place belongs to a handsome, dreamy teenager named Joseph, whom "Israel loved...more than any other of his sons, because he was the son of his old age" (37:3).[6]

Having grown up in a household in which Mom and Dad played favorites (Rebekah loving Jacob and Isaac loving Esau [Gen. 25:28]) and having witnessed the turmoil that such preferential treatment caused, Jacob should have known better. Obviously, he *did* know better. But knowing X is bad and avoiding doing X is not high on a sinner's list of noteworthy moral achievements. Our problem, generally speaking, is not ignorance of "shoulds, musts, and oughts" but the willful refusal to do what would actually be best for ourselves and everyone else concerned. It is a commonplace truth, as well, that children often grow up to replicate the foibles and failures of their parents. This does not always happen (thank God!), but one does not need a Ph.D. in psychology to realize the unavoidable impact, for good or for ill, that our parents make on us when we ourselves begin trying to figure out the vocation of child-rearing.

Jacob, who never seems to do anything halfway, does appear to out-Isaac Isaac and out-Rebekah Rebekah in the specific way that he showed favoritism. He didn't just spend a little extra time playing baseball with Joseph at the park or take him fishing on more weekends than the other boys. No, Jacob basically hung a brightly flashing neon sign on Joseph that shouted the words, "MY FAVORITE BOY," for all to see. This was the well-known "coat of many colors" or, in Hebrew, the *k'tonet passim*, which is also translated as "ornamented tunic" (R. Alter) or "long-sleeved robe" (CSB).[7] Jacob, who earlier had robed himself in his brother's clothing to conceal the truth, now robed his son in clothing that revealed the truth *all too clearly*. And

---

[6] The stated reason for Jacob's favoritism is odd: "because he was the son of his old age." If that were the only determining factor, then not Joseph but Benjamin would be his real favorite, since he was not only from the same chosen wife (Rachel) but also the last-born son. Perhaps because Joseph was the firstborn of Rachel, he was accorded preferential treatment.

[7] As I explain elsewhere, "A *k'tonet* is a long robe. *Passim* is less clear. It may be connected to *pas* ('the palm of the hand of sole of the foot'). If so, it's a long-sleeved tunic reaching down to the feet," *Unveiling Mercy: 365 Daily Devotions Based on Insights from Old Testament Hebrew* (Irvine, CA: New Reformation Publications, 2020), 49.

Joseph's siblings, who were already irritated at their seventeen-year-old brother for being their father's little tattletale (37:2), were now positively incensed: "But when his brothers saw that their father loved him more than all his brothers, they hated him and could not speak peacefully to him" (37:4). It's the cycle of Cain-and-Abel, Jacob-and-Esau, all over again.

If we think of Genesis 37-50 as a novella, what a riveting opening scene we have. A foolish father, a spoiled son, and the acrid smell of smoldering hatred that might burst into a fratricidal flame at any time. All the ingredients of a gothic-like story are in play. Bring on the blade. Bring on the blood. Bring on the ghoulish ending.

But not so fast. Broken humans are the actors in this account, yes, but a merciful God authored the narrative. Sinners are doing what sinners do best—messing everything up—and God is doing what God does best. He's weaving events, replete with hatred and horror and a vestige of hope, into a finished product of redemption that we could never have foreseen.

How often in my own life have I acted selfishly, parented stupidly, or simply made a series of colossally bad decisions, surveyed the aftereffects, and thought, "There's no way something good can come out of this." And how often have I pronounced that same judgment when I have run up against families that seem red in tooth and claw; marriages that reek of decomposing love; or churches that are riven asunder by factionalism, power-posturing, or pharisaical legalism. The oh-ye-of-little-faith part of me sizes up these situations and pronounced them D.O.A. No life. No hope. All we have here is an existential crisis of hellish proportions.

Yet there stands God, who peers down at me, grins mischievously, and says, "Oh yeah, Chad? Just hide and watch." And sometimes—some blessed times—I am privileged to see radiant flowers growing out of the sidewalk cracks of human existence. Good, and often even beauty, arises from the cold and gray death. Such "resurrection moments," if we can call them that, are ongoing reminders that we serve the God who brought an entire universe out of nothing, a new start after a cosmic flood, a new Adam-like Abraham and Eve-like Sarah out of the mass of unbelieving humanity, and redemption for Jacob and his family out of a string of unfortunate events that culminated in Joseph sitting alongside Pharaoh as the savior of Egypt.

Do we, as Christ's disciples, dare to imagine that he will do less for us? He will do profoundly more than we think or can even imagine. Joseph's "coat of many colors," though an asinine gift that prompted naked hostility, was also one thread in the tangled narrative that led, finally, to Joseph emerging from a prison to shave and change his clothes before going in to interpret the dreams of the king of Egypt (Gen. 41:14). Similarly, over a millennium later, a young man named Saul, who guarded the robes of those who stoned Stephen (Acts 7:58), became the apostle who wrote, "Clothe yourselves with the Lord Jesus Christ" (Rom. 13:14 NIV).

Never underestimate our Lord's willingness and ability to take betrayals, disasters, and all manner of brokenness, and to squeeze something good out of them. As with the Bible, so in our lives as followers of Jesus, a merciful God is the true author of the narrative of our lives.

He who hung naked upon the cross knows a thing or two about weaving the bright hope of resurrection out of the shadow threads of a Good Friday afternoon.

DISCUSSION QUESTIONS

1. As you think about your own life, do you have any stories like Tim Keller's where, in hindsight, you were able to see the Lord providentially at work? What good were you able to see emerge from the bad?

2. Read Genesis 37:1-11. How is Jacob repeating the errors of his parents? How did his father, Isaac, do the same regarding the error of his father (Gen. 12:10-20 and 26:1-11)? What are some commonly repeated mistakes, sins, and failures that pop up in generation after generation of families? How can these patterns of sin be broken?

3. Read Genesis 49:19-21 and Acts 2:22-23. What do these verses say about human sinning and divine planning? What do they teach us about God's providential care of us?

4. Talk about this statement and apply it to the life of discipleship: "Never underestimate our Lord's willingness

and ability to take betrayals, disasters, and all manner of brokenness, and to squeeze something good out of them. As with the Bible, so in our lives as followers of Jesus, a merciful God is the true author of the narrative of our lives." How is the Lord "authoring" our lives?

CHAPTER 26

Wunderkinds and Word-Keepers

> His father kept the saying in mind.
>
> Genesis 37:11

One of the greatest joys in studying the Scriptures is that, no matter how deeply we dig, there are always more jewels to find, buried here, buried there, awaiting our interpretive excavation. Part of the reason for this is that the biblical authors, being masterful storytellers, stuck to the elementary rule for writers, "Show Don't Tell." They let us readers do our part in coloring lines from A to Z which they only faintly traced. Or detecting subtle wordplays, double entendre, foreshadowing, and the like. The NT authors mimic their older, Hebrew counterparts in this way. We see this especially in the Gospels, where OT themes and images are whispered within narratives about Jesus so as to lead us to listen with rapt attention—and to trail the NT whisper back into the OT shout.

Case in point: St. Luke's adroit portrayal of Mary as Jacob-like and Jesus as Joseph-like.

Remember that time that Mary and Joseph couldn't find Jesus? This was a headline-worthy event: "Local Nazareth Couple Lose Track of God's Son for Three Days." The loss culminated in the distraught parents locating him finally in the courts of the temple. There, in his Father's house, he was carrying on like a rabbinic wunderkind, "sitting among the teachers, listening to them and asking them questions" (Luke 2:46).

Now pay careful attention to what transpires next:

1. Mary rebukes Jesus: "And his mother said to him,
   'Son, why have you treated us so? Behold, your father
   and I have been searching for you in great distress'"
   (Luke 2:48).
2. After Jesus responds, we are told that "his mother
   treasured up all these things in her heart" (2:51).

The Greek verb for "treasured up" is *diatereo* and the noun for
"things" is *rhema*. Now, tuck those two words into your back pocket
and let's trot back to Genesis 37:6, where we left off in our last chapter.

What's going on? Joseph is about to relay one dream, then
another, to his father and brothers. These twin dreams fit within a
recognizable pattern in the Joseph story, where doublets routinely
occur: the two servants of Pharoah have dreams; the king himself
has two dreams; the brothers travel twice to Egypt; etc. In Dream
#1, there's a terrestrial focus: sheaves in the field (=brothers) bow
down to another sheaf (=Joseph). In Dream #2, there's a celestial
focus: stars (=brothers) along with the sun and moon (=parents),
bow to Joseph. Just as sometimes "heaven and earth" are called upon
to witness something in Scripture (e.g., Isa. 1:2; Ps. 50:4), so here the
celestial and terrestrial affirm the prophetic truth of what will come
to pass.

Little brother's dreams were not warmly welcomed by his
already-jealous siblings—no shock there—and they ended up hating
"him even more" (37:10). Notice the precise language: they hated him
"for his dreams and for his words." His dreams alone were not cause of
accelerated hatred, but also "his words." Twin reasons. Joseph insisted
on talking about his dreams instead of keeping them to himself.

Now, remembering what we saw with Mary and Jesus in Luke 2,
notice what happens next in Genesis:

1. "[H]is father rebuked him and said to him, 'What is this
   dream that you have dreamed? Shall I and your mother
   and your brothers indeed come to bow ourselves to the
   ground before you?'" (37:10).[1]

---

[1] Commentators have long noted that Rachel, Joseph's mother, had long
been dead (35:19), so there is a seeming temporal incongruity here. The most

2. "And his brothers were jealous of him, but his father kept the saying in mind" (37:11).

These words were originally written in Hebrew, of course, but later translated into Greek in the Septuagint, with which Luke would have been familiar. The Greek verb used in the Septuagint for "kept…in mind" is *diatereo* and the noun for "the saying" is *rhema*. These are the same words we saw in Luke 2! In other words, both Jacob and Mary *diatereo* ("treasured up" or "kept in mind") the *rhema* ("things" or "the saying") concerning their respective young sons.

This allusion to Genesis in Luke's Gospel is the evangelist's way of teaching us to press our ear onto the scroll of the Bible, to listen for echoes and whispers that summon us back to earlier Scriptures. The two scenes are not the same, of course, but there are plenty of similarities to pique our interest. One, both Jacob and Mary, upset by what their sons say or do, verbally rebuke or chide them. Two, the sons are surrounded by those who, though family or fellow countrymen, will one day become their adversaries (i.e., the brothers in the case of Joseph and the teachers of the law in the case of Jesus). Three, as the dreams foretell Joseph's future royalty, so Christ's precocious understanding presages his adult wisdom. Four, both sons are sold or betrayed for a few pieces of silver (Gen. 37:28; Matt. 26:15). And five, both Joseph and Jesus will, through suffering and betrayal and time in the pit/tomb, arise to be their people's savior. We could go on with more parallels, but these few will suffice for now.[2] These shared themes, along with the linguistic links of *diatereo* and *rhema*, encourage us *to read the life of Joseph as Jesus-like and the life of Jesus as Joseph-like.* For this reason, in his lectures on Genesis, Martin Luther calls Joseph "the image of God's Son."[3]

It seems entirely reasonable that, when Luke was doing the research to prepare his "orderly account" for Theophilus (Luke 1:3), he sat down with Mary and interviewed her.[4] After all, the mother of

---

likely explanation is that the "mother" to which Jacob referred was Leah, who would have become Joseph's step-mother after the death of Rachel.

[2] For more on this subject, see Jeffrey Pulse, *Figuring Resurrection*.

[3] AE 6:385

[4] Arthur A. Just Jr., commenting on Mary "treasuring up" all these things, both in Luke 2:51 and earlier in 2:19, writes, "This strongly suggests that she is a source for the historical information in the infancy narrative in Luke."

Jesus was active in the early church (Acts 1:14). And who better to tell the story of the early years of Jesus' life? I can imagine her saying something like this to Luke: "That whole scene in the temple when Jesus was a boy....I couldn't get it out of mind and heart. I mulled over it. Treasured it like gold or a precious stone. As I watched Jesus grow up, I would lie awake in bed at night, hearing and rehearing every word, reliving every moment, wondering what it all meant. Only after everything happened, of course, with his death and resurrection, did I truly begin to understand." Likewise, many years after Jacob listened to young Joseph recount his dreams, when the patriarch was finally reunited with the grown son, the one whom he had thought dead all those years, I can imagine elderly Jacob reminiscing, "Ah, how many times, over those long and dark years when I was bereft of my beloved boy, did my mind and heart drift back to those two dreams he had as a teenager. Even in my sorrow, I guarded and treasured those strange, unforgettable dreams. They were nailed to the wall of my memory like portraits from the past."

What both Mary and Jacob shared was an unwillingness to let go of something, even though they did not fully grasp the truth of it. They knew that it was important, worth treasuring and pondering. Eventually, the fog cleared and they saw the message clearly. But that took time, almost the same amount of time for both of them: for Mary twenty-one years, and for Jacob twenty-two years.[5] But for over two decades these disciples held fast to the mystery. They treasured a word they did not fully understand.

In so doing, Mary and Jacob remind us that, as followers of Jesus, we hold fast to a word that we do not always, or cannot always, understand. And that is 100% OK. Now please don't misunderstand me. I'm not talking about mental laziness (God preserve us from more of that). I don't mean leaving our brains in the car when we walk into church (of which Christians are sometimes accused). What I mean

---

Luke 1:1-9:50, in the series *Concordia Commentary: A Theological Exposition of Sacred Scripture* (St. Louis: Concordia Publishing House, 1996), 128.

[5] Jesus was twelve years old in the temple scene and about thirty-three when he was crucified and resurrected. Joseph was seventeen years old around the time of his dreams (Gen. 37:2). He was reunited with his father when he was thirty-nine, since Gen. 41:46 puts him at thirty when he became "Vice Pharaoh," followed by seven years of plenty and two years of famine (cf. 45:6).

is that, even after we have heard, read, studied, and grappled with some parts of Scripture and theology; pored over commentaries and learned tomes; discussed the topic with friends and scholars; prayed about it; and used every ounce of our God-given reason and education to grasp their import, sometimes we are left saying, "God said this. God did this. God gave this. It is therefore important. And I think that maybe, just a little, I get the meaning of it, but I feel like I've only scratched the surface. Nevertheless, I treasure this divine word and action—and always will."

C. S. Lewis famously wrote of the Lord's Supper, that the command of Jesus "was Take, eat: not Take, understand."[6] The Lord tells us, "This is my body" (Matt. 26:26). I first began wrestling with the meaning of those four words when I was eighteen years old. I am currently fifty-one and still, to this day, they remain to me a beautiful mystery. The bread I eat from the Lord's table looks nothing like a human body. It looks and tastes like bread. Yet Jesus clearly said, "This is my body." So, to those words I cling. I have read them in Greek. I have studied multiple books about the Lord's Supper. I have preached, taught about it, and received it thousands of times. But do I understand it? No. Do I believe it? Yes. It is the body of Jesus that we eat when we eat the bread. Do not ask me to give you a philosophical—let alone scientific—explanation for how this is possible. It simply is because Jesus said it is. It is a blessed, divine mystery that I receive but do not come close to comprehending. I take and eat; I do not take and understand.

And that is but one example among a host of others we might put forward. How is Jesus both divine and human? How is God three persons who share one essence? What does it mean that the Lord has predestined people to believe? What do all the numerical, animalistic, humanoid, and astral symbols in Daniel and Revelation mean? Oh, sure, I can partially answer some of these questions, as I'm sure you can as well. We can go into dogmatic detail about the Trinity and Christology and Eschatology. But though you and I may walk along, discussing and debating these issues and teachings and verses, eventually we will leave the bright light of understanding, walk through dusky corridors of uncertainty, and finally step into capacious rooms

---

[6] *Letters to Malcolm, Chiefly on Prayer* (San Francisco: HarperOne, 2017), 141.

cloaked in mystery too dark for human intelligence to see. There we stop and simply say, Amen.

Being disciples of Jesus means treasuring his words, holding fast to his truth, living by faith in his promises, even when, like Mary and Jacob, we're confused. Uncertain. Wrestling with what it all means. Maybe, twenty or thirty years down the road, we will understand some things, as Mary and Jacob did. Or maybe we never will.

Either way, our faith is in a loving and gracious Lord of mystery who said, "Follow me; not Analyze me."

DISCUSSION QUESTIONS

1. Read Genesis 37:11 and Luke 2:41-52. What are the connections between these two stories? How do these connections urge us to listen more closely, more attentively, to the Scriptures?
2. Neither Jacob nor Mary fully understood what happened with their children. Only years later did the words of the Lord become clear. Talk about something from the Word of God that once was unclear to you, but became clearer over time.
3. Discuss some examples of biblical stories, prophecies, or parts of theology that are still baffling or mysterious to you.
4. Read 2 Peter 3:14-16. What does Peter say about the writings of Paul? As we read, study, and reflect upon the Bible, how do we approach writings that are "hard to understand"?

CHAPTER 27

Dear Lord, Go Away
and Leave Me Alone

Jacob refused to be comforted.

Genesis 37:35

The poet and undertaker, Thomas Lynch, began operating a mortuary in Milford, Michigan, in the early 1970's. In his collection of essays, *The Undertaking*, he contrasts the burial of the old with the burial of the young:

> When we bury the old, we bury the known past, the past we imagine sometimes better than it was, but the past all the same, a portion of which we inhabited. Memory is the overwhelming theme, the eventual comfort. But burying infants, we bury the future, unwieldy and unknown, full of promise and possibilities, outcomes punctuated by our rosy hopes. The grief has no borders, no limits, no known ends, and the little infant graves that edge the corners and fencerows of every cemetery are never quite big enough to contain that grief. Some sadnesses are permanent. Dead babies do not give us memories. They give us dreams.[1]

I read this book when it was first published, well over a quarter century ago. I was a rookie pastor at the time. Unschooled in suffering. That

---

[1] *The Undertaking: Life Studies from the Dismal Trade* (New York City: W. W. Norton and Company, 2009), 51.

line, "We bury the future," inked itself within my memory because, merely on an intellectual level, it seemed brilliantly and succinctly accurate.

Alas, I really was clueless at the time. I had no idea how painfully true it was. A year later, when my wife and I lost our first unborn child, then two years later, when we lost our second unborn child, I began to understand, on a deeper, emotional level, what Thomas Lynch meant. As more years rolled by and I sat with moms and dads in darkened rooms furnished with empty cradles, or listened to the silence around a parishioner's kitchen table on the morning when the police knocked on the door with news that changed everything, "burying the future" seemed almost a biblical maxim. Here was a grief that "has no borders, no limits, no known ends."

Such was the unfathomable grief into which Jacob sank. His older sons, to whom Jacob had sent Joseph, pulled their own double version of *carpe diem* by seizing not only the day but that hated "dreamer" when he showed up in their camp (Gen. 37:19). They ripped off his robe, lobbed him like garbage into a waterless pit, and callously fed their faces while their little brother pleaded for mercy from the bowels of the earth (42:21). Then, spotting some Midianite traders passing by, they became cool businessmen. They sold their own flesh and blood for "twenty shekels of silver," a slave's price (cf. Lev. 27:5). As the proverbial cherry on top of this satanically inspired dessert of revenge, the brothers smeared Joseph's cloak with the gushing veins of a slaughtered goat. They transmogrified Joseph's "coat of many colors" into the "coat of the color of violence." And this stained garment, with frigid malice, they dropped in the lap of their father, saying, "This we have found; please identify whether it is your son's robe or not" (37:22).

The brothers could not have carried out their plans with greater accuracy. When they had spied Joseph coming from afar, they said, "Come now, let us kill him and throw him into one of the pits. Then *we will say that a fierce animal has devoured him*, and we will see what will become of his dreams" (37:20; italics added). But they had no need to say it; Jacob himself mouthed the words. When he saw the robe and recognized that it was Joseph's, he said, "*A fierce animal has devoured him*. Joseph is without doubt torn to pieces" (37:33; italics added).

In a fashion, the father was right: Joseph was torn to pieces. The Hebrew verb for torn, *taraf*, is used elsewhere to describe the manner in which the wolf-like tribe of Benjamin (Gen. 49:27) and the lion-like tribe of Gad (Deut. 33:20) *taraf* their prey. The patriarchs of these tribes, along with the other brothers, acted like beasts instead of brothers. They *taraf* Joseph, ripped his life in shreds, and left him ragged and forlorn. And, as if this were not sufficiently barbarous, they also tore their father's soul into pieces. Then, oozing with hypocrisy, they "rose to comfort"—to comfort!—their grieving dad as he robed himself in sackcloth and "mourned many days" (37:34-35). I wonder: was there still goat blood under their fingernails as they gently patted the back of their weeping father? But Jacob was having none of their proffered consolation. He was burying the future. So, he "refused to be comforted and said, 'No, I shall go down to Sheol[2] to my son, mourning'" (37:35).

Were we first-time readers of Genesis, we might wonder if in fact that is exactly what Jacob did: go down to Sheol. Die of a broken heart. Because, as we read on in the book, for a long time—four chapters, to be precise—this grieving father completely vanishes from the narrative (37:35-42:1). He had been the main actor on this Torah stage for quite some time, of course. We have read of his conception and birth, confrontations and deceptions, exiles and returns. And now, as his life is eclipsed by grief, as his tears become floods and his hopes dry into desert sands, the narrator gently closes the curtain around this shattered man.

Jacob needed that. Have you ever watched an interview in which the interviewee begins to sob uncontrollably as she relates some painful memory? If they keep the camera on the person too long, I get angry. Do you? It makes me want to yell at the television, "Good grief! Show some compassion! Take the camera off her and let her cry in peace." In a way, that is what is happening here. The director of the Genesis movie pivots the camera away from Jacob, first to Judah (in a rather twisted, R-rated scene involving father-in-law and daughter-in-law "prostitution" [Genesis 38]), and then onto Joseph in Egypt (39:1ff). Jacob, however, he leaves alone, off camera. To weep. To

---

[2] "Sheol" is a general Hebrew designation for the grave, literally or metaphorically. It frequently refers to a place of suffering, sadness, loss, or despair.

grieve. And, for an indeterminate amount of time, to "refuse to be comforted."

This stubborn refusal of consolation reminds me of some of the audacious language of the psalms, especially the lament psalms, when those who pray (implicitly, if not explicitly) tell the Lord they are not ready to hear a word of comfort. Not yet. They need to squeeze some screams out of their battered souls first. They need to howl and question and bawl their eyes out, till snot runs down their face and they collapse in a heap of exhausted emotional ruin. Those kinds of prayers. The kind you gasp and whimper on the bathroom floor at 2 A.M. after you've puked your guts out because the losses of life have made you physically ill. Sometimes, the best you can manage is to assume a Job-like posture and say, "Look away from me, that I may smile again, before I depart and am no more!" (Ps. 39:13; cf. Job 10:20-21). Leave me alone, God. Look away from me. My future lies buried six-feet-under and I'm in no way ready for you to sit me down, pat my knee, and talk to me in your grandfatherly way about how everything is going to be okay. Because it's not okay. Everything sucks. It hurts. Go away. I refuse to be comforted.

Job's friends, you might recall, only did good work when they sat there with their lips sewn shut. "They sat with him on the ground seven days and seven nights, and no one spoke a word to him, for they saw that his suffering was very great" (Job 2:13). There is "a time to keep silence, and a time to speak" (Eccl. 3:7). And often silence is its own peculiar language. The grammar of grieving can be eloquent when mute. Ah, words, words, words! Ironically, too many of them can deafen us to the healing speech of silence. Of letting be. Of giving ourselves time. Of refusing, for today, for tomorrow, for perhaps longer, to be comforted.

We live in an "Amazon Prime" world, where we can tap a button on our phone and, *Voila!*, running shoes or coffee filters or a new book lands on our doorstep within 24 hours or less. In many ways, that's fine and a very cool thing. But it has a tragic side effect: we become acclimated to acceleration. Schooled into thinking all of life could, or at least should, work that way. Our souls do not. Mourning cannot be microwaved. The healing of the soul—from grief, from shame, from loss, from despair, from the razored shards of broken dreams—may take months, years, or even decades. Who knows how long? And almost all of the time, those wounds will leave scars as iconic reminders of dark days that cannot be unlived.

So, what are we to do? Let's first learn to be comfortable with being mad at or disappointed with God. We all have been, are, or certainly will be. If you think that's wrong, put this book down immediately and go read Job. All of it. And note God's decree at the end, where he says that, unlike Job's friends, the sufferer who shouted chapter after chapter at heaven, had "spoken of [God] what is right" (42:7). Then, go read the Psalms. All of them. Then we can talk. Disciples don't sit around campfires all the time, strumming guitars and praising sweet Jesus. Sometimes we cry out, "Why? Where are you? How long? Leave me alone!" from the ashes of despair.

Second—and this is going to sound weird but hear me out—wait for the past. Something has already happened to which we, in our darkest days, are totally oblivious. Jesus has tracked us down, where we're curled up in fetal position in our dark and dank alleys of hopelessness, and he's picked us up to hold us there. Now all we still smell is the stench of garbage. Now all we still feel is unforgiving concrete. Eventually, however, ever so slightly, things will begin to change. The past—the past action of Jesus, his gentle and healing embrace of us before we were ever aware of it—will become more palpable. One day we'll open our eyes and the first thing on our minds will not be the death of our child, five years, four months, two weeks, six days, and one hour ago. Halfway through our morning coffee, yes, we will remember. But progress is progress. Healing is healing. And we will sense, with a growing awareness, that our refusal to be comforted has slipped ever so slightly.

Christ is doing what Christ does: healing and helping. No, more than that. He is working within us, with all our brokenness and fear and hurt, to show us that he has always been there. As close as our wounds. As near as our scars. And his past presence, for which we have waited, will arrive from yesterday into the today of our lives to show us that, in him, tomorrow's hope always dawns.

DISCUSSION QUESTIONS

1. Read Genesis 37:12-36. Review the story of Joseph with his brothers, noting the details. Did all the brothers hate Joseph? What did they do to him? What did they do to their father? How would you characterize the actions of the brothers? What words come to mind?

2. Review Genesis 37:35. Talk about what it means to "refuse to be comforted." Discuss also why our culture seems so intent on speeding up the grief process. Why is this so counterproductive?

3. Read some of the lament psalms like Psalms 13 or 88. How would you characterize the language of these prayers? What kind of strange comfort is found in being so raw and honest in prayers?

4. As we suffer as disciples, what does it mean for us to "wait on the past"? How is our Lord "working within us, with all our brokenness and fear and hurt, to show us that he has always been there"?

CHAPTER 28

Jacob and Clint Eastwood

> Jacob said to his sons, "Why are you staring at one another?" (NASB).
>
> Genesis 42:1

Near the top of my list of favorite movies is "Gran Torino." As the film begins, we meet Walt Kowalski (played by Clint Eastwood), who is a Korean War vet, retired auto worker, and all around cantankerous old fart. You know the type. The "get off my lawn!" kind of guy. With his characteristic sneer, Eastwood plays the part masterfully. Kowalski embodies the man who has been beaten by the calendar and kicked to the curb. Xenophobic. Bitter. A man who stands aghast at the audacity of change. If you've seen the movie, you know the alterations, both internally and externally, that overtake Kowalski as his story progresses. But in the beginning, as we become acquainted with the man, we quickly recognize the face of one whose happy days have long since gathered dust.

Walt Kowalski, meet Jacob.

Jacob, meet Walt Kowalski.

You guys should get along just fine.

About twenty years have come and gone since last we heard from Jacob. Then he was weeping, covered in sackcloth, refusing consolation because he supposed his beloved boy, Joseph, had been attacked and torn to pieces by a wild beast (Gen. 37:33). The last Hebrew word out of Jacob's mouth was, quite fittingly, "Sheol" (37:35).

What has transpired over the last two decades in Joseph's life? Plenty. Take a deep breath and race through this list of highs and lows: taken to Egypt as a slave, sold to Potiphar, stiff-armed the amorous advances of his boss's wife, falsely accused of attempted rape by the aforementioned woman, incarcerated, interpreted dreams, was forgotten then remembered, introduced to Pharaoh as a top-notch dream-explainer, skyrocketed to the king's powerful right hand, and implemented massive national plans to prepare for the forthcoming seven years of famine (Genesis 38-41). Quite the resumé, eh? All those years that Jacob assumed Joseph was dead and gone, he was actually being used by God to prepare for saving everyone else's life. Our Lord often does his best work when we suppose all hope is lost.

And what has transpired over the last two decades in Jacob's life? I wish we knew. We're told basically nothing. But as we discussed in the previous chapter, perhaps that is for the best. Jacob needed time "away from the camera" to hurt, weep, complain, question, sit in silence, and hopefully inch toward healing. That being said, given what we are about to see, I don't know that he made much progress.

"Why are you staring at one another?" (42:1; NASB).[1] This was Jacob's first recorded speech after his twenty-year silence in Genesis. In my imagination, I hear it spoken with the sneer of a Walt Kowalski. He was addressing his sons (minus Benjamin, to whom he never would have spoken so roughly). Hard times had fallen on the family because the famine wasn't isolated in Egypt; it "was severe over all the earth" (41:57). Picture the "Dust Bowl" days of America's past. The patriarch, however, had "learned that there was grain for sale in Egypt" (42:1). Presumably he wasn't the only member of the family privy to this information, so his words come across in the tone of "What's wrong with you numbskulls? Why are you lollygagging around here? Get! Go! Pack some clean underwear, saddle your donkeys, and take your shopping bags down to Egypt before our cupboards are completely bare." I wonder if the brothers were hesitant because the mere mention of that dreaded name "Egypt" caused

---

[1] The particular Hebrew verbal form of "staring at one another" (a Hithpael of *ra'ah*) is reciprocal or reflexive: not just looking but looking at each other. Picture the brothers, looking left and right, scanning each other's faces, none willing to act first.

the Joseph-bones in the closet of their memories to rattle with guilt (cf. Gen. 42:21).

Hunger overcoming hesitation, however, they said "Yes, sir," to the patriarch. They headed south, as generations before, also in search of food, great-grandpa Abraham had journeyed to the land of the pyramids (Gen. 12:10). Moreover, as Abraham had landed himself in a heap of trouble with Egyptian overlords, so did his great-grandsons. Only they didn't find themselves on the wrong side of the king but the king's dream-interpreter. He bore the Egyptian name, Zaphenath-paneah (Gen. 41:45). We know him better by his Hebrew name, Joseph.

Let's telescope the events. The brothers, clueless as to Joseph's true identity, prostrated themselves before him, thus fulfilling his dream from two decades prior. The fact that they bow before him, needing grain for food, also perfectly comports with the first dream in which they are represented by "sheaves" of grain (Gen. 37:7). Joseph fingers them as spies. They protest their innocence. He interrogates them. They tell him all about their family—including, in a "Road to Emmaus" kind of irony, talking *about* their dead brother *to* that same brother who stood alive before them (Gen. 42:13; Luke 24:19-21)! In the end, Joseph forces them to leave Simeon behind as collateral until they return with their "youngest brother" (i.e., Benjamin) whom they mentioned in the family description (Gen. 42:13-20). Then they head homeward, only to discover along the way that the money with which they had purchased the grain had been, lo and behold, deposited back inside their sacks of grain. Verse 28 says it all: "Their hearts failed them." Or, literally in the Hebrew, "their hearts went out." It was a heart-stopping moment, we might say. They were scared stiff. Turning to face one another, they exclaimed, "What is this that God has done to us?" (42:28).

Once home, after the sons reported to Jacob what happened, the aged patriarch speaks yet again. If he sounded gruff before, now he sounds like "the prima donna of paternal grief," as Robert Alter describes him.[2] Worse yet, he basically charges his sons with killing their brother(s). He says, "Me you have bereaved. Joseph is no more and Simeon is no more, and Benjamin you would take! It is I who bear

---

[2] *The Hebrew Bible*, 1:166.

it all" (42:36; R. Alter). In Hebrew, the "me" is uncharacteristically stuck at the front of the sentence. "*Me!*" We can almost see Jacob poking himself in the chest as he spits out the words: "*Me* you have hurt. *Me* you have deprived. *I* am the one who has to shoulder all the pain." The Hebrew verbal form for "bereave" carries the connotation of killing.[3] As Victor Hamilton says, "[In using this verb,] Jacob is tacitly accusing his sons of Joseph's murder."[4] When Reuben, with complete unsuccess, attempts to change his father's mind, he replies, "My son [Benjamin] shall not go down with you, for his brother is dead, and he is the only one left. If harm should happen to him on the journey that you are to make, you would bring down my gray hairs with sorrow to Sheol" (42:38). This statement is a total slap in the face to his other sons: "he [Benjamin] is the only one left." His other sons must be thinking: "Wow. What are we, Dad, chopped liver? Are we nothing to you? Just because it was our unlucky fate to be born *not* of your Oh-so-precious Rachel but of your *three other wives*, do we not qualify as sons?"

Finally, when the family was scraping the bottom of the barrel, Jacob attempted to get his sons to make a second international grocery run. He sounds much less gruff this time: "Go again, buy us a little food" (Gen. 43:2). I suspect he knew what their response would be: "Sorry, not happening unless little Ben goes with us." Judah becomes the spokesmen of the brothers, as he will be in the rest of the story. This also is Judah's moment to redeem himself, as it were. Remember: whose idea was it to sell Joseph into slavery (37:26-27)? Judah's. Now, twenty years later, as he speaks to his father, he volunteers to protect the life of Joseph's brother, Benjamin: "Send the boy with me, and we will arise and go, that we may live and not die, both we and you and also our little ones. I will be a pledge of his safety. From my hand you shall require him. If I do not bring him back to you and set him before you, then let me bear the blame forever" (Gen. 43:8-9).

Out of options, Jacob's hand is forced. He has to relent. But he does not resign himself to what might happen in a Stoic, whatever-fate-has-determined sort of way. No, first, he acts practically: he sends his sons back to Egypt laden with gifts for "the man" and returns the

---

[3]   The Piel of *shakal*.
[4]   *The Book of Genesis: Chapters 18-50*, 531, footnote 16.

silver which they had found in their grain sacks (43:11). Second, he acts prayerfully: he says, "May God Almighty grant you mercy before the man, and may he send back your other brother and Benjamin. And as for me, if I am bereaved of my children, I am bereaved" (43:14).

Unbeknownst to Jacob, God has Jacob right where he wants him: out of options. That is, out of options except for (1) the necessity of relying, not upon himself, but upon *mercy* and (2) the necessity of relying, not upon himself, but upon *others*. Not only for Jacob but for all of us, that is a highly unsettling place to be.

One of the many pseudo-gods in my personal pantheon is Control. Control is the love child of Ego and Fear. I (Ego) am afraid (Fear) of what might happen in my life, so I keep a white-knuckled grip on the reins of my existence (Control). Others will let me down— *have* let me down—so I will take care of things myself. And reliance upon mercy? Give me a break. Mercy may be heaven's gift but it's scary as hell. Mercy means I must lose my false god, Control, and rely on the true God, Jesus Christ. Mercy means that *I am not enough*. Mercy means I am inadequate, mortal, grossly unprepared for all that life will throw my way. Mercy means I need another. I need Christ.

Here's the problem, however: none of us willingly place ourselves in situations where we are out of options, where we must rely upon divine mercy and our neighbor's actions on our behalf. We're too busy playing divinity in our juvenile galaxies of self-determination. So, in ways sometimes small and sometimes big, the Master of providence picks us up by the scruff of our necks and drops us there. We can't go into Egypt, so we send our sons, along with our beloved Benjamin. We can't manipulate the events in Egypt, so we pray for mercy and compassion. We are empty. We are at our wits' end. And we are thus precisely in a situation ripe for divine work in our lives.

There we Jacobs wait. As our sons ride away, Benjamin in tow, we are left standing there alone. We put our hands to our eyes, shielding them from the sun, and strain our vision until the last dim hint of their figures is swallowed by the horizon. There's no texting or calling them to find out how things are going. We're in the dark. All we can do is wait, hope, and pray.

It's a terrible place for disciples to be. And it's a blessed place for disciples to be. Terrible, obviously, because we cannot shepherd events or pull the strings to get what we want. We can't even get updates. It's a gut-wrenching reminder that we are not in charge of this world, masters of our own destiny. Far from it. We are servants of a King.

But it's also a blessed place to be for all those reasons, and more. A vacuum is created within us that the Spirit of God begins to fill. Less of me, more of God. Less of control, more of Christ. I am never more fervent in prayer than when I realize that the most important person I need to be talking to is Jesus.

And Jesus, he is all ears. He is all mercy. Jesus isn't a cat that wants us mice at his mercy. He is the friend who sees what we cannot see: that mercy is all we have. All the time. In every circumstance of life. Christ is revealing to us, his disciples, that mercy is our daily bread and daily drink, which he lavishes upon us, whether we realize it or not.

Therefore, we sit in the dirt with Jacob and fix our eyes on the horizon. We place ourselves under the mighty and merciful hand of a compassionate God. We wait. We hope. And we trust that, no matter what happens, we do not really sit there alone. Jesus is right there beside us. For if there's one truth we know about Christ, beyond any doubt, it's that hell and all its demons cannot make him budge one inch from those whom he calls his friends.

DISCUSSION QUESTIONS

1. Review everything God does with Joseph in Genesis 38-41. Discuss this statement: "All those years that Jacob assumed Joseph was dead and gone, he was actually being used by God to prepare for saving everyone else's life. Our Lord often does his best work when we suppose all hope is lost." How have you found that to be true in your own life?
2. Read the dialogues between Jacob and his sons in Genesis 42:1-4 and 29-38. Does the relationship between Jacob and his sons seem to have improved during the absence of Joseph? Why or why not? Why are the wounds between family members often so difficult to heal?
3. Read Genesis 43:1-14. How does Judah begin to "redeem" himself? How does this episode exemplify the Lord's use of our past sins to move us into paths of righteousness?

4. Talk about Jacob's reactions in Gen. 43:11-14. How does he act practically and prayerfully? How do we, as disciples, also do the same? Give examples.
5. Discuss how being out of control, at the mercy of God, is both a terrible and blessed place to be. Why does the Lord place us in these situations?

CHAPTER 29

Jacob's Eucatastrophe

And Israel said, "It is enough; Joseph my son is still alive.
I will go and see him before I die."

Genesis 45:28

I wonder if there was a comical wink in Luke's eye when he penned Acts 12. The scene always makes me chuckle. Jerusalem is bathed in darkness. A solitary man strolls through the streets, looking like he's sleepwalking. And, in a sense, he is. It's Peter. The previous day he had been arrested, jailed, and shackled between two soldiers for a very non-Tempur-Pedic variety of shut-eye. That night, however, an angel shows up, Peter's chains fall off, and he is escorted out of the prison, not knowing if this is even real or if he is experiencing a vision (Acts 12:9). It's real, alright. Peter is free.

Meandering through the streets of Jerusalem, the apostle finds his way to the home of Mark's mother, Mary. Inside the church has gathered, fervently interceding to God for him (12:5). His knuckles rap on the gate. A young servant girl named Rhoda tiptoes out to investigate. Upon hearing the well-known voice of Peter, she is ecstatic, so much so that, rather than unbolting the gate and letting Peter inside, she sprints back in the house with the astonishing news. "It's Peter! It's Peter! It's Peter!" But everybody thinks she's lost her everliving mind. Peter's in jail, you crazy girl. Inside Rhoda and the doubters engage in "a shouting match"[1] over whether it's actually Peter, his angel (whatever

---

[1] *The NET Bible First Edition Notes.* Biblical Studies Press. (Dallas, TX: Biblical Studies Press 2006), Acts 12:15.

that means),[2] or whether the servant has turned mad as a March hare. Outside, poor Peter, well, he just keeps on knocking and knocking, no doubt wondering what in tarnation the holdup is.

Finally, when the group cracks open the door to peek out and see if it really is Peter, there he stands, in all his liberated glory. In typical biblical understatement, we read that, "they saw him and were amazed" (12:16). I'm sure they were! Now check this out: the Greek word for "amazed [*existemi*]" is the same word used by the Emmaus disciples when they reported that "some women of our company amazed [*existemi*] us" when they reported the resurrection of Jesus (Luke 24:22). It also just so happens that, when the Hebrew of Genesis was translated into Greek in the Septuagint, as the scholars were deliberating upon the best Greek word to describe Jacob's reaction to the news that Joseph was still alive, they also chose *existemi*: "And [Jacob's sons] reported to him, saying, 'Your son Joseph lives, and he rules the whole land of Egypt.' And the mind of Jacob was confounded [*existemi*], for he did not believe them" (Gen. 45:26).[3]

There's nothing like thinking someone is dead (Jesus and Joseph) or unreachable (Peter), who turns out to be very much alive and standing in front of you, to cause the light of amazement to blaze inside the human soul. In fact, as we also see from these examples, the initial report of this good news strikes the hearers as so breathtaking, so contrary to their every expectation, that they can't believe it. They are, we might say, joyfully incredulous. In Jacob's case, his "heart stopped, for he did not believe them" (Gen. 45:26; R. Alter). Ironically, the good news of Joseph still being alive almost killed the old man! A similar reaction is recorded by Luke when Jesus suddenly appeared to his disciples on the day of his resurrection: they "disbelieved for joy and were marveling" (24:41).

Jacob "did not believe" his sons. The disciples "disbelieved for joy." It was all "too good to be true," but in the best possible sense of that expression.

---

[2] "His angel" probably refers to the angel who watched over him, his "guardian angel," as they are sometimes called. A similar expression, "their angels," is used in Matthew 18:10, where Jesus warns, "See that you do not despise one of these little ones. For I tell you that in heaven their angels always see the face of my Father who is in heaven."

[3] Brannan, R., Penner, K. M., Loken, I., Aubrey, M., & Hoogendyk, I. (Eds.). *The Lexham English Septuagint* (Bellingham, WA: Lexham Press, 2012).

What all these people were experiencing is best captured by a delightful word coined by J. R. R. Tolkien: eucatastrophe. The word is formed by prefixing the Greek word "*eu*," which means "good" (as in "eulogy [good word] or euphoria [good feeling]) to the word "catastrophe." Tolkien himself defines a eucatastrophe as "the sudden happy turn in a story which pierces you with a joy that brings tears."[4] Samuel P. Schuldheisz writes that "the eucatastrophe in a story is a good catastrophe; it is the surprise twist or turn you never see coming or least expect," as "when the eagles rescue Bilbo and the company of Dwarfs out of the trees in *The Hobbit*, or when the eagles deliver Frodo and Samwise from the fires of Mt. Doom in *The Lord of the Rings*."[5] When the last few grains of sand in the hourglass of hope are about to fall, when the tragic end is at hand, then suddenly the hourglass is flipped over, the hole stopped up, and no more grains can fall again: that's a eucatastrophe. It leaves one disbelieving for joy, weeping and laughing all at the same time.

Jacob experienced a kind of double eucatastrophe in Genesis 45, which we will talk about momentarily. First, let's take stock of what happened leading up to this. In our last scene with Jacob, he stood alone, watching his remaining sons, especially Benjamin, fade into the horizon as they traveled to Egypt a second time. In this father's mind, Joseph was long dead. Simeon might be dead. And now, forced by extreme circumstances, he was obliged to send his youngest and favorite son into mortal danger as well. His last recorded words, spoken with a kind of prayerful resignation, are, "If I am bereaved of my children, I am bereaved" (Gen. 43:14).

Between this speech and the next time we see Jacob, some of the most scintillating drama in the Bible transpires. In scene after scene, Joseph keeps his brothers vacillating between confusion and happiness, dismay and sheer terror. One moment this strange Egyptian is feeding them a noonday feast at his home, and the next he's accusing them of grand ritual larceny for stealing his silver divination cup. Finally, after a humble and eloquent speech by Judah in which he volunteers to forfeit his own life and freedom in place of Benjamin's,

---

[4] J. R. R. Tolkien, *The Letters of J. R. R. Tolkien*, ed. Humphrey Carpenter (New York: Houghton Mifflin, 2000), 100.

[5] https://www.1517.org/articles/the-great-eucatastrophe

Zaphenath-paneah the Egyptian finally reveals himself to be none other than Joseph the Hebrew (45:3).

At first, the brothers are so shocked, they just stand there, mouths agape. No doubt a thousand different questions flashed through their minds in an instant: Is this really Joseph? How do we know? If it is, are we dead men walking? Will he enact mercy or exact revenge? And how on God's green earth did our kid brother—if this really is our kid brother—manage to climb the Egyptian ladder from slave to vice-regent? Wisely, though, they just stood there, mute as statues of stone. Joseph beckoned them closer. Their feet shuffled forward. Then, with a speech Joseph had probably rehearsed many times in the solitude of his heart, he told them the whole truth. *Am I your brother? Yes, Joseph, whom you sold into slavery. Am I angry with you? No, and neither should you be with yourself. Why am I really here? Because God sent me here, to save you, our whole family, and many others. So, it's time to bring our father to me, here, so I can care for you all* (cf. Gen. 45:4-13). The verses that follow glisten with smiling tears. Brothers embrace. Brothers kiss. Brothers weep. All's well that ends well.

Now, back to Jacob. He hasn't a clue about all these joyful events, of course. While his sons have been on cloud nine, he's been in the slough of despond. *But, wait! What is that on the horizon? Wagons? Yes. Dozens of donkeys? It seems so. And the men with them; they look familiar. Is that Judah...Levi...Dan? Yes, yes. And, oh, good God in heaven above, it's Simeon! He's okay. It's Benjamin! He's alive. My boys, my boys are home, safe and sound!*

Welcome to Eucatastrophe #1. Not only does Jacob get his sons back, including the one whom he feared was dead, but, wonder of wonders, they come home looking like they have won the Egyptian lottery. In a kind of backshadowing of what happened when Abraham left Egypt (Gen. 12:16-20), and a foreshadowing of what will happen when all Israel leaves Egypt (Exod. 12:35-36), Joseph sent his brothers home laden with Egyptian goods, food, wagons, clothing, silver, and livestock. What a shock this all must have been to the old patriarch!

But he had no idea—how could he?—of the greater shock that was about to drop.

In a mere nine Hebrew words, the sons of Jacob upend what their father had believed all these many sad and broken years: "Joseph is still alive, and he is ruler over all the land of Egypt" (45:26). In my mind's eye, I see the brothers gathered before their father. His brow is furrowed as he scans all the wagons, donkeys, and wealth. Looking from face to face, his hands are spread, palms upward, in the international sign of "What in the world is going on?" And notice that *they said* those nine startling words to their dad. Not "Judah said." Not "Simeon said." Not even "Benjamin said." No, they said it. Fraternal unity spoke. And if Jacob's heart didn't temporarily stop when he heard, "Joseph is still alive," then certainly it did when he heard, "and he is ruler over all the land of Egypt."

Welcome to Eucatastrophe #2. As the sons begin to tell their tale of shock and surprise in Egypt, expanding those nine words into nine hundred sentences of color and detail, "the spirit of their father Jacob revived" (45:27). His heart began to beat again. A smile erupted on that wrinkled face. And taking a deep breath, shedding his joyful incredulity, he said, "It is enough; Joseph my son is still alive. I will go and see him before I die" (45:28).

Every year, when springtime rolls around, little boys and girls hunt for Easter eggs and sanctuaries splash with the colors and scent of white lilies. Then, I am reminded that we as followers of Jesus live in the unfading light of the greatest eucatastrophe the world has ever, and will ever, experience. There was a man who was more than a man. And we killed him. He was the greatest man who ever lived. And we killed him. He was the kindest, most gentle, most truthful and upright and compassionate man who ever lived. And we killed him. Hands that healed, we wounded. The face that glowed, we spit upon. The heart that beat with love, we pierced. There was a man who was more than a man; he was God. And we—you and I and all of lost and hopeless humanity—we killed him.

Wrapped in cloths and laid in a borrowed tomb was the only chance our world ever had of redemption and life. And we went, all of us together, and ruined it all.

Or so we thought. Suddenly, in the pitch black darkness of a world gone wrong, a tiny flicker of light began to shine. A flicker that became a flame. A flame that became an unsetting sun. The rock that had been rolled against the tomb began to hum with excitement. Grass began to dance in the music of the wind. Rivers clapped their hands and hills girded themselves with rejoicing. Because outside that tomb stood a man who was more than a man. He was the greatest man who ever lived. He was the kindest, most gentle, most truthful and upright and compassionate man who ever lived. His hands gripped once more. His face smiled. His heart beat. This man who was more than a man, who was God in flesh, was alive again.

And one of the first words out of his mouth to us was, "Peace" (John 20:19). Not "you killed me." Not "you dirty, rotten sinners." But peace. Jesus is alive, and he is ruler over all the land of this once bleak and forlorn world. And that, my friends, changes everything.

As we seek to follow Jesus in our lives and vocations, his resurrection becomes the universal "but" to every heartbroken fact of our existence.

-When we watch our beloved parent or child or friend lowered into the grave, we say, "*But*, Christ is risen."

-When we see our families or communities torn asunder and wonder if there is any hope for the future, we say, "*But*, Christ is risen."

-When our churches are plagued by scandals, frozen by despair, or shrink into a few scattered and gray-haired worshipers, we say, "*But*, Christ is risen."

-When we stumble and fall, get up only to stumble yet again, limping our way along as mortal, weak, weary disciples, we say, "*But*, Christ is risen."

And because of that "but," because of that divine and joyful rebuttal, Julian of Norwich is right: "All shall be well, and all shall be well, and all manner of things shall be well." Jesus is alive and well and reigning over us as King of kings and Lord of lords.

It's no exaggeration to say that makes all the difference in the world.

Discussion Questions

1. Scan the events in Genesis 43:15-45:24. What must have been the thoughts of Joseph's brothers when he finally revealed himself to them? How does Joseph give a theological interpretation of his sufferings in 45:5-8?

2. What is a eucatastrophe? What are some biblical and/or literary examples of this? Have you ever experienced a kind of eucatastrophe in your own life?

3. Read Genesis 45:25-28. What are the two eucatastrophes that Jacob experiences in these verses? How do you envision this whole scene? Talk about Jacob's reactions and response.

4. How is the resurrection of Christ the greatest eucatastrophe the world has ever, and will ever, experience? Discuss how his resurrection becomes the universal "but" to every heartbroken fact of our existence. Apply that "but" to examples in our lives as followers of Christ.

CHAPTER 30

Turning the Page and Looking Fear in the Face

"Do not be afraid to go down to Egypt."

Genesis 46:3

We have, over the course of these pages, walked through one hundred and thirty years of Jacob's life. He was once relatively young and highly ambitious. A take-the-tiger-by-the-tail kind of guy. He made some rash and foolhardy decisions along the way, as we all do, and landed himself in quite the pickle on more than a few occasions. For many years now, however, that younger version of Jacob has undergone the kinds of alterations that all people go through as time catches up with them. Hair grays. Skin wrinkles. Joints make eerie noises when we crawl out of bed.

Along with all those physical taps on the shoulder, reminding us that we're not getting any younger, is the heightened presence of fear, all varieties of fear, in our lives. Some of these fears are healthy, or at least useful. Aging brings perspective, and perspective wisdom, and wisdom fear. Once you've lived a few decades, for instance, you realize that driving 90 mph down the interstate, slithering in and out of traffic, just so you can get somewhere a whopping two minutes early is an activity that we should be afraid to do. For one, it's dangerous. For another, it's just dumb. You're not Vin Diesel in "Fast and Furious." So some fears are well and good.

Other fears, however, rather than enabling a safer, healthier life are debilitating; they diminish instead of enrich our lives. Fear of any change. Fear of trying new things. Fear of travel. Fear even of leaving the house. In addition, if you're a parent (as I am) or a grandparent (as I also am), then you also know that, no matter how old your children or grandchildren might be, you also fear for their safety, well-being, and happiness. We might liken all these fears to water: some of it is healthy and sustains our lives; some is dirty and will make us sick; some is salty and, if consumed, will kill us. Not all fears are created equal.

"Do not be afraid to go down to Egypt" (Gen. 46:3). So says the Lord to elderly Jacob. Was he actually afraid? Scholars are divided on this, but my own hunch is that he was. Some ancient Jewish writings certainly agree. Jubilees, for instance, a second century BC retelling of the Old Testament, says that Jacob was so afraid to go down to Egypt that he was on the verge of begging Joseph, instead, to come visit him in the promised land (44:2-3). The first century AD Jewish historian, Josephus, echoes and expands upon this sentiment. When he wrote about this account in *The Antiquities of the Jews*, he said that Jacob was afraid his family would fall in love with Egypt and want to stay there permanently, and he feared that going there might be contrary to God's will.[1] After all, the Lord had expressly told Jacob's father, Isaac, "Do not go down to Egypt; dwell in the land of which I shall tell you" (Gen. 26:2). Although Jacob desperately wanted to see his son, Joseph, and had even loaded the U-Haul and begun the trek to Egypt (46:1), it does appear that, once he pulled into Beersheba, on the southern edge of the promised land, he was still trepidatious as to whether he should go on.

Were Jacob able to pick up a copy of the Bible at the local Beersheba Bookstore and read about the next few chapters in his life, as well as to see what was on the horizon for his people, he would have reasonable cause to experience a rise in blood pressure. Unbeknownst to him at the time, he stands at a major crossroads in biblical history. As Nahum Sarna says, "With this narrative [in Genesis 46], the patriarchal period in the history of Israel comes to an end."[2] Winds of change are blowing in. The last patriarch is fading fast. Israel will be exiled from the holy land for centuries. Their erstwhile "home away

---

[1] Book 2:170-171.
[2] *Genesis*, The JPS Torah Commentary, 312.

from home" will eventually oppress and enslave them. And for the entire time, God will be silent. No theophanies. No prophets. Nothing but the word that he once swore to Abraham, "Know for certain that your offspring will be sojourners in a land that is not theirs and will be servants there, and they will be afflicted for four hundred years. But I will bring judgment on the nation that they serve, and afterward they shall come out with great possessions" (Gen. 15:13-14). Although we are still in Genesis, we could just as well read these final few chapters as the Preface to the book of Exodus.

When the Lord says to Jacob, "Do not be afraid to go down to Egypt," (Gen. 46:3), we might think to ourselves, "Easy for you to say, God!" The Lord has nothing and no one to fear. But Israel's list is long: exile, old age, death, suffering, taskmasters, infanticide, chains. The horrors of Egypt are the stuff of nightmares not Disney movies. But, of course, the Lord is also well aware of this. He knows that existence in a world fraught with danger and deprivation is no utopia. So, as a kind of preemptive promise, he appears to Jacob, speaks words of comfort, and establishes the immovable foundation of hope for the patriarch—and for us.

> And God spoke to Israel in visions of the night and said, "Jacob, Jacob." And he said, "Here I am." Then he said, "I am God, the God of your father. Do not be afraid to go down to Egypt, for there I will make you into a great nation. I myself will go down with you to Egypt, and I will also bring you up again, and Joseph's hand shall close your eyes." (Genesis 46:2-4)

Let's stop and let these words sink in for a few moments.

One of the truths this divine visitation underscores is the consistency of the Lord's mercy. We observe here "an emphatic recapitulation" of what happened to the earlier patriarchs.[3] Jacob offered sacrifices in Beersheba (46:1), likely on the very altar that his father, Isaac, had built and used a generation earlier (26:25). At that time, the Lord told Isaac, "I am the God of Abraham your father" (26:24), as now he tells Jacob, "I am God, the God of your father [Isaac]," (46:2)." To Isaac, God said, "Fear not, for I am with you" (26:24) as

---

[3] R. Alter, 181, footnote 3.

now he tells Jacob, "Do not be afraid to go down to Egypt…I myself will go down with you to Egypt" (46:3-4). And, as with other momentous occasions in Scripture, the Lord spoke the patriarch's name twice, "Jacob, Jacob" (46:2), as earlier he said, "Abraham, Abraham" (Gen. 22:11), and would say in the future, "Moses, Moses" (Exod. 3:4); "Samuel, Samuel" (1 Sam. 3:10); and "Saul, Saul" (Acts 9:4). By making sure this episode "rhymes" with the others, God is also affirming his unflagging commitment to Jacob and his offspring.

Note, too, the "I" language that God employs. When reading Scripture, it's always a good idea to pay close attention to who does the verbs. The threefold doer here is God: (1) "*I will* make you into a great nation"; (2) "*I myself will* go down with you to Egypt"; and (3) "*I will* also bring you up again" (46:3-4; emphasis added). I, I, I. The chronological order is out of sequence, since the Lord must first go down with Jacob before he makes him into a great nation. Perhaps the promise of "making great" is fronted so as to highlight it. Not in Canaan but in Egypt, "the people of Israel were fruitful and increased greatly; they multiplied and grew exceedingly strong, so that the land was filled with them" (Exod. 1:7). Moreover, "the more they were oppressed [by the Egyptians], the more they multiplied and the more they spread abroad" (1:12). Contrary to what one might expect, in hard circumstances, Israel did well. Why? Because they were all ancient versions of David Goggins, who thrive off of and laugh in the face of pain and adversity? No. Rather, because of God's gift. He made them into a great nation. The more they were emptied of themselves, the more the Lord could do with them.

Jacob himself, of course, would not live to see all of these promises come to fruition. Joseph's hand would close his father's eyes as they dimmed in death. Nevertheless, Jacob was privy to the end of the story while still stuck in the middle of it. God allowed him to scan the last chapter, as it were, by telling him what was to come. And what was to come was the valley of the shadow of suffering and death which would one day, by God's grace, issue forth into a bright new horizon of freedom and light. Exile would be a tremendous cross for his people to bear, but that cross would end as Israel stepped out of their Egyptian tomb to walk toward the promised land.

Now that's the way to speak to people's fears. Not by downplaying the reality of future suffering. Not by some vapid and generic promise of "I'm sure things will get better someday" or "Just hang in there, buddy." Rather, Jesus bids us face our fears by banking our future hope on the present reality of his divine promises. When, like Jacob, we are staring down the road at some time in Egypt, when the journey ahead is certain to be littered with pitfalls, when life as we know it is about to slide into the twilight zone of uncertainty, the Lord does *not* tell us to take a leap of faith. Rather, he bids us step forth onto the solid rock of his promises. Christ does not say, "Just trust me." Instead, he says, "Trust me *because* I am your God; I will be with you wherever you go; I will bless you; and one day I will bring you forth from Egypt."

As disciples of Jesus, we do not face an uncertain future. Granted, we do not know what will happen to us tomorrow or next week or over the next few years. Nor do we know when or how our earthly lives will end. We're not prophets or soothsayers. But our future is far from uncertain. We can open up the Bible, any time we choose, and read about the last chapter of world history. It's right there in Revelation, in black-and-white. And the message? The Lamb of God is victorious! Jesus wins! And in Jesus, we win. The resurrection is coming. All tears will be wiped away. All cancer will die. All abuse will cease. All hatred will end. That is not a wish or a good guess or a probable eschatological forecast. It's a divine fact, grounded in the resurrection of our Lord Jesus from the grave. His ultimate victory at the end of time—which is also *our* victory—is as solid and certain as is the glory of his resurrected flesh.

When fears begin hissing at me, taunting me, wooing my fickle heart away from Christ, I often respond very simply with a three-word prayer, "Lord have mercy." When I or a loved one are sick, "Lord have mercy." When I hear of persecutions of God's people, "Lord have mercy." When I am forced into uncomfortable situations, "Lord have mercy." When I think of the day of my own death, "Lord have mercy." It's not an eloquent prayer. It's not flowery. But it grounds me in Jesus, the resurrected King, and reminds me of why all disciples of Jesus can trust in him: because he who holds the past, present, and future in his hands, is mercy incarnate.

DISCUSSION QUESTIONS

1. Are some fears more prevalent among the young and others among the old? Are all fears bad? Distinguish between good, unhealthy, and deadly fears.

2. Read Genesis 46:1-4. Why did the Lord reassure Jacob that there was nothing to fear? Compare the doubling of Jacob's name (v. 2) with other doubling of names in Scripture. What precisely did the Lord promise Jacob? Why did he need this comfort?

3. How and why do we tend to ignore or downplay people's fears? Talk about how Jesus bids us face our fears by banking our future hope on the present reality of his divine promises. What kinds of promises did the Lord give to others, as well as to us, as we face fears (Deut. 31:6-8; Ps. 23:1-6; Ps. 91:1-16; Isa. 43:1-2)?

4. As disciples of Jesus, we do not face an uncertain future. We can open up the Bible, any time we choose, and read about the last chapter of world history. How does knowing the future help us in the present as we follow the Lamb of God?

CHAPTER 31

Christians are Israelite Disciples

All the persons of the house of Jacob who came into
Egypt were seventy.

Genesis 46:27

Of the various jobs I've had as an adult—from roofing houses to
teaching Hebrew—in only one did I need, on a regular basis, to draw
upon my mathematical training: as a truck driver in the Texas oil and
gas fields. Quite frequently, my dispatcher at Turner Energy would
send me to do an oil transfer. The oil, which was resting on top of
waste water, had to be moved from one tank to another. I'd climb the
ladder to the top of the tank, pop the cover, and drop in my measuring
device (basically a fancy tape measure). It was coated with a special
paste which turned different colors for oil and water respectively. On
the basis of the tank size, and the respective depths of the two liquids,
I'd use the simple arithmetic of adding, subtracting, multiplying, and
dividing to get the job done. Now this was a far cry from algebra or
trigonometry. And if I was off by a few gallons, well, no sweat. That
was mighty good news as far as I was concerned. With apologies to
Mr. Bryant, my high school algebra teacher, precision with numbers
was never my forte.

That is one reason why I like *biblical* numbers: precision doesn't
matter nearly as much as typology. In Genesis 46, we encounter an
example of this typology or numerical symbolism in the size of Jacob's
expansive family. At the end of a long genealogy, we read, "All the
persons of the house of Jacob who came into Egypt were seventy"

(46:27). Why seventy? What does it symbolize or typify? And how does this number, in a surprising way, help us better to understand our identity as disciples of Jesus? To get to that answer, let's first do a survey of representative occurrences of seventy in the Bible.

In the post-flood world of Genesis 10, the descendants of Noah's three sons are grouped into seventy peoples or families (the so-called "Table of Nations"). As James Jordan points out, "Although the number of nations in the world soon grew beyond seventy, the symbolic number of the nations remains seventy in the Bible."[1] If seven is the number of completeness on a "small scale," then take seven and multiply it times ten (another number of completeness) and you get seventy. This number is "'typological'; that is, it is used for rhetorical effect to evoke the idea of totality, comprehensiveness on a large scale."[2] Because the world is envisioned as comprised of seventy peoples, this number therefore stands for the entire human race.

Now let's look at a couple of examples that focus on Israel. When God's people were camped at Sinai, God said to Moses, "Come up to the LORD, you and Aaron, Nadab, and Abihu, and seventy of the elders of Israel, and worship from afar" (Exod. 24:1). So they did. "Then Moses and Aaron, Nadab, and Abihu, and seventy of the elders of Israel went up, and they saw the God of Israel" (24:9-10). These seventy elders were the representative body of leaders for Israel (cf. Ezek. 8:1). Thus, once more, the number seventy is typological for "the whole"—in this case, the whole of Israel. As such, these seventy elders embodied every individual Israelite standing before the Lord.

In Numbers, the Lord tells Moses, "Gather for me seventy men of the elders of Israel, whom you know to be the elders of the people and officers over them, and bring them to the tent of meeting, and let them take their stand there with you. And I will come down and talk with you there. And I will take some of the Spirit that is on you and put it on them, and they shall bear the burden of the people with you, so that you may not bear it yourself alone" (11:16-17). When Moses gathers them, "the LORD came down in the cloud and spoke to him, and took some of the Spirit that was on him and put it on the

---

[1] *Through New Eyes: Developing a Biblical View of the World* (Eugene, OR: Wipf and Stock, 1999), 175.
[2] Nahum Sarna, *Genesis*, The JPS Torah Commentary, 69.

seventy elders. And as soon as the Spirit rested on them, they prophesied" (11:25). Here, too, the number seventy is typological; these
Spirit-filled men will be, as it were, the feet and legs which support
the entire body of Israel.

There are many other occurrences of seventy in the OT (e.g.,
seventy sons [Judges 8:30; 2 Kings 10:1] and seventy years [Jer. 25:11;
Daniel 9:2, 24]), but let's move forward to investigate how this Hebrew
background impacted the use of seventy in the NT and later rabbinic
tradition. Then we will circle back to Jacob's family of seventy in
Genesis.

The explicit NT use of seventy symbolism is in the number of
disciples that Jesus sent out in Luke 10 to heal the sick and proclaim
the kingdom of God.[3] Our Lord's choice of twelve apostles and these
seventy disciples could hardly be coincidental. The twelve apostles
correspond to the twelve patriarchs and twelve tribes since these men,
chosen by Jesus, are the foundation of Israel, which is continued and
expanded in the church. Likewise, the seventy disciples, correspond-
ing both to the seventy elders of Israel as well as the seventy members
of Israel's family who migrated to Egypt, represent Israel, under the
Messiah, furthering the kingdom of God by healing and proclamation.

In Acts 2, on the day of Pentecost, we find an implicit NT reference to seventy. Luke writes, "Now there were dwelling in Jerusalem
Jews, devout men from every nation under heaven" (2:5). The phrase,
"every nation under heaven," echoes almost exactly the language in
Deuteronomy 2:25 and 4:19, both of which refer to the peoples of
the world. As we saw in Genesis 10, "every nation under heaven"
would be, in the typological imagination of Israel, seventy nations.
In Acts 2, because the devout men from these "seventy" nations were
Jews, dwelling in Jerusalem, they represented the entire world, present
at Pentecost. As God gave his Spirit to the seventy elders of Israel in
Numbers 11, so in Acts 2 these seventy "world representatives," as
it were, witnessed this pouring out of the Spirit at Pentecost on his
church.

Likely hidden in the background of Luke 10 and Acts 2 are also
Jewish traditions that were voiced in later, post-NT rabbinic writings.

---

[3] Because some ancient Greek manuscripts of the NT have "seventy" and
others have "seventy-two," English translations will differ at this point.

In Aramaic paraphrases of the Bible, known as Targums, as well as in Jewish biblical commentaries and legal writings, phrases such as "the seventy nations" and "the seventy languages" were commonly used. This was a type of biblical, literary shorthand that referred to "humanity in its entirety."[4]

So, let's pull all this together: in the OT, NT, and later Jewish literature, the number seventy typologically represents the whole of humanity and/or the whole of Israel. These two groups, however, were by no means completely separate entities. Rather, God's chosen people, as those who had inherited the promises made to Adam of the coming Seed, were the ongoing "corporate Adam" in a fallen world.[5] In them "all the families of the earth" were to be blessed (Gen. 12:3). *We might say the "seventy-ness" of Israel was to become the epicenter of divine blessings that were to ripple out to the "seventy-ness" of all nations, to all those who, by faith, "are Abraham's offspring, heirs according to promise" (Gal. 3:29).*

With all this biblical background in mind, let's return to Jacob and his family as they make the journey to Egypt. Judah, who has become the unofficial leader of the brothers, stands at the head of their group (Gen. 46:28). Behind him are Jacob's sons and daughters,[6] grandsons and granddaughters, livestock, and all their property. They are, as we have seen, seventy in number.[7] Here is a picture of the total-

---

[4] Nahum Sarna, *Genesis*, The JPS Torah Commentary, 69. See his footnote 2 for a full list of rabbinic references.

[5] For more on this theme of Israel as the "corporate Adam," see G. K. Beale's chapter on "The Redemptive-Historical Storyline of the Old Testament," in *A New Testament Biblical Theology: The Unfolding of the Old Testament in the New* (Grand Rapids: Baker Academic, 2011), especially pp. 83-88. I also discuss this in *The Christ Key*, pp. 109-129.

[6] Dinah is the only daughter of Jacob who is named, but that the patriarch had other daughters is evident in Genesis 34:9, 16, and 24.

[7] Commentators point out that exactly how we get to the number seventy is not easy to determine. Yes, the total number of descendants of the matriarchs is seventy, but Joseph was already in Egypt, and Judah's sons, Er and Onan, died before the nation entered Egypt (38:6-10). And is Jacob himself to be counted or not? Robert Alter is correct when he notes that the "interpretive acrobatics" that are used to get the exact number of seventy are misguided: biblical numbers are "symbolic approximations" rather than "arithmetically precise measures" (*The Hebrew Bible*, Volume 1, Note 27, p. 183).

ity of the people of God, on the move in this world, led by Judah, into an exile from which the Lord will eventually redeem them.

This relatively small group, which traces its origin to one man, which in its "seventy-ness" is a kind of priestly representative of the "seventy-ness" of all people, is iconic of the church. They had Judah at their head; we have the descendant of Judah, Jesus the Messiah, at our head. They are called Israel because they all originated from the man Israel; we are called Christians because we all have our new birth from above in Christ the Lord. And we, in the church, having been filled with the Spirit of God at that "seventy-ish" Pentecost, are now led by the Spirit into all the world to spread the good news of Jesus to the "seventy nations".

This means that we, the followers of Jesus the Israelite, are ourselves Israelite disciples. When the Messiah came, he did not replace Israel with the church. Nor did he build the "church house" next door to the "Israel house." The people of God do not have a Jewish address on Law Street and a Gentile address on Gospel Street. No, whatever barriers were between Jew and Gentile before, Jesus "has broken down in his flesh" so that "he might create in himself one new man in place of the two [Jew and Gentile], so making peace, and might reconcile us both to God in one body through the cross" (Eph. 2:14-16). Christ entered the "Israel house" with a hammer, saw, and pickup load of wood from Home Depot. He added rooms, floors, and wings. He made the "Israel house" bigger, cosmically bigger, to include all Jews and Gentiles who confess him as Messiah. As such, we who are Gentiles become Israelites in the womb of baptism, individual members of the Israelite seventy.

This also means that we, Israelite disciples, can confess things like: "Our father, Jacob, went down into Egypt," or "our fathers were brought through the Red Sea," or "our father, David, ruled over Israel." In other words, the OT is *our* story, not another person's or another religion's story.

This story is of the God who used our family of seventy to preserve the promise of the Seed in Egypt. He used our holy nation of seventy to intercede for the unholy seventy nations of the world. And he still uses our church—the one, holy, Christian, apostolic, "seventy-ish" church—to witness boldly before all the world.

DISCUSSION QUESTIONS

1. What are some biblical numbers that often have symbolic value? For instance, how is the number twelve used in the OT and NT?

2. Read Gen. 46:27; Exod. 24:9-10; Num. 11:16-25; and Luke 10:1. Which groups does "seventy" designate? What is the symbolism of this number?

3. Read Genesis 12:3 and Gal. 3:29. Talk about what this means: we might say the "seventy-ness" of Israel was to become the epicenter of divine blessings that were to ripple out to the "seventy-ness" of all nations, to all those who, by faith, "are Abraham's offspring, heirs according to promise."

4. Sometimes a wedge is driven between Israel and the church, as if these are two different bodies of believers. How does this chapter describe their union? How does Ephesians 2:11-22 describe this union? What does it mean for us to be Israelite disciples? And how does this help us to read the OT as our book, our story?

CHAPTER 32

Living in Tents of Faith

"Few and evil have been the days of the years of my life."

Genesis 47:9

Already at the age of twenty-three, my daughter is an experienced world traveler. Between 2017 and 2020, she visited or studied in eight foreign countries: Spain, France, Switzerland, Germany, Argentina, Peru, Singapore, and Thailand. Me? At the age of fifty-one, I'm lagging way behind her, though I have twice traveled to Siberia and once to Canada. That's ten countries between father and daughter. Both of us have seen vastly more of the world than 99.9% of people would have dreamed of seeing a century ago. We do something that, before the 20th century, was unthinkable: we roll out of bed in Texas or Utah, climb inside a huge flying object, and in less than 24 hours, lay our heads on a pillow in Novosibirsk, Siberia or Bangkok, Thailand. We overhear people speaking in languages that were only the stuff of far-flung legend in previous generations. Should I wish, I can float in the Dead Sea, dip my feet in the blue waters of the Maldives, or swim in the Amazon. I can lift my eyes to the Egyptian pyramids or gaze down upon the geoglyphic Nazca Lines in southern Peru. If I have the time to travel, and a little extra money to make it happen, I can drink deeply of the beauty, mystery, and marvels of this world.

To me, that is a gift. It's a way of experiencing the work of our Creator. It's also, in a bizarre way, full of both hope and danger.

It's full of hope because this world is the handiwork of a wise, benevolent, and careful Father. He is the divine Philocalist, a lover of the beautiful. When he crafted the heavens and the earth, he didn't grunt, "Well, I suppose that'll have to do." Rather, he smiled and sang over them the songs of "good" and "very good." And that is *good* news for us, too, because this creation, old as it is, showing the wear and tear of countless generations, is also a foreshadowing of the new creation yet to come. "I saw a new heaven and a new earth, for the first heaven and the first earth had passed away," John says (Rev. 21:1). Peter, too, echoes this when he writes that "according to [God's] promise we are waiting for new heavens and a new earth in which righteousness dwells" (2 Peter 3:13).

Three times I have stood on the rim of the Grand Canyon; each time it seemed so surreal that it took my breath away. Yet, in the new creation, I expect there will be canyons that make that grand one seem but an ungrand hole in the ground. The mountains will be taller. The waters clearer. The snow whiter. I am using my imagination, of course, but how could the new creation not be infinitely better than the old? So, this world is an eschatological icon, that is, a window into the better world to come. As such, our old earth is pregnant with hope of the new earth yet to be. When we behold, therefore, the beauty, mystery, and marvels of this world, let us exclaim, "Thanks be to God!" and also knowingly whisper to ourselves, "But we ain't seen nothin' yet."

But there's also the flip side: this world is simultaneously full of danger. I don't mean the dangers of human violence, real as they are, or even the dangers of fires, floods, or hurricanes. I mean the danger of forgetting that, as wonderful as this world is, it is not our home. Not really. We are, in the language of Jacob, sojourners. Resident aliens. Outsiders. For the disciples of Jesus, this is our permanent status in this world.

Hold on to that thought for a moment; let's return to it and expand upon it. But first, let's see what's happening with Jacob.

In the last chapter, we saw how Jacob and his household of seventy began their journey to Pharoah's land. Centuries later, as the people of God exit Egypt, a hardhearted Pharaoh will prepare his chariot to meet and fall upon Israel (Exod. 14:6). Now, as the people of God enter Egypt, the opposite happens: Pharaoh's right-hand man, Joseph, "prepared his chariot and went up to meet Israel his father in Goshen. He presented himself to him and fell on his neck and wept on his neck a good while" (Gen. 46:29). The last time this father saw his son, the boy was about seventeen years old (37:2). Over two decades have come and gone. The boy is now a man, indeed, a powerful ruler and savior of Egypt. Jacob is 130 years old and will die at the age of 147 years (47:9, 28). *It is, therefore, remarkably fitting that Joseph was with his father seventeen years before his disappearance, and will be with his father for seventeen more years after their reunion.* Jacob will not quite be made "glad for as many days as [God] afflicted" him (Ps. 90:15), but it will be in the ballpark. That long, dark night of twenty-plus years of affliction will recede before the rising sun of a much happier seventeen more years with Joseph.

When the parents of Jesus brought him to the temple as an infant, a man named Simeon took the child in his arms and sang, "Lord, now you are letting your servant depart in peace, according to your word; for my eyes have seen your salvation that you have prepared in the presence of all peoples, a light for revelation to the Gentiles, and for glory to your people Israel" (Luke 2:29-32). Often known by its Latin name, *Nunc Dimittis* ("Now let depart"), this canticle almost sounds like the NT version of Jacob's words when he holds Joseph in his arms, "Now let me die, since I have seen your face and know that you are still alive" (Gen. 46:30). Simeon could go joyfully to the grave, knowing that the Lord's Messiah had arrived. Likewise, Jacob, after all those years of thinking his son was dead, that he would never see his face again, could smile at the grave since he had arrived in Joseph's presence once more.

Now that Joseph was reunited with his family—and what a surprise it must have been to see how much that family had grown over the last two decades!—he needed to take care of some practical concerns. Land and jobs, to be precise. So, he handpicked five of his brothers, coached them on what to say to pharaoh, and introduced them to the king. The ruler of Egypt, in royal munificence, let the family of Joseph live in the rich land of Goshen and even put them in charge of his livestock (47:6).

Then it was the turn of the patriarch, Jacob, to appear before the king:

Then Joseph brought in Jacob his father and stood him before Pharaoh, and Jacob blessed Pharaoh. And Pharaoh said to Jacob, "How many are the days of the years of your life?" And Jacob said to Pharaoh, "The days of the years of my sojourning are 130 years. Few and evil have been the days of the years of my life, and they have not attained to the days of the years of the life of my fathers in the days of their sojourning."[1] And Jacob blessed Pharaoh and went out from the presence of Pharaoh. (47:7-10)

Jacob characterizes his 130 years as "few." This might strike us as odd, if not humorous. None of us today would say that even a sixty or seventy-year-old had lived "a few years." But in Egyptian culture, the ideal lifespan was 110 years—not coincidentally, the length of Joseph's life (Gen. 50:22).[2] Jacob, therefore, in downplaying his lifespan to "only" 130 years, could have been coyly engaging in a little Hebrew one-upmanship. It certainly wouldn't be contrary to his nature, even at this late age, to still be flexing.

Leaving aside the word "few," however, notice how else Jacob depicts his life: as "evil [ra]" and his time in this world as years of "sojourning [magor]." The ESV translates ra as "evil," but, given the context, this seems an unsuitable rendering. The word ra has an extremely wide range of meaning, including "bad, poor, injurious, hard, painful, evil," etc. Given what we know of Jacob's life, his choice of ra probably means, in colloquial English, "he's had it rough."[3] Of course, we know that much of the responsibility for this "rough life" lay squarely on the shoulders of Jacob himself. In the memorable words often (wrongly) attributed to John Wayne: "Life is hard; it's harder if you're stupid." And, let's be honest, Jacob, while not stupid, did make his share of stupid decisions. Even if you've only been paying half attention to this book, you can recount a number of those decisions. And we've also seen how all of us, in Jacob fashion, have made similar ones ourselves.

Jacob's description of his life as a "sojourning [magor]" brings us back to how we began this chapter. The patriarch had been around the

---

[1] Jacob will live to be 147 years, which, of course, is a lot of years to us. His grandfather, Abraham, however, lived 175 years (Gen. 25:7) and his father, Isaac, 180 years (35:28).

[2] See K. A. Kitchen, *On the Reliability of the Old Testament* (Grand Rapids: Eerdmans, 2006), 411.

[3] Other translations have "difficult" (NIV), "unpleasant" (NASB), and "hard" (CSB).

block a time or two. His steps had carried him from southern Canaan all the way north and east into Mesopotamia, then back again. Now, even with a head full of gray hair and a face full of wrinkles, he was forced to uproot his life once more and transplant his entire family south and west to Egypt. When my wife, Stacy, and I retire, our plan is to buy ten or twenty acres in east Texas, built a log cabin, and—God willing—remain there as long as the good Lord grants us life and health. Jacob would not have that leisure. His mail was always being forwarded to the next town. Like his father, Isaac, and grandfather, Abraham, so Jacob too knew all about *magor*, that rootless life of sojourning.

Writing about these ancient believers, the preacher in Hebrews says, "By faith [Abraham] went to live in the land of promise, as in a foreign land, living in tents with Isaac and Jacob, heirs with him of the same promise. For he was looking forward to the city that has foundations, whose designer and builder is God" (11:9-10). That God-built city is "Mount Zion and...the city of the living God, the heavenly Jerusalem" (12:22). It is the end-time city of which we are already citizens, to which we were granted liquid passports in baptism. We visit there every Lord's day as we gather for worship as the body of Christ, then disperse to our various vocations as resident aliens in this beautiful but doomed and dying world. Like our forefathers, we too live in tents of faith in this world that is our Egypt, our Babylon, our Rome.

So hold on loosely to this world, dear disciple. It's rife with danger. The siren calls of sexy and powerful religions ring out from every direction, but especially within the echo chambers of our own hearts. Of course, it's always been this way. Well before OnlyFans on Instagram there were peep shows in seedy circuses and cult prostitutes in Canaanite shrines. The religion of sex has always sold. The religions of money, nationalism, and power, as well as the seemingly "good religions" of family and work, have never and will never go out of style, wooing hearts to a "Christ and (fill-in-the-blank-with-your-pet-god)" kind of faith. As Orthodox theologian, Fr. Thomas Hopko, once wrote, "Have no expectations, except to be fiercely tempted to your very last breath."[4]

---

[4] This is one of his famous "55 Maxims," which, to my knowledge, are not found in any of his printed writings. The full list can be found at https://christ thesavioroca.org/files/Hopko-55Maxims.pdf.

While graphically describing how this current world will be dissolved, the heavens set on fire, and the heavenly bodies will melt to give way to the new heavens and new earth, Peter says, "What sort of people ought you to be in lives of holiness and godliness!" (2 Peter 3:11). Using this same language of "godliness [*eusebeia*]" earlier in his letter, Peter says, "His divine power has granted to us all things that pertain to life and godliness [*eusebeia*], through the knowledge of him who called us to his own glory and excellence, by which he has granted to us his precious and very great promises, so that through them you may become partakers of the divine nature, having escaped from the corruption that is in the world because of sinful desire" (1:3-4).

Our gracious Father has made us "partakers of the divine nature" by uniting us, through the body of his Son, to himself, in the communion of the Holy Spirit. We are, quite factually and everlastingly, the sons and daughters of God. This is not metaphor; it is reality. As Peter says, he has called us to his own glory and excellence. He has granted us precious and great promises. We are a new creation in Christ Jesus. We are in this world, to be sure, but we await a better one.

In the meantime, we pray. We labor. We witness. We love. Fail we will, of course, sometimes gravely. Our lives are a constant repentance and renewal by the Holy Spirit, for holiness and godliness, while perfect in Christ, will always be imperfect in us.

One day, like Jacob, we too will stand before a king. But he will not be the king of Egypt but of heaven and earth. The King above all kings who bears the name above all names. On that day, it will not be time for us to say, like Jacob, "Few and evil have been the days of the years of my life" or even "Many and great have been the days of my life." Rather, it will be time for us, the baptized citizens of heaven's kingdom, to lift up our heads and hear our King say, "Well done, good and faithful servant" (Matt. 25:21).

Welcome home. Your sojourning is over.

Discussion Questions

1. How is our world full of both hope and danger? How is this world a preview of the one to come? In what ways can we become too attached to this old and dying world?

2. Read Genesis 46:28-47:10. How was the reunion of Jacob with Joseph like the Song of Simeon (Luke 2:29-32)? Talk about what Jacob said to Pharaoh in Gen. 47:7-10. Why would he characterize his years as "few" and his life as "evil" or "rough"?

3. Read Hebrews 11:8-16; Rom. 12:2; John 15:18-21; 1 Peter 2:9. What is the overall message of these verses about how Christians relate to the unbelieving world? What does it mean to be a resident alien?

4. Discuss how this passage defines our lives as followers of Jesus: "We are in this world, to be sure, but we await a better one. In the meantime, we pray. We labor. We witness. We love. Our lives are a constant repentance and renewal by the Holy Spirit, for holiness and godliness, while perfect in Christ, will always be imperfect in us."

CHAPTER 33

Jacob, the Preacher of the Gospel

> Then Jacob called his sons and said, "Gather yourselves together, that I may tell you what shall happen to you in days to come."
>
> Genesis 49:1

We looked at Hebrews 11 in our previous chapter. The preacher moves through the history of the Old Testament, highlighting various individuals to describe how they did this or that "by faith." For instance, "by faith Abel offered to God a more acceptable sacrifice than Cain..." (11:4). And, "by faith Abraham obeyed when he was called to go out to a place that he was to receive as an inheritance..." (11:8). Besides these two individuals, included on the author's list are Enoch, Sarah, Isaac, Joseph, Rahab, and many others. Jacob, too, makes his appearance.

Now let's pretend for a moment. Imagine that you are good friends with the author of Hebrews (whoever that was). You happen to be walking through his neighborhood, so you stop by for a quick visit. He has a scroll unrolled in front him and he's working on this sermon.[1] You ask how it's going and he says, "It's going well. Very

---

[1] As Albert Vanhoye has noted, the "Epistle to the Hebrews" is not a letter or epistle but a sermon. It "would be better called 'Preaching on the Priesthood of Christ' or, more briefly, 'The Priestly Sermon.'" *Structure and Message of the Epistle to the Hebrews*, Subsidia Biblica 12 (Rome: Editrice Pontificio Instituto Biblico, 1989), 5.

well, thank you. But I'm here in the middle of a section where I'm talking about our forefathers. How they lived by faith. I've already covered Abel, Enoch, Noah, Abraham, Sarah, and Isaac. Now I'm deliberating on what to say about Jacob. I'm keeping it short. One verse max. What's your opinion? What episode from his life should I address and relate it to faith?"

Interesting question to ponder, isn't it? So, how would you respond? Perhaps, "By faith Jacob went forth into Haran with only his staff in his hand." That would work. Or, "by faith Jacob wrestled with God on the banks of the Jabbok River." You certainly could say that, too. Or you could describe how, by faith, Jacob grieved for Joseph, traveled to Egypt, and spoke to Pharaoh. Perhaps you suggested all of these possibilities to your author/preacher friend. He listened politely, then responded, "Thanks for the ideas. And, yes, I suppose any or all of those would indeed work. But, you know what? I'm actually thinking about focusing on something else."

That "something else" is a detail from Jacob's life that I daresay neither you nor I would have ever guessed. It's not unimportant, but it hardly seems like *the one and only thing* about Jacob's life that reaches out and grabs our attention. What is it? In Hebrews 11:21 we read this: "By faith Jacob, when dying, blessed each of the sons of Joseph, bowing in worship over the head of his staff."

That is a curious choice, isn't it? To what exactly is the preacher referring? And what is so significant about this incident? Let's take a look at the later years of Jacob's life, especially in Genesis 47-49, to find out.

In the last couple of chapters, we covered how Jacob and his family arrived in Egypt, the long-separated father and son were reunited, and the aged patriarch appeared before Pharaoh and blessed him. We are given sparse details about what happened during the next seventeen years. We do know that the family of Israel lived and prospered in the good land of Goshen, where "they gained possessions in it, and were fruitful and multiplied greatly" (Gen. 47:27). Presumably, during these years, Joseph got reacquainted with his long-lost family, and introduced his Egyptian wife, Asenath, and their two sons, Manasseh and Ephraim, to his relatives (41:45, 51-52).

We have many more details, however, about what happened at the close of those seventeen years. It was the year of Jacob's death.

God had granted him almost a century and a half of life—147 years, to be precise (47:28). Summoning Joseph, he had his son take an oath that he would not bury his body in Egypt. Instead, the patriarch said, "Let me lie with my fathers. Carry me out of Egypt and bury me in their burying place" (47:30). After Joseph swore to this, "Israel bowed himself upon the head of his bed" (47:31).

This last detail is one of the events to which Hebrews 11:21 refers. In Genesis 47:31, the Greek text of the Septuagint (echoed in Hebrews 11) says that Jacob worshiped "upon the top of his staff"[2] while the Hebrew text says he worshiped "upon the head of his bed." These slight differences aside, we get the meaning.[3] Jacob is dying. Jacob knows he's dying. So he makes this last request. He does not want to be buried on foreign soil.

But in broader context of Genesis, there's more going on than simply an old man's dying wish to be laid to rest "back home." In Genesis 48-49, we have two stories about blessings pronounced by Jacob. The patriarch takes up the mantle of a prophet and preacher. First, he blesses his grandsons, Manasseh and Ephraim (48:1-22), then he blesses his sons (49:1-27). The blessing of his grandsons is the event to which the preacher explicitly refers when he says that Jacob, "when dying, blessed each of the sons of Joseph" (Heb. 11:21). It seems plausible that the author of Hebrews, even though he refers only to the blessing of the grandsons, also has in mind the blessing of Jacob's sons. After all, the two events are thematically identical and follow one another sequentially in Genesis 48-49. If so, we might expansively paraphrase Hebrews 11:21 this way: "By faith Jacob, during the last year of his life, inspired by the Spirit to see what lay in the future, blessed his sons and grandsons as he bowed in worship over the head of his staff."

A detailed examination of these two chapters is not our concern here, but there are two details we want to focus on. One, Jacob draws our attention to the Son of God, calling him "God" and "Messenger."

---

[2] *The Lexham English Septuagint.*
[3] Keep in mind that the original Hebrew text was not written with vowels but only consonants. The vowel sounds were supplied orally when the text was read. The Hebrew consonantal text is *m-t-h*. This could be vocalized one of two ways: as *mittah* ("bed") or *matteh* ("staff"). Either translation is therefore possible.

And, two, enlarging upon this theme, Jacob tells us from which tribe the Son of God will be born "in days to come" (Gen. 49:1).

When Jacob blesses his grandsons, Manasseh and Ephraim, he crossed his hands to give the greater blessing to the second-born Ephraim over the firstborn Manasseh. As he did so, he pronounced these words:

> The God before whom my fathers Abraham and Isaac walked,
> the God who has been my shepherd all my life long to this day,
> the angel [Hebrew: *malak*] who has redeemed me from all evil,
> bless the boys;
>> and in them let my name be carried on,
>> and the name of my fathers Abraham and Isaac;
>> and let them grow into a multitude in the midst of the earth.
> (Gen. 48:15-16)

As I have pointed out elsewhere, "angel" is an ill-chosen, easily misleading translation of the Hebrew noun, *malak*, which means "messenger"—a human messenger, an angelic messenger, or a divine messenger.[4] In this case, the *malak* is obviously a divine Messenger. The Jewish scholar, Nahum Sarna, notes that "the God" and "the messenger" do not refer to God *and* a messenger *but to the God whom Jacob calls the messenger.*[5] The Hebrew grammar underscores that the God/God/Messenger are all the same designee because the Hebrew verb for "bless" (in the phrase "bless the boys") is singular in form. If Jacob had meant God *and* his messenger (plural subject), then the verb would be a grammatical plural as well.

Who is this divine Messenger who is also called God? Who is he before whom Abraham and Isaac walked? Who is this shepherd and redeemer of Jacob? Who is this one who will bless the grandsons? This Messenger is the same Messenger of Yahweh who appeared to Hagar (Genesis 16), who spoke to Moses from the burning bush (Exodus 3), who has the divine name in him (Exodus 23:21), whom people call and who calls himself *Elohim* (=God [e.g., Exod. 3:6]). This Messenger

---

[4] *The Christ Key*, 26.

[5] Sarna writes, "The capitalization [of Angel] reflects the fact that the parallelistic structure of verses 15-16 strongly suggests that 'angel' is here an epithet for God." *Genesis*, The JPS Torah Commentary, 328.

of God is the Son of God, who himself will one day become incarnate as the bearer of the Father's word to all humanity.

Near the end of his life, therefore, Jacob preaches Jesus. He proclaims the Son of God to us. The patriarch, by faith, as he worshiped, spoke of the divine Messiah, who is the Shepherd and Redeemer of Israel.

Second, in Genesis 49, Jacob also specifies which of his twelve sons will carry on, in his family tree, the promise of the Messiah-Seed. Based on what we know of Genesis 37-48, we might assume the most likely candidate would be Joseph. After all, he is Jacob's favorite son of his favorite wife. By Joseph's wisdom, he delivered Egypt and the surrounding nations—including his own family—from death by starvation. As a regal figure, people take the knee before him. And he is gracious and magnanimous. But as he is wont to do, the Lord does not choose the candidate that we expect. Rather than Joseph, his older brother, Judah, is the one designated by God, through Jacob, to be the bearer of the ongoing promise of the Seed.

Judah's name in Hebrew is Yehudah, which means "he will be praised," formed from the verb *yadah* ("to praise"; Gen. 29:35). Punning off this, Jacob says of his fourth-born son, "Judah, your brothers shall praise [*yadah*] you; your hand shall be on the neck of your enemies; your father's sons shall bow down before you" (Gen. 49:8). Giving rise to the later designation of the Messiah as the "Lion of the tribe of Judah" (Rev. 5:5), Jacob adds, "Judah is a lion's cub; from the prey, my son, you have gone up" (Gen. 49:9). Highlighting his leadership and the tribe from which David and the messianic Son of David will come, Jacob says, "The scepter shall not depart from Judah, nor the ruler's staff from between his feet, until tribute [or 'Shiloh']⁶ comes to him; and to him shall be the

---

⁶ The words "until tribute [or 'Shiloh'] comes to him" are a notoriously difficult clause to translate and interpret. Not surprisingly, it has generated countless explanations by Jewish and Christian commentators throughout the centuries. The ESV's translation of "tribute" is made by splitting the one Hebrew word *shiloh* into two words and vocalizing them as *shai lo* ("tribute to him"). Other translations, like the KJV and NASB, read *shiloh* as a proper name, Shiloh, which could refer to a person (i.e., the Messiah) or a city (e.g., Josh. 18:1). Its unknown meaning does not detract, however, from the overall regal theme of the verse: Judah's descendant will hold the ruling staff or scepter.

obedience of the peoples" (49:10). Finally, picturing the luxuriant blessings of his kingdom, Jacob says of Judah, "Binding his foal to the vine and his donkey's colt to the choice vine, he has washed his garments in wine and his vesture in the blood of grapes. His eyes are darker than wine, and his teeth whiter than milk" (49:11-12). This hyperbolic description means basically this: "He'll have so many vineyards that he can randomly tie his donkey to a vine and be unconcerned if the animal munches on the grapes. He'll have so much wine, it'll be like the water he uses to wash his shirt." In short, the Seed of Judah, the Messiah, will be acclaimed by others, victorious over foes, a king over the nations, and his kingdom will be lush and lavish.

To return to Hebrews 11, Jacob, in the year of his death, while worshipping, by faith spoke these blessings of what was to come. He blessed each of the sons of Joseph, and he spoke prophetic words over his sons and the tribes of which they were patriarchs. We read, at the beginning of Genesis 49 that the patriarch prophesied what was to happen "in days to come" (49:1). The Septuagint translated "in days to come" as "at the last of days,"[7] which is virtually identical to the phrase used at the opening of Hebrews, "[I]n *these last days* he has spoken to us by his Son...." (Heb. 1:1; italics added). In Jacob's own "last days," he spoke of the coming "last days," when the Messiah, the Messenger of the Father, would be the chosen mouthpiece of God.

Old man Jacob became a preacher of the gospel. Imagine that. Not the first image—or second or third or fourth image!—that we have of Jacob. But, after a long life, full of ups and downs, deceits and deaths, he ended the best possible way: talking, by faith, about Jesus. I suppose, in highlighting this singular incident from Jacob's life, the author of Hebrews did indeed choose wisely. What better way to be remembered as an exemplar of faith?

Several years ago, someone told me about a pastor who died, in the pulpit, while preaching the Gospel, on Easter day. I can think of no better way to wave goodbye to this world and to be carried by the angels into the presence of Christ. Just think of having these words on your gravestone: "He died while preaching the Gospel." It is not

---

[7] *The Lexham English Septuagint.*

the action itself that matters so much as the one whose name and life and saving ministry are on our lips.

If I am remembered, let it be said of me, "That Chad, he sure talked about Jesus a lot." Let my enemies rejoice at my death and complain of me, "All he could talk about, teach about, preach about, write about, was Christ this and Christ that, all the blasted time." Disciples are all about keeping first things first. And there is no greater first than he who is the true Alpha. Christ first, Christ always. To "seek first the kingdom of God and his righteousness" is to seek Jesus (Matt. 6:33). To decide "to know nothing…except Jesus Christ and him crucified" is to give him, his wounds, and his saving life preeminence in everything (1 Cor. 2:2). To live by faith is to die and rise in Jesus, so that it is no longer we who live but Christ who lives in us. The life we now live in the flesh, we live by faith in the Son of God, who loved us and gave himself up for us (Gal. 2:20).

Most of the time, Jacob was not a great model disciple for us to emulate. But on his deathbed, as he talked about Jesus—the Father's Messenger, the Redeemer, the Shepherd, the King, the Lion of the Tribe of Judah—we can truly say, "Lord, make me as Jacob. Let your name, your work, your love, and your life, never be far from my lips, as you are the overflow of my heart."

DISCUSSION QUESTIONS

1. If you were that friend of the author of Hebrews, which episode in Jacob's life would you have recommended as an example of him living "by faith"? As you reflect back on the ups and downs in his life, what makes you think of his trust in the Lord?

2. Read Genesis 48, especially vv. 14-16. Who is this "angel" or "messenger"? What does Jacob say that he did for him? How does this fit with the work of the Son of God as both redeemer and shepherd? See Gal. 3:13-14; Titus 2:11-14; Ezekiel 34:23-24; John 10:11-18.

3. Read through and discuss the details about Judah in Genesis 49:8-12. How do these verses prophecy the Messiah?

4. How does Jacob, at the end of his life, become a model disciple for us? What are the ways we can talk about Jesus with friends, coworkers, strangers, and others? How can you "always being prepared to make a defense to anyone who asks you for a reason for the hope that is in you," and to do so "with gentleness and respect" (1 Peter 3:15)?

CHAPTER 34
Lord, Teach Us to Number Our Days

> When Jacob finished commanding his sons, he drew up
> his feet into the bed and breathed his last and was gath-
> ered to his people.
>
> Genesis 49:33

Not a day goes by when I don't think about the day of my death. I don't know if that makes me normal or abnormal, but it certainly makes me keenly and consciously aware of my own mortality. And that's one of the reasons I practice the daily remembrance of death. There is nothing morbid or macabre about this. To actively contemplate one's mortality is to position oneself in a place of awareness, readiness, and opportunity.

First, awareness prevents us from being deluded into the juvenile tendency of assuming we are invincible. We are aware that sickness, accident, or violence can end our earthly lives at any moment. We are not gods, but humans, whose days—the Scriptures constantly remind us—"are like a passing shadow" (Ps. 144:4) for "they are soon gone, and we fly away" (Ps. 90:10). Second, readiness positions us for the unpredictability of when we will draw our last breath, so that when that moment comes, we are not like the foolish virgins or unfaithful servant in the parables that Jesus told about his second coming (Matt. 24:45-25:13), but on the alert. "Happy and wise is he who now strives to be such in life as he wishes to be found at death."[1] And how do we wish to be found

---

[1] Thomas à Kempis, *The Imitation of Christ*, Book 1, Chapter 23 (Uhrichsville, OH: The Christian Library), 26.

at death? Full of faith, hope, and love. Alert and readied by the Spirit. And, third, contemplation of our mortality fires within us countless opportunities to make the most of our lives now, by laying down our lives in service for others, by giving, praying, laboring, witnessing, and forgiving. With Paul we acknowledge that "we would rather be away from the body and at home with the Lord," but until that day arrives, "we make it our aim to please him. For we must all appear before the judgment seat of Christ, so that each one may receive what is due for what he has done in the body, whether good or evil" (2 Cor. 5:8-10).

Jacob had certainly known, and made preparations for, his upcoming death. To his sons he said,

> "I am to be gathered to my people; bury me with my fathers in the cave that is in the field of Ephron the Hittite, in the cave that is in the field at Machpelah, to the east of Mamre, in the land of Canaan, which Abraham bought with the field from Ephron the Hittite to possess as a burying place. There they buried Abraham and Sarah his wife. There they buried Isaac and Rebekah his wife, and there I buried Leah— the field and the cave that is in it were bought from the Hittites." (Gen. 49:29-32)

Having said these words, Jacob "drew up his feet into the bed and breathed his last and was gathered to his people" (49:33). The Hebrew phrase, "drew up his feet" is unusual. The impression is that Jacob, on his bed, assumes a kind of fetal position. He whom we met at the beginning of this book, while still in utero, at the start of his life, now finishes his life in much the same way. Then, he was already wrestling with his twin brother; now, his fights are over, his race is run, and he is "gathered to his people" (cf. Gen. 25:8, 17, 35:29). He is dead but not dead, for, as Jesus says, the God of Abraham, and the God of Isaac, *and the God of Jacob*, is "not God of the dead, but of the living" (Matt. 22:32). Jacob, while dead, lives on in the God of life, together with the believers who have preceded him in death.

And what a period of mourning, what a funeral procession, the dearly departed Jacob had! There is no service of death in Scripture more elaborately described than what this patriarch received. First, his body was embalmed over a period of forty days, per Joseph's command. This father and son are the only two Israelites whom we know underwent this Egyptian mummification process (Gen. 50:2, 26). "The Egyptians wept for [Jacob] seventy days," either after the forty days of embalming or, more likely, meaning that there was official mourning for thirty more days, totaling seventy (50:3). Some ancient evidence says that Egyptians mourned for seventy-two days at the death of a king, thus implying that Jacob was treated as a royal personage.[2] Following this long period of grieving, a huge entourage of Egyptians and Israelites, complete with horsemen and chariots, carried the body of Jacob from Egypt to Canaan (50:4-14). After another seven days of "very great and grievous lamentation," which captured the attention even of the Canaanites, the sons of Jacob "buried him in the cave of the field at Machpelah, to the east of Mamre, which Abraham bought with the field from Ephron the Hittite to possess as a burying place" (50:10-13). Having done this, the sons left again for their homes in Egypt, leaving behind the body of Jacob to await, as it were, the return of his people, many years in the future, under the leadership of Moses.

Speaking of Moses, in his prayer, recorded for us as Psalm 90, he asks the Lord to "teach us to number our days that we may get a heart of wisdom" (90:12). What a fitting prayer that is for a disciple of Jesus.

Teach us to number our days, O Lord, that as we rise to meet each day, we might do so in your name. An ancient Christian practice is to make the sign of the cross—as a reminder of the cross itself, Christ, and our baptism into Jesus—and to say, "In the name of the Father and of the Son and of the Holy Spirit." Making the sign of the cross is not a "Catholic thing." Like folding our hands in prayer, closing our eyes to pray, bowing our heads or kneeling, when we trace the cross upon ourselves, we incorporate our bodies in prayer itself. We were made disciples when, according to Christ's own words, we were baptized "in the name of the Father and of the Son and of the Holy Spirit" (Matt. 28:19). To begin the day in this way is to remind

---

[2] The Greek historian, Diodorus of Sicily, in his *Histories* 1.72, says that when an Egyptian king died, the citizens celebrated no festivals, recited dirges, fasted from certain products, and grieved for seventy-days as if their own child had died. We have to bear in mind, however, that Diodorus was a historian of the first century BC, so even if he were recording ancient traditions, he is separated by well over a millennium from the time of Jacob.

ourselves that, whatever this day might bring, however hot and fiery a trial we might face, that heat will not evaporate the water of baptism by which we have been clothed with Christ. Teach us, O Lord Jesus, to number our days by first numbering ourselves among your brothers and sisters.

Teach us to number our days, Jesus, that we might remember that "this is the day that the LORD has made," so that we might "rejoice and be glad in it" (Ps. 118:24). It was no mistake, no accident, that we awoke on this particular day. This is a day to rejoice because it is another day to follow Jesus, wherever he might lead us. To make breakfast for our children? Yes. To bring a cup of coffee to our sleepy spouse? Yes. To go to work? Yes. To speak a word of encouragement to a stressed coworker, a word of forgiveness to someone who hurt us, a word of wisdom to a friend who is confused? Yes. This is the day that the Lord has made, for us to make something of it, even in the normal and underwhelming ways that populate most of the hours of our lives. We are disciples on this day, right now, to be conduits of divine love for those whom the Lord has placed in our lives, in our vocations, for us to serve. Lord Jesus, teach us to number our days, especially this day, as the twenty-four hours we live and serve by grace.

Teach us to number our days, O Lord, as well as our nights. When our work is done and we retire for the evening, let us remember that, even as the sun is setting, "the darkness is not dark to you; the night is bright as the day, for darkness is as light with you" (139:12). At night, Jacob dreamed of the God who stood beside him, at the bottom of the ladder, promising never to leave him or forsake him. At night, Jacob wrestled with the Son of God, who let himself lose that Jacob would win and limp away with a new name. At night, as we ourselves dream, let us remember that the Lord who keeps us will not slumber, that "he who keeps Israel will neither slumber nor sleep" (Ps. 121:3-4). As we go to bed, bearing our own wounds and scars, may the Lord teach us to be good stewards of our painful moments, and to remember that we bear the name "Christian," for we belong to Christ. On his own bed, Jacob "drew up his feet...and breathed his last and was gathered to his people" (Genesis 49:33). Since none of us are promised a tomorrow, what better way to end our day than, lying in bed, to pray the Lord's Prayer, Psalm 4 (an evening psalm), or a simple "Lord Jesus Christ, Son of God, have mercy on me, a sinner," as we fade off to sleep. Lord, teach us to number our days, as well as our nights, that we might rest in you.

Finally, Father, teach us to number our days, as we joyfully reflect upon the fact that, because of Jesus, you are not numbering, not counting, our trespasses against us (cf. 2 Cor. 5:19). The Lord is not a celestial accountant, who keeps an exact tally on our sins, hourly and daily adding them up and sending us the bill to show us how indebted we are to him. What a joyless monster of a deity that would be. To be a disciple of Jesus is live completely and perfectly covered by divine love, even as, in ourselves, we incompletely and imperfectly follow him. We limp. We stumble. We fall. And we confess, repent, and pray. As we do, the Lord's hand is never withdrawn from our own, nor is his heart ever, even for a moment, turned from us. "As a father shows compassion to his children, so the LORD shows compassion to those who fear him. For he knows our frame; he remembers that we are dust" (Ps. 103:13-14). Dust, to be sure, but dust that is as precious to him as gold. Lord, teach us to number our days, as days lived solely by your mercy, at the foot of the cross and empty tomb, overshadowed by your love.

Such a life will probably not end, as Jacob's did, with a spectacular funeral and international march to the cemetery. It will most likely conclude not with a bang but a simple last breath. One more exhalation of the air that we have long breathed in his world. A humble funeral. A final goodbye (for now) from our grieving family and friends. But inside us will be that "heart of wisdom," of which Moses spoke (Ps. 90:12). A heart formed by the very hands that fashioned the world, that were fastened to the cross, and that filled us with the Holy Spirit that we might follow him. Lord, create in us such a heart of wisdom, that running or walking or limping or crawling or lying on our deathbed, we might, along with Jacob, be your disciples, chosen, beloved, and precious in your sight. Amen.

DISCUSSION QUESTIONS

1. Do you think often of the day of your death? Why or why not? How can such contemplation position us in a place of awareness, readiness, and opportunity?

2. Read Genesis 49:29-33. How is the death of Jacob described? What instructions did he give? How were these carried out in 50:1-14?

3. Read Psalm 90. What does it teach us about life, death, and the numbering of our days? How can we incorporate the prayer, "Teach us to number our days," into the daily rhythm of our lives?

4. As you think back on the life of Jacob, what are three or four of the major takeaways? In one or two sentences, how would you describe this man? How has studying his life, and God's actions in his life, enabled you to see more clearly who Jesus is, what he has done for us, and how we follow him?

Afterword

At the beginning of *The Ragamuffin Gospel*, Brennan Manning makes it clear that his book is not for "muscular Christians" or "legalists" or "the fearless and the tearless," but "for earthen vessels who shuffle along on feet of clay" and "for inconsistent, unsteady disciples whose cheese is falling off their cracker."[1]

Jacob fits that description. So do I. And, if you've made it all the way through this book without throwing it against the wall or shelving it to shift to more law-oriented "How To" books on discipleship, there's a high likelihood you fit that description, too.

We are limping with God. But it's the "with" part that matters most, isn't it? We are not alone. We are not flying solo, fueled by self-confidence, leaning on me, myself, and I to make a name for ourselves in this world. That may sound like the foundation of the American dream but it's a biblical nightmare. Nor are we, like the rich young ruler in the Gospels, so self-delusional as to boast that we've kept all the divine commandments and are shopping for even more "shoulds" and "musts." We are painfully aware that we have not even begun to keep one of the commandments, much less all ten of them.

So, No Thank You, we do not desire a list of more rules and how-to-be-a-saint guidelines that we will likewise bend and break and besmirch.

---

[1] *The Ragamuffin Gospel* (Colorado Springs, CO: Multnomah Books, 2005), 13-14.

The God with whom we limp, alongside of whom we limp, who is constantly holding us up and carrying us through—he is what we need and desire. And, thanks to the Father, that is who we have in Jesus the Messiah.

"Come, follow me," he said to his first disciples.

"Come, follow me," he still says to us, his disciples.

So we do. There are times—rare though they are—when it feels like we're running. More often than not, while bearing the burdens of this life, stiff in soul and weak in resolve, we just manage to "shuffle along on feet of clay."

But, to quote Julian of Norwich once more, "all shall be well and all shall be well and all manner of things shall be well." They shall be well because being a disciple means, above all else, being loved by the Father, embraced by the Son, and filled with the Holy Spirit.

What could be better than that?

So, let us limp onward, borne by the one whom we follow, Jesus our Lord, the God of Jacob and the Friend of sinners.

General Index

Scripture Index